# Revolution
# in the Village

# REVOLUTION
# IN THE
# VILLAGE

Tradition and Transformation

in North Vietnam, 1925–1988

·

HY V. LUONG
with the collaboration of Nguyen Dac Bang

UNIVERSITY OF HAWAII PRESS
HONOLULU

Library of Congress Cataloging-in-Publication Data
Luong, Hy V.
Revolution in the village : tradition and transformation in North
Vietnam, 1925–1988 / Hy V. Luong with the collaboration of Nguyen
Dac Bang.
    p.    cm.
Includes bibliographical references and index.
ISBN 0–8248–1382–0.—ISBN 0–8248–1399–5 (pbk.)
1. Son Duong (Vietnam)—History.   2. Vietnam—History—20th
century.   I. Title.
DS559.93.S66L86     1992
959.7—dc20             91–40031
                CIP

# CONTENTS

88114

# ILLUSTRATIONS

## Maps

## Photographs

## Figures

# TABLES

# ACKNOWLEDGMENTS

I FIRST LEARNED of Son-Duong village in 1984, when my colleague Sidney Mintz introduced me to Nguyen Dac Bang. Mr. Bang, an octogenarian exile living in Toronto, had received two death sentences from the French regime in Vietnam for having participated in an anticolonial uprising in 1930 organized by the Vietnamese Nationalist Party. Both sentences were commuted, and he was subsequently sent to French Guiana together with other Vietnamese inmates to open up the interior of this sparsely populated French colony in South America. Mr. Bang eventually escaped to Georgetown, Guyana, where he became heavily involved in the mobilization of local support for Ho Chi Minh's government in the period from 1946 to 1975. His political activities in South America led to an official visit to Cuba in 1962. Sidney Mintz had met Bang in 1966 at an academic conference in Georgetown, Guyana.

In interviews in Toronto in 1985–1986, Bang discussed his life history with me in depth. Despite his advanced age, he was able to provide valuable information on the structure of his village before 1930 and on his prison experiences in Vietnam. Bang also introduced me to his relatives in Vietnam to facilitate my field research in Son-Duong village in the summer of 1987. Although I conducted all of the research and analysis in this book myself, without Nguyen Dac Bang, this book on the village of Son-Duong would not have been written.

The relative depth of the oral history and archival materials in Can-

ada and France notwithstanding, the book was considerably enriched
by my field and library research in Vietnam in the summers of 1987 and
1988. I am grateful to many individuals for assistance during those
trips. Professor Ngo Vinh Long encouraged me to submit a research
visa application to the Vietnamese government and actively supported
my application. During my research in Vietnam in summer 1987, the
late professor Pham Huy Thong of the Social Science Committee of
Vietnam asked Professor Le van Lan of the Institute of History and Mr.
Nguyen van Ku of its Department of International Cooperation to
assist me. Mr. Ku helped to untangle the bureaucratic red tape in
Hanoi, and Professor Le van Lan coordinated my fieldwork in Son-
Duong magnificently. Dr. Ngo Quang Nam, director of the Office of
Cultural Services in the province of Vinh-Phu, and Mr. Nguyen Duc
Quy, a Son-Duong native and a nephew of Nguyen Dac Bang, introduced me to the village leadership and the rest of the village population. Professor Diep Dinh Hoa coordinated my revisits to Son-Duong
in 1988 and 1991, and Mr. Le Huong took Photos 1–5 and 8–10 for
this book in 1991. Had it not been for the tolerance of Son-Duong villagers and the village leadership for an anthropologist's intrusion into
their lives, this study could not have been completed. To all these individuals I am truly indebted.

Sidney Mintz has been supportive of my project from its inception,
and he offered valuable advice on the first draft of the manuscript. Pro-
fessors Christine White, David Marr, David Hunt, Dr. Vu Huy Phuc
(Vietnam Institute of History), and a remaining anonymous reader for
the University of Hawaii Press made many useful and detailed comments on earlier versions of the book. It was a challenge to respond
adequately to the advice these scholars offered from different disciplinary and theoretical perspectives. Claudia Vicencio, Pamela Kelley, and
Susan Stone made useful editorial suggestions. I also benefited from the
comments of several students in my course on Vietnam at Johns
Hopkins University. I am solely responsible for any remaining errors.

During my archival and library research in France and Vietnam, the
staff at the Bibliothèque nationale (Paris), the Archives nationale, Section d'outre-mer (Aix-en-Provence), the Centre des études de l'Asie du
sud-est et du monde insulindien (Valbonne), and the Vietnamese
National Library (Hanoi) kindly provided a large amount of material
on short notice. I also benefited from Le Vinh Phuc's preliminary

translation of Nguyen Dac Bang's Vietnamese-language account of the major political events in his life. My sisters Therese Kim-Trang Luong and Yvonne Kim-Cuc Luong provided valuable assistance in transcribing the tapes of my interviews with Bang. The discussion of Vietnamese kinship in this book is based on my previously published article "Vietnamese Kinship: Structural Principles and the Socialist Transformation in Northern Vietnam," which appeared in the *Journal of Asian Studies* in 1989 (vol. 48, pp. 741–756).

The research on which this book is based was assisted by a grant from the Joint Committee on Southeast Asia of the American Council of Learned Societies and the Social Science Research Council with funds provided by the National Endowment for the Humanities and the Ford Foundation.

Finally and most important of all, this book would not have been completed without the sacrifices by my family. My wife, Tuyet, endured my research schedule, which involved long summer absences from home. I revisited Son-Duong in summer 1988 only two months after the birth of our daughter, Jennifer Hong-Tam Luong. My mother volunteered with childcare to allow me to make the trip. I greatly appreciate their understanding.

# ABBREVIATIONS AND UNITS OF MEASUREMENT

## Abbreviations

| | |
|---|---|
| AOM-P-NF | Archives nationales, Section d'outre-mer, Paris, Indochine–Nouveaux fonds |
| AOM-AP-I | Archives nationales, Section d'outre-mer, Aix-en-Provence, Indochine |
| AOM-AP-RST | Archives nationales, Section d'outre-mer, Aix-en-Provence, Résidence supérieure du Tonkin |
| DRV | Democratic Republic of Vietnam |
| GGI-DAP | Gouvernement général de l'Indochine, Direction des affaires politiques et de la sûreté générale, *Contribution à l'histoire des mouvements politiques de l'Indochine française* |
| ICP | Indochinese Communist Party |
| VNP | Vietnamese Nationalist Party |

## Vietnamese Units of Measurement

*dau*   1 liter, or 0.91 quart (dry)
*mau*   3600 square meters, or 0.9 acre
*sao*   360 square meters, or 0.09 acre

# CHRONOLOGY

| 1881 | Chinese troops move into northern Vietnam to "protect" Vietnam from the French threat |
| 1882–1883 | French attack on Hanoi, Hue, and Hon-Gay coal mine areas |
| 1883 | Tonkin and Annam become French protectorates |

**Vietnam and Son-Duong Village, 1884–1988**

| | *Vietnam* | *Village of Son-Duong* |
|---|---|---|
| 1884–1896 | First major wave of anti-colonial resistance in Tonkin and Annam | Son-Duong becomes an anticolonial base |
| 4/1885 | | Massacre of three hundred villagers by Chinese troops |
| 6/1885 | Withdrawal of Chinese troops from Vietnam under the Tientsin agreement | |
| 1890 | Birth of Ho Chi Minh | |
| 1907 | Tonkin Free School movement | |
| 1908 | Tax protest movement in Annam | |
| 1925 | Formation by Ho of Vietnamese Revolutionary Youth League | |
| 1927 | Formation of Vietnamese Nationalist Party | |
| 2/1930 | VNP movement in Tonkin; formation of Indochinese Communist Party | Participation of villagers in VNP uprising against French colonialism; massive arrests and burning of village houses by the French |
| 5/1930–8/1931 | ICP-led Nghe-Tinh soviet movement | |
| 1936–1938 | Popular Front rule in France | |

| | | |
|---|---|---|
| 9/1940 | Arrival of Japanese troops in Indochina; modus vivendi with French colonial administration | |
| 5/1941 | Formation of Communist-led Vietminh Front | |
| 1942 | | Spread of Vietminh influence |
| 10/1943 | | French repression of Vietminh influence |
| 3/1945 | Formal end to French rule; Vietnam under Japanese influence | |
| 8/1945 | Surrender of Japan; Vietminh seizes power | Formation of Vietminh administration |
| 9/1945 | Ho's Declaration of Independence | |
| 1946 | | Merger with Dung-Hien, and Thuy-Son into one village |
| 12/1946 | Outbreak of Franco-Vietnamese war | |
| 1948 | France creates "State of Vietnam" under former emperor Bao Dai | Separation of Party membership of Son-Duong from neighboring Ngu-Xa; first village Communist Party cell founded |
| 1950 | Major defeat of French by Vietminh along Sino-Vietnamese border; direct U.S. military aid to French in Vietnam | |
| 1951 | | French bombing (four incidents) |
| 5/1954 | Victory of Vietminh at Dien-Bien-Phu | |
| 6/1954 | | Arrival of land reform team |

| | | |
|---|---|---|
| 7/1954 | Geneva Agreements: temporary division of Vietnam into two parts | |
| 1956 | Rectification of land reform errors in the north | |
| 1958 | | Formation of labor exchange teams |
| 1959 | | Formation of hamlet-level cooperatives |
| 12/1960 | Formation of the National Liberation Front of South Vietnam | |
| 1965 | Introduction of U.S. ground combat troops to South Vietnam | |
| 3/1965 | Beginning of sustained U.S. bombing of North Vietnam | |
| 6/1965 | | U.S. bombing |
| 1968 | End of sustained U.S. bombing of the north | Son-Duong becomes part of the new province of Vinh-Phu; creation of villagewide cooperative; short-lived experiment with household contracts in agriculture |
| 4/1975 | Collapse of Saigon government | |
| 1976 | Unification of Vietnam | |
| 2/1979 | Chinese invasion of Vietnam | |
| 1979 | Limited introduction of the household contract system in agriculture | |
| 1/1981 | Directive 100 on the nationwide application of the household contract system | |

| | | |
|---|---|---|
| 11/1982 | | Reintroduction of the household contract system in agriculture |
| 6/1987 | | Third-class labor medal awarded by the state |
| 1988 | Further agricultural reforms (Directive 10) | Application of Directive 10 (new contract system in agriculture) |

# SIGNIFICANT PEOPLE IN SON-DUONG VILLAGE AND ANTICOLONIAL HISTORY

ACCORDING TO Vietnamese naming practice, personal names follow family names and middle names. Most Vietnamese are referred to by their personal names. The following figures, with the exception of Ho Chi Minh, are listed in the alphabetical order of their personal names. Titles used in the text are given in parentheses.

Bang, Nguyen Dac *(Giao)*   A French-trained village teacher and a leader of the Vietnamese Nationalist Party (VNP) organization in Son-Duong village, exiled to French Guiana in 1930; currently residing in Canada.

Bich, Nguyen Quang   The Vietnamese governor of Hung-Hoa to 1884 and a leader of the anti-French movement in North Vietnam in the late nineteenth century.

Bon *(Doi)*   The leader of the anti-French guerilla movement in Son-Duong village during the late nineteenth century.

Chau, Phan Boi   A Confucian scholar and leader of the activist school of Vietnamese anticolonialism in the first quarter of the twentieth century.

Chinh, Pho Duc   Deputy leader of the Vietnamese Nationalist Party; executed in 1930.

| | |
|---|---|
| Dien, Bui Huu | A Communist Party member and a leader of the Vietnamese inmates of Guiana prison camps. |
| Duong, Pham Thanh | A major traitor to the Vietnamese Nationalist Party leaders on the eve of the Yen-Bay uprising in 1930. |
| Gia, Nguyen Khac | Bang's senior brother. |
| Giap, Nguyen van | Treasury director in Son-Tay to 1883 and a leader of the anti-French movement in the Hung-Hoa area in the late nineteenth century. |
| Ho Chi Minh | The most important anticolonial leader in post-1925 Vietnam; leader of the Vietnamese communist movement and president of the Democratic Republic of Vietnam from 1945 to 1969. |
| Hoc, Nguyen Thai | President of the Vietnamese Nationalist Party, 1927–1930; executed by the French in 1930. |
| Lap, Bui Khac | A leader of the VNP organization in the village of Kinh-Ke, neighboring on Son-Duong. |
| Linh, Bui Kim | A major Vietminh organizer in Son-Duong village in 1942–1943. |
| Ngu *(Doc)* | A major anti-French guerilla commander in the Hung-Hoa area from 1888 to 1892. |
| Nhu, Nguyen Khac *(Xu)* | A Confucian scholar and vice-president of the VNP on the eve of the Yen-Bay uprising; committed suicide after being captured by the French in 1930. |
| Tang, Nguyen Doan | Bang's senior brother; a French-trained teacher, a VNP movement participant and later a Vietminh cadre. |
| Te, Nguyen Doan | A landless peasant in the colonial period, later a Communist Party member and the first president of an agricultural cooperative in Son-Duong. |

Thanh (Old Lady)         A landless laborer in Son-Duong during
                         the colonial period.

Tiem, Le van             A French-trained teacher and Bang's for-
                         mer student; president of the Communist
                         Party cell in Son-Duong during its forma-
                         tive period (1948–1950).

Toai, Nguyen van *(Do)*  A Confucian scholar and a leader of the
                         VNP organization in Son-Duong village;
                         executed by the French in 1930.

Trinh, Phan Chu          A Confucian scholar and leader of the
                         reformist school of Vietnamese anticol-
                         onialism in the first quarter of the twenti-
                         eth century.

# Introduction

LIKE VIRTUALLY all other rural communities in the Red River delta of North Vietnam, the village of Son-Duong is well hidden from the paved provincial highway, lying behind a bamboo hedge. In order to get to the village, one has to turn off the provincial highway onto a pothole-ridden dirt road. A one-mile ride along this road into the village leaves a vehicle completely covered either with dirt or with red mud from the potholes, depending on whether the road has been baked in the hot sun or watered by a tropical summer downpour. The dirt road continues well beyond Son-Duong, plowing through the rice fields of this small fertile plain and turning back toward Viet-Tri, the provincial capital of Vinh-Phu and one of the three major industrial centers of the north. Familiar eyes can recognize the village of Son-Duong from afar among other bamboo clusters dotting the rural landscape by tracing the road against a background of mountain peaks rising in the west on the other side of the Red River. Arriving in Son-Duong, one leaves behind the main delta of North Vietnam to enter the midland district of Phong-Chau (formerly Lam-Thao) in the heartland of the first Vietnamese kingdom, the kingdom of the Hung dynasty (which lasted up to the third century B.C.).[1] In the courtyards of many houses in the village are huge haystacks for oxen and buffalo, the draft animals used in the rice paddies. Towering over the cultivators' dwellings are the areca palm trees. These provide the highly valued nut, chewed with betel leaves in a long-existing practice that

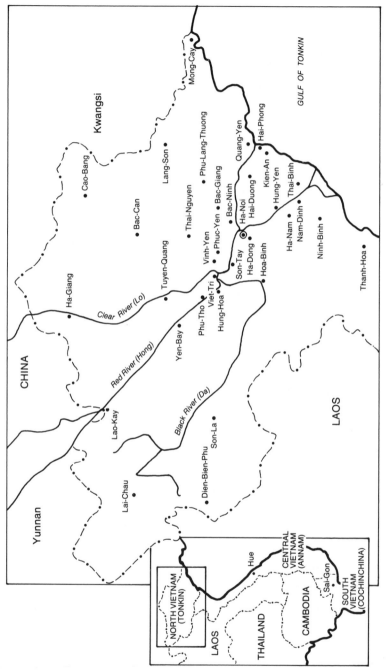

MAP 1. North Vietnam

MAP 2. Province of Vinh-Phu (modern)

is widespread in the southeastern part of Asia. The physical landscape may seem at first glance to have been frozen since time immemorial.

Such an impression is misleading. Events behind the bamboo hedge have been partly shaped by Chinese and Western capitalist world systems in the course of their economic, political, and ideological expansion. Son-Duong has withstood repeated foreign ravages throughout the past century: first by the Chinese, then by the French, and finally by the Americans. At the same time, it has undergone fundamental ecological, demographic, socioeconomic, and political changes in one of the most important revolutions of our time.

As early as June 1965, three months into the sustained U.S. air war against North Vietnam, many young Son-Duong villagers experienced for the first time the bitter taste of modern technological destruction:

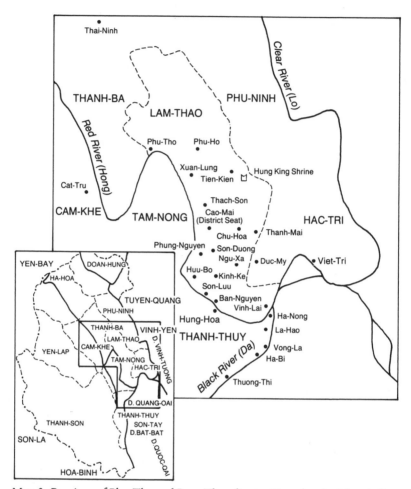

MAP 3. Province of Phu-Tho and Lam-Thao district (French colonial period)

The sky was vividly blue above the village of Son-Duong, Lam-Thao district, on the afternoon of June 24, 1965. Members of the [agricultural] cooperative all prepared to leave for the field, when two American "pirate" planes zoomed into sight. Incomprehensibly, bombs exploded in the village. Fires instantly erupted. Smoke billowed into the blue sky. The burning smell of bomb powder filled the air. The earth shook.

. . . [as soon as the bombing was over] the ground surrounding bomb craters became the informal meeting place for almost 200 people

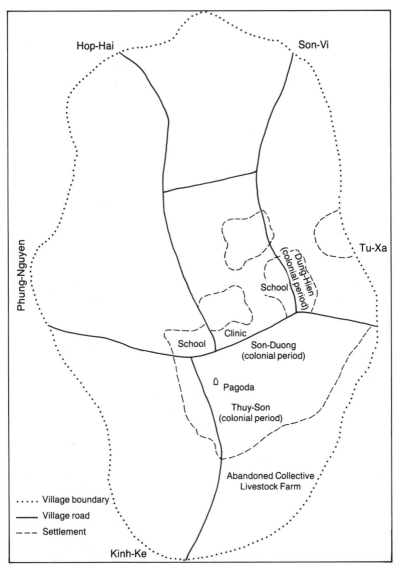

Hop-Hai

Son-Vi

Phung-Nguyen

Tu-Xa

Dung-Hien
(colonial period)

School

School          Clinic

Son-Duong
(colonial period)

◊  Pagoda

Thuy-Son
(colonial period)

Abandoned Collective
Livestock Farm

····· Village boundary
——— Village road
— — — Settlement

Kinh-Ke

MAP 4. Son-Duong village, 1987

denouncing the crime of American "pirates." The mourning cries of little Ho's father [over his bombing victim son] and sister Ai's five small children, now rendered motherless . . . registered deeply in the hearts and minds of every villager. (*Phu-Tho,* July 9, 1965)

The July 9, 1965, article in the provincial Communist Party newspaper *Phu-Tho* was a harbinger of tough days ahead for Son-Duong villagers. They had heard of the U.S. bombing along the North Vietnamese coast in the summer of 1964. On June 24, 1965, the intensified second Indochina War struck home in Son-Duong (estimated 1965 population 2700). Bombs heavily damaged the village's junior high school and a few nearby houses. They also left deep craters in the surrounding rice fields. In the eleven years of the intensified armed conflict to follow (1964–1975), the village sent to the front, in both the north and the south, 360 of its own sons. How many returned remains a secret well guarded from Westerners, at least until the village administration realizes its plan for a war memorial cemetery. The bitter memory undoubtedly lives on in the minds of many villagers. During my research in the village in the summer of 1987, for example, a ranking village cadre referred obliquely to the unforgettable devastating impact of B-52 bombing on his battalion in the south during the war. He remained openly suspicious and hostile to my research throughout my visit. To this day, villagers still wonder why Son-Duong became a U.S. bombing target on June 24, 1965.

Son-Duong had endured many other foreign ravages in the seven decades of French colonialism in North Vietnam (1883–1954), and certainly many others well before that. Firmly supporting Ho Chi Minh's Vietminh forces during the first Indochina War (1946–1954) against the French, the village was bombed four times in 1951 by the French colonial airforce. Over thirty villagers died and seventy-eight houses were reportedly destroyed in those bombings. In early 1930 the village had been a hotbed of anti-French activity in then Phu-Tho province. In retribution, the majority of its houses were burned after an abortive anticolonial uprising in the provinces of Phu-Tho and Yen-Bay. A native son was beheaded in an open guillotine in the town of Phu-Tho, then the provincial capital. Nineteen others were sent to colonial penitentiaries, some as far away as French Guiana in South America. Earlier, in the first wave of resistance to French colonialism (1884–1895), Son-Duong villagers had also been active participants. In the turmoil of the first anti-French resistance movement, a movement in which Chinese troops initially participated against the French at the request of the Vietnamese court, three hundred villagers were reportedly massacred by Chinese troops out of personal animosities between the anti-French guerilla leader in Son-Duong and certain other anticolonial leaders (Son-Duong 1987).

Son-Duong has not only endured the ravages of war. Within a precarious balance of a rapidly expanding population and millenium-old rice fields, its socioeconomic structure has also undergone a fundamental transformation. Despite the impression of a physical landscape frozen in time, the irrigation canals along the provincial highway and the road leading into the village were constructed only three decades ago. Before this major water-control project, large portions of the low-lying village fields had been inundated in the tropical summer and fall monsoons, and the high-lying sections were too dry for winter and spring cultivation. Before the completion of the canals in 1957, most village fields yielded only one staple crop annually, and some even lay fallow for the entire year. By 1987 the same land had yielded at least two, if not three, crops. These ecological changes came not a moment too soon. From 1954 to 1987 the cultivated area shrank from 1009 *mau* (363 hectares or 908 acres) to 820 *mau* (295 hectares or 737 acres). In the same period the village population increased from 2144 to 3828, not counting the increasing number of villagers temporarily residing elsewhere for advanced schooling, armed service, or other government service.[2]

The most significant changes remain the land reform campaign and the cooperative program that Ho Chi Minh's government launched after its 1954 power consolidation in the north. The land reform of 1954 redistributed approximately 300 *mau* (108 hectares or 270 acres) of rice fields from landlord and rich peasant households in Son-Duong to other members of the village.[3] The formation of agricultural cooperatives five years later was the first step toward the communal ownership of virtually all the cultivable land in Son-Duong. Despite a significant policy shift in 1981—a radical decentralization of the production process, which has raised rice crop yield by more than 100 percent in the 1982–1988 period—this collective ownership of land remains the fundamental principle in the socioeconomic structure of the village.

The following study examines the revolutionary processes in the vil-

lage of Son-Duong during the past six decades partly through the
voices of elderly villagers and partly through the findings of archival
and field research in France and North Vietnam. As the only study on
the interplay of structure and history in a Vietnamese community from
the colonial to the socialist era, it differs from the few Western-language village studies done in Vietnam in certain important respects.[4]
Previous studies have examined a Vietnamese community either in ethnographic or sociological-statistical terms without an in-depth historical dimension (Hickey 1964; Houtart and Lemercinier 1981) or from a
historical perspective without a detailed microscopic investigation of
structure in the colonial or socialist era (Pham-Cuong and Nguyen-
van-Ba 1976; Trullinger 1981).[5]

I was not aware that anticolonial resistance had simmered in Son-
Duong for a large part of the past century when I selected the village
for study. I chose the community on the basis of a chance encounter
with an exiled octogenarian revolutionary from Son-Duong village,
Nguyen Dac Bang. Originally a member of the Vietnamese Nationalist
Party (VNP), Bang had participated in the VNP-organized uprising in
North Vietnam in 1930. Having obtained a copy of Mr. Bang's memoir on the major events of his political career, I found fascinating his life
trajectory that spanned different corners of the French and British
empires and bridged the colonial and socialist eras of twentieth-century
Vietnam. With Bang's collaboration and with his memoir as my starting point, I decided in 1985 to undertake a study of how historical
events in Bang's life in particular and in Son-Duong in general inter-
played with both the microstructure of Son-Duong village and the
French colonial system. With the encouragement of Vietnamese diplomatic authorities, I planned a research visit to Bang's native village in
order to complement archival research in France and interviews in Canada in the summer of 1985. I hoped to combine the life-history method
and archival research in order to illuminate the interplay of local tradition and history—an interplay seen both in the continuity and discontinuity of a community and in the lives of community members.

My field research in Son-Duong was eventually conducted in the
summer of 1987 under difficult circumstances. Although the U.S. war
in Vietnam had officially ended twelve years earlier, tension and hostility lingered on both sides of the conflict. For a variety of reasons, the
United States continued to maintain a trade embargo on Vietnam, had

refused to normalize relations, and had exerted pressure on its allies and international organizations for widespread economic sanctions. As a researcher from the United States, I was viewed with suspicion by certain cadres within the local community as well as by Vietnamese officials in Hanoi responsible for national domestic security. Vietnamese academic authorities were also cautious, although more understanding. Through the arrangements of Vietnamese social science authorities a member of the provincial party leadership personally introduced me to the party leaders of Son-Duong village and informed the latter of the provincial authorization of the study. Although I had visited the village earlier in the summer as a fictive kin of Nguyen Dac Bang, with this formal introduction I was able to gain research access to a wider network of villagers, including the party leaders. I selected most of my interlocutors through informal consultations with acquaintances and through my past research on the village. The interview sample included both male and female villagers of different class backgrounds whose lives involved different degrees of political activism. Despite the hostility of one ranking party member, the village leadership consented to all my interview requests. A ranking party leader was assigned to coordinate my research and to introduce me to the requested villagers in their homes. After an initial acquaintance or a formal interview, I visited many interviewees again on an informal basis, at times unexpectedly, for follow-up inquiries. The duration of my field research in 1987 was limited by national security officials as well as by the common practice among Vietnamese ethnologists and sociologists of spending no more than six weeks in any particular community at a time. I extended my research briefly to include a two-day research revisit to the village in the summer of 1988. In my three visits to Son-Duong, relying primarily on the life-history approach, I interviewed in some depth sixteen and mostly elderly villagers.

The elderly villagers' vivid narratives were especially enriching because their lives bridge different historical eras of twentieth-century Vietnam and coincide with the transition from French colonialism to nationalistic socialism. Their significant others range from the French colonial masters and the last generation of Vietnamese Confucian literati to the Marxist cadres of socialist formation. Their narratives are used at some length to provide a detailed ethnographic portrait of village structure as it bears upon the major historical events of the past six decades, especially since no non-fictive in-depth accounts were available on the structure of any Vietnamese community in the French colonial period. Although shaped by the historically constituted context of the narration and inextricably linked to the narrator's reconstruction of his self, the narrative of the major interlocutor (Nguyen Dac Bang) is substantiated by available archival and newspaper accounts, except for a small number of details to be noted (see also Luong 1991; cf. Knudsen 1990). Other Son-Duong villagers related the events of their lives within a tightly knit community where their life histories constituted a part of public knowledge. However, in the context of a sharp conceptual distinction between village members and outsiders, a few influential members of the Son-Duong community were concerned that villagers might relate politically sensitive developments to a researcher whom they considered a part of the alien outside world. In order to protect those narrators, their stories are not presented in full. For the same reason, many interlocutors of the postcolonial period cannot be identified except in terms of socioeconomic backgrounds.

The goal of the following study is twofold. First, in examining socioeconomic structure and historical events in a north Vietnamese village through half a century of Western encounter, the study seeks to highlight the dynamics of a major revolution of our time. Given the research objective, the short fieldwork period, and the life-history method, the book does not attempt to provide a full ethnographic description of Son-Duong village. It is not concerned with the structure and events of a microtemporal order presented in standard ethnographies as much as with the interplay of tradition and events in historical time. In the metaphor of the well-known French historian Fernand Braudel, the book attempts to situate historical events, the surface ocean waves, in the major undercurrents of socioeconomic formations, more specifically, in terms of the encounter between Western colonialism and capitalism, on the one hand, and a Chinese-influenced indigenous system, on the other. Second, since the ethnohistorical data bear upon the debates on the dynamics of the Vietnamese revolution, the study also seeks to make a small contribution to the refinement of theoretical models of modern revolutionary processes in agrarian societies— theoretical models that are firmly embedded in the major traditions of contemporary Western social theory represented by John S. Mill, Karl Marx, Emile Durkheim, and Ferdinand de Saussure. The following survey of these major theoretical traditions provides the background for my analysis of tradition and historical events in the 1925–1988 period in the village of Son-Duong in particular and in Vietnam in general—an analysis that is most critical of the Millean tradition of inquiry.

## REVOLUTIONARY PROCESSES IN AGRARIAN SOCIETIES: THEORETICAL MODELS OF STRUCTURE AND HISTORY

In the Millean tradition of inquiry, structure is assumed to be derived from the goal-directed acts of self-interested individuals. The significance of structure is thus rendered peripheral in the analysis of historically embedded revolutionary processes and of human action in general. In the literature on revolution and agrarian unrest, the political scientist Samuel Popkin's rational choice model offers a good example of this theoretical framework (Popkin 1979). The human act and historical events are examined not in systematic relation to the structure of the capitalist world system and the native sociocultural framework but primarily in terms of the logic of individual self-interest. In his study of the Vietnamese revolution, Popkin examines the behavior of the peasantry and the elite in their search for individual material gains. He emphatically rejects the view that modern agrarian movements involve defensive reactions to the violation of precapitalist normative structures by the colonial and capitalist order. In Popkin's argument the incorporation of indigenous agriculture into the capitalistic world market, the establishment of the colonial regime, and the expansion of state power are not necessarily deleterious to peasants' welfare. The single-stranded relations of the market actually free peasants from dependence on monopolistic local lords. According to Popkin, colonialism brings vital stability and an improved communication system that keeps prices from fluctuating widely and thus keeps peasants alive in times of local famine.

Along the same line of analysis, Popkin argues that modern revolutionary movements such as the Vietminh do not succeed because of the decay of an old normative order. Rather, these movements succeed because, as political entrepreneurs, their leaders can offer peasants concrete welfare improvements and effective organization against marauding lords and notables. Popkin's analysis of revolutionary movements develops as a direct corollary to Olson's neoclassical thesis that "class-oriented action will not occur if the individuals that make up a class act rationally" (1965:105). According to Olson, since the provision of collective good as by land reform benefits all the members of a group (i.e., the peasant class), rational individuals will not incur the heavy cost of that collective good in order to further group interests unless there also exist selective incentives available only to active contributors to the collective cause. Popkin's rational peasant actors are primarily projected as Hobbesian men who act in an environmental and sociocultural vacuum and who, beyond family circles, engage in a war of all against all for maximum personal gains. Underlying Popkin's model of revolutionary processes and his analysis of the Vietnamese revolution is the tradition of Western thought that has dominated economics and shaped major theoretical endeavors in sociology (e.g., Homans), political science (e.g., Riker, Frohlich), and anthropology (e.g., Malinowski, Barth).

In contrast, the Marxist tradition seeks to situate revolutionary movements and historical events in general within the structure of conflict-ridden class relations.[6] The Marxist analyses of class relations and revolutionary dynamics in the past century were strengthened by the development of Immanuel Wallerstein's world system theory, which seeks to situate them within a broader international context—the context of unequal exchange between the core and the periphery of the world capitalist system. A new phase of the core-periphery relation emerged in the nineteenth century, when the different states within the capitalist core began to compete with one another on a global scale as they sought territorial expansion. The competition did not necessarily arise because of the immediate profitability of colonial conquests: it arose at least in part out of the concern of many states that they would be denied access to potential markets and resource bases in Asia and Africa (Murray 1980:10–15).

Instead of defining capitalism in terms of one particular method of labor control (wage labor), Wallerstein views capitalism as essentially involving "the maximization of surplus creation" (Wallerstein 1979: 285). Since wage labor is more costly in the capitalist core than in the periphery, within the context of unequal exchange relations between the core and the periphery, the capitalist world system utilizes a variety of labor methods in the periphery, including coercive labor, in order to maximize surplus appropriation.[7] In the context of the capitalist world system, the proletariat is either largely located in the periphery or composed of "ethnicities" originating in the periphery; the bourgeoisie is heavily concentrated in, although by no means restricted to, the core. Within the world-system framework, class conflict takes on an international dimension, and revolution is seen as originating in the periphery, where proletarian class interests emerge most clearly. As Wallerstein puts it, "The primary contradiction is between the interests organized and located in the core countries and their local allies on the one hand, and the majority of the population on the other. In point of fact then, an 'anti-imperialist' nationalist struggle is in fact a mode of expression of class-interest" (Wallerstein 1979:200). In other words, ethnonationalism can serve the interests of the oppressed classes within the capitalist world system despite its frequent manipulation by an indigenous elite. On the relationship between class interest and ethnonationalism outside the capitalist core, Wallerstein suggests:

> It is no accident that the great social revolutions of the twentieth century (the Russian, Chinese, Vietnamese, Cuban) have been at one and the same time "social" and "national." To be "social," they had to be "national," whereas those "revolutions" which claimed to be "national" without being "social" (for example, that of the [Chinese] Kuomintang) could not in fact defend "national" interests. . . . The fundamental political reality of that [capitalist] world economy is a class struggle which however takes constantly changing forms: overt class consciousness versus ethno-national consciousness, classes within nations versus classes across nations. (Ibid.:230; see also Ngo-Vinh-Long 1978b)

Within the same Marxist framework, although he does not explicitly adopt Wallerstein's key concepts of core and periphery, the sociologist Jeffery Paige examines in depth the greater historical probability of revolution outside the capitalist core, especially in areas of the underdeveloped world that export agricultural products:

> The expansion of the [agricultural] export sectors led to vast population movements, including the international slave trade, massive appropriations of traditional landowners, the creation of armies of agricultural laborers, and the replacement of traditional communal social ties with commercial market relations. The new forms of export agricultural organization created new social classes and destroyed old ones and introduced new patterns of class conflict. Conflict developed between the foreign owners of the new agricultural organizations and their

wage laborers, between the new agrarian upper class and the old pre-
industrial landlords it replaced, and between landlords converted into
commercial entrepreneurs and their former tenants now bound by ties
of wages and rent. The strength of colonial and imperial political controls long prevented the political expression of these conflicts, but with
the decline of colonial power in the postwar era, the commercial export
sectors of the underdeveloped world have become centers of revolutionary social movements. (Paige 1975:3)

Assuming inherent conflicts between agricultural producers and the
dominant class, Paige attempts to construct an overall model of the
forms that class conflict takes (Paige 1975; 1983). Paige deduces behavior patterns and the form of agrarian unrest from the income sources of
the involved actors. More specifically, he proposes, on the one hand,
that the economic base of the landed dominant class is narrower, more
static, and less efficient than that of its commercial and industrial counterparts. The former's economic weakness gives rise to zero-sum class
conflict as well as to its tyrannical political control of the means of production (both land and labor). On the other hand, the broader, more
dynamic and efficient capital base of the commercial or industrial upper
class can expand nonproducers' resources. This factor facilitates the
adoption of more compromising solutions by the dominant class. In
this context class conflict involves the economic distribution of goods
and products rather than the political control of labor and land. Adopt-
ing Marx's theoretical arguments in his analysis of the French peasantry
(Marx 1963; cf. Mitrany 1951), Paige further hypothesizes that cultivators' dependence on land as their main source of income gives rise to a
conservative, competitive, and structurally dependent peasantry. In
contrast, their dependence on wages would result in a more radical,
solidary, and structurally interdependent cultivator class.

Based on the premise of inherent class conflict and with its focus on
the structure of class relations at the expense of both individual choices
and the native sociocultural universe, Paige's model predicts that agrarian unrest will only take the form of rebellion when both cultivators
and noncultivators derive their incomes from land, as is the case in
north and central Vietnam. Furthermore,

A combination of non-cultivators dependent on income from land and
cultivators dependent on income from wages leads to revolution. Such
a combination of income sources is typical of sharecropping and migra-

tory labor estate systems. . . . In sharecropping systems [as in South Vietnam] the dominant ideology is likely to be Communist, while in migratory labor systems [e.g., Kenya] the dominant ideology is likely to be nationalist. Revolutionary socialist movements are most likely in decentralized sharecropping systems, and revolutionary nationalist movements are most likely in colonial settler estate systems. (Paige 1975:71; also Paige 1983:706)

In contrast, although they have been influenced to varying degrees by the Marxist approach, anthropological analyses of agrarian revolutions and of historical events in general have paid closer attention to the dynamic interplay between capitalism and indigenous noncapitalist social formations as *sociocultural systems* (Wolf 1969; Smith 1984; see also Scott 1976). For example, Carol Smith suggests that political unrest involves not necessarily and not only class conflict within the local system but a clash between Western capitalism as a sociocultural system and native organizational frameworks. In her examination of the ongoing Guatemalan revolution, Smith argues, "It cannot be accidental that wherever closed corporate peasant communities have formed, the social formations holding them have been plagued by the 'agrarian problem'—peasantries that refuse to be easily proletarianized —as well as by countless peasant rebellions, control of state apparatus by powerful landed oligarchies, and persistent ethnic divisions that shape the way in which regional and national political processes operate" (Smith 1984:195; cf. Luong 1985).

In James Scott's moral economy model, agrarian unrest is examined in terms of the reactive response of the peasantry in a precapitalist social formation to capitalism and colonialism. In the context of the world market and the colonial state, the subsistence ethic of the precapitalist order by which lords and the state are supposed to respect peasants' right to subsistence in exchange for legitimacy is often violated. Given peasants' concern with subsistence and the precarious relations between nature and the production process, they are hypothesized to prefer a variable to a fixed tax and rent policy. Scott's framework defines exploitation not merely in terms of the amount of resources extracted but, more important, also in terms of the nature and timing of this extraction from the peasantry. The expansion of Western capitalism and the establishment of European colonies eventually lead to the violation of the subsistence ethic through the erosion of patron-client ties and the existing welfare mechanisms in the relation between cultivators and noncultivators. As a corollary, Scott suggests that peasant rebellions essentially involve a conception of social justice. Peasant movements are seen as quintessentially defensive reactions of a moral nature —defensive reactions against the violation of the subsistence ethic and the increasingly serious threat to peasants' survival during subsistence crises. Under this threat and violation, any significant natural or human-induced disaster can spark agrarian unrest. The prominent role of third-world peasants in twentieth-century political movements, Scott argues, involves a dynamic interplay between a precapitalist sociocultural order, on the one hand, and colonialism and capitalism, on the other. Unrest is thus defined, within the Durkheimian tradition of social thought, in terms of a breakdown of the normative framework during a period of transition (cf. Gran 1975).

From a different analytical angle, while still situating modern anticolonial movements in the context of the structure and processes of Western colonial expansion, the political scientist Rupert Emerson deemphasizes the significance of class conflict:

> Save in the sense that Western-inspired changes in the economic structure underlay much of the disruption of the older societies, it is doubtful that the economic aspects were as significant as the political and social in turning the new colonial elites to nationalism. . . . [The ample grounds for hostility to colonial economic systems, such as the favoring of metropolitan interests over indigenous enterprises] were not generally the original source from which the more basic hostility sprang. . . . The more fundamental elements were the sense of inferiority inherent in colonialism, the indignation aroused by determination of status on racial grounds, and the gnawing consciousness of being a second-class citizen in one's own country.   (Emerson 1962:54–55)

Emerson suggests two major conditions for the rise of nationalism in the colonial context: the disruption of the precolonial order and the emergence of a Westernized bourgeois elite—an elite who are particularly sensitive to the incongruity between Western egalitarian and democratic ideals and the colonial structure of racial and ethnic inequality.

> In the first place, the greater the disruption of the old society under the impact of the intruding Western forces—assuming that the disruption takes the form of a development of modern enterprise and administra-

tion and not merely the suppression of the native population—the speedier and more complete the assertion of nationalism is likely to be. . . . The elements of . . . population which have been most drastically divorced from the close-knit pattern of their traditional society are the most susceptible to the appeal of nationalism.    (Ibid.:44)

Emerson suggests that it is nationalism that serves as the major basis for both the emergence of anticolonial movements and the integration of the modern nation-state. If the colonial encounter initially provokes a xenophobic reaction on the part of the indigenous system, the anticolonial movements of a later stage tend to involve both a nationalist ideology and a progressive orientation (ibid.:11). Emerson proposes that the nationalism emerging from colonial contexts has stronger democratic roots than that in comparable noncolonial societies for two reasons. First, the modern anticolonial and nationalist leadership comes not so much from the traditional elite but from the ranks of the Western-educated intelligentsia whose world view is shaped, at least to a certain extent, by Western democratic ideals. Second, democratic emphases enable the anticolonial leadership to gain greater legitimacy and mass support (ibid.:213–237).[8] According to Emerson, Marxism owes its appeal among the anticolonial leaders in the (former) colonies of European empires not to the inherent class conflict between workers and the owners of the means of production, but to the nationalist ideology onto which it is grafted. To the extent that Emerson's thesis centers on the notion of an integrated normative order—an order that colonialism disrupts and nationalism serves to achieve—it is also under a Durkheimian influence.

On a general theoretical level both the Marxist and Durkheimian approaches stand in sharp contrast to J. S. Mill's utilitarian framework in that they examine historical events and revolutionary dynamics in structural terms, either in terms of the structure of class relations or the disjuncture between an expanding Western capitalism and local indigenous systems. In this respect, all the models in which the notion of structure constitutes a fundamental analytical concept are generally congruent with Fernand Braudel's situation of historical events within deeper socioeconomic undercurrents. The critical difference among these models of the relationship of structure to historical events lies in the extent to which they pay attention to the structure of native categories. Paige's model, for example, focuses almost exclusively on the structure of class relations at the expense of the ideological dimensions of capitalism and indigenous noncapitalist formations. In contrast, within the Saussurean-Durkheimian tradition, Marshall Sahlins, for example, situates historical events in the conjuncture of different systems of meanings. In the case of the early period of contact between Westerners and the Hawaiian kingdom, he analyzes how the arrival of Captain Cook was metaphorized within the supposedly integrated Hawaiian scheme of conceptual categories (Captain Cook as the Hawaiian god Lono) and how the historically specific conjuncture of Western and Hawaiian systems shapes the latter through the mediation of events and practice (e.g., the murder of Captain Cook in accordance with Hawaiian categories; see Sahlins 1981 and 1985).[9] The theoretical issues emerging in the three major theoretical approaches to historical events constitute the background for the following analysis of tradition and history in the village of Son-Duong in the 1825–1988 period.

Part 1 of the present study examines in microscopic detail the interplay of anticolonial events in the 1884–1930 period and the colonial social structure in the village of Son-Duong and the district of Lam-Thao. The second part of the book analyzes the rise of Marxist power and the socialist revolution in the village in the past half a century. I argue that the events in Vietnam during the most violent phases of the Western colonial and capitalist encounter (1930–1975) cannot be fully understood by applying a narrow cost-benefit analysis to historical agents as emphasized in Popkin's model and the Millean tradition of inquiry. As emphasized respectively in Wallerstein's work and the aforementioned anthropological analyses of agrarian unrest, those events should instead be situated both in the structure of Western capitalist imperialism and in the indigenous sociocultural framework—a framework in which the kinship-centered model of hierarchical relations exists in a dialectical tension with the collectivistic ideology. More specifically, the Vietnamese revolution is rooted in two sets of conditions of the native system. First are the fundamental inequality and contradictions in the relationship between the European metropolis and the capitalist core, on the one hand, and the colonies and the periphery of world capitalism, on the other. It is a relation in which the racial diarchy of the colony stands in sharp contrast to the discourse of "liberty, equality, and fraternity" of the European metropolis. It is a system in which, at least in the perception of anticolonial leaders, the policy of the colonial state is geared more often than not toward the process of capital accumulation by and for the capitalist core. Second, and equally significant, is the degree of divergence of local tradition from the practice of capitalist imperialism as well as the strength of this tradition in providing the ideological support and organizational resources for revolutionary movements. Against Paige's analysis of the Vietnam case (Paige 1975 and 1983), I argue that, throughout the past century, the greater divergence of local tradition in northern and central Vietnam from the imperialist capitalist framework accounts both for the generally greater intensity of armed unrest against French and American intervention and for the greater receptivity to a mild form of collectivism there than in south Vietnam. In other words, the greater degree of armed unrest and receptivity to collectivism relate to the greater strength of both the collectivistic ideology and the kinship-centered model of hierarchical relations in the local tradition of the center and the north. In sum, I suggest that the structures of both the capitalist imperialist system and the indigenous social formation have powerfully shaped historical events in Vietnam in the past century. These structures are in turn shaped by historical events themselves.

# PART ONE

.

# Historical Events and Village Structure in Colonial Northern Vietnam

CHAPTER 1

•

# Vietnamese Anticolonialism, 1884–1930: A Microscopic Perspective of Historical Events

On February 10, 1930, the Ministry of Colonies in Paris received a "most urgent" cable reporting that two Vietnamese companies in the colonial infantry had revolted in Yen-Bay, a town located 153 kilometers northeast of Hanoi (AOM-P-NF, 322-2614). Other "urgent" cables reported armed violence in the northern provinces of Phu-Tho, Thai-Binh, and Hai-Duong, as well as bombing incidents at colonial government buildings in Hanoi. The initial report of three casualties among the ranking French officers in Yen-Bay was subsequently revised upward to ten. The revolt received heavy coverage in the press of both the French metropolis and the Far Eastern colony. Most accounts initially blamed the uprising on communist agitation.[1] However, it was not until three months later that the Indochinese Communist Party (ICP) launched its own movement—a fifteen-month insurrection in which half a million Vietnamese in twenty-five provinces actively participated.[2] The short-lived Yen-Bay precursor of the ICP-led soviet movement was actually organized by the Vietnamese Nationalist Party (VNP, Viet Nam Quoc Dan Dang). It marked the beginning of a period of unrest in which members of the French-educated intelligentsia played, for the first time, an active role in Vietnamese anticolonialist movements.

The unfolding of the Yen-Bay drama had a profound significance for the members of the village of Son-Duong, at that time in the province of Phu-Tho. It was in this village that a large number of the bombs for the Yen-Bay uprising were manufactured. It was also at Son-Duong that the VNP vice-president, the Confucian scholar *Xu* Nhu, established his command post for the armed movement in the provinces of Phu-Tho and Yen-Bay.[3]

According to French reports, on February 9, 1930, many male and female villagers from Son-Duong and some other villages in the district of Lam-Thao pretended to make a pilgrimage to a well-known pagoda in the town of Yen-Bay.[4] They carried bombs, scimitars, flags, bandoliers, and badges in suitcases and baskets. The baskets were covered with fruit, flowers, votive paper, and incense. The "pilgrims" got off the train at three different stations near the town in order to avoid attracting the attention of the local police. From these stations, they were led to temporary hideouts by soldiers in the colonial forces stationed in Yen-Bay (Report 78 c.s. of the Résident Supérieur of Tonkin to the Governor General of Indochina, pp. 28–29, AOM-P-NF, 323-2626; also AOM-P-NF, 322-2614). Over one hundred bombs as well as revolutionary leaflets had been produced at the Son-Duong house of a French-trained school teacher, Nguyen Dac Bang. Bang and his wife's cousin, the local Confucian teacher Toai (*Do* Toai), had actively organized Son-Duong villagers in preparation for the armed movement in Yen-Bay and Phu-Tho.

Not only did the village of Son-Duong become a bomb factory, a major point of political mobilization, and the command post for the Yen-Bay insurrection; a large number of its members also actively participated in the armed attacks on the local colonial headquarters in Phu-Tho. On the evening of February 9, 1930, according to a French Sûreté report,

> Around eight or nine o'clock . . . the rebels gathered in three locations in Son-Duong, some at Toai's house, some at Bang's residence, and others in the fields of Son-Duong where they would soon be joined by the other two groups. Around eleven or midnight, *Xu* Nhu divided the contingent into two groups, one [heading for the district seat of] Lam-Thao, the other led by *Xu* Nhu himself to [the native guard barrack in] Hung-Hoa, with Toai as second in command. Each rebel received two bombs and a scimitar, with the exception of *Xu* Nhu, who armed himself with a pistol. Some wore khaki uniforms and sashes. The two groups departed around one o'clock in the morning.
>
> Of the *Xu* Nhu–led contingent heading for Hung-Hoa . . . one

group crossed the river on the public ferry, the other on sampans. . . .
They gathered on the sand bank of Ban-Nguyen, where it seems that
other participants had arrived in sampan from the Ha-Bi and Vong-La
areas of Thanh-Thuy district. . . . [With additional participants from
nearby villages, the rebel ranks swelled to thirty-three to forty men,
and] *Xu* Nhu ordered an arms redistribution, gave final and detailed
instructions to his men [and waited for the attack signal from the Lam-
Thao district seat]. . . .

As a glimmer of light was finally detected from Lam-Thao, *Xu* Nhu
gave the order to march to the native guard post of Hung-Hoa by skirt-
ing the administrative building and passing the town post office. It was
around three in the morning then. Arriving at the foot of the complex,
the revolutionaries exhorted the sentry guards to open the doors and
join them. They had expected the defection of the guards and an easy
achievement of their objective. But they were greeted with rifle shots.
The rebels soon threw bombs into the yard of the post, the barracks,
and the residence of the commanding officer. They burned gasoline
near a side door and forced open the gates. Some entered the yard and
attempted an entry into the residence of the commanding officer.
Together with his wife, he managed to [flee to] the blockhouse. . . .
The attack lasted about forty-five minutes. As the attackers encountered heavy fire, they quickly retreated and fled toward the river, carrying with them the unused arms. Some dispersed into the surrounding
areas. Three arrests were subsequently made and seventeen nonexplod-
ing bombs were found in the yard of the post.

The same night, a group of approximately twenty individuals
showed up at the house of the instructor Nguyen Quang Kinh of Kinh-
Ke village [next to Son-Duong]. He lived with his two wives, the two
sisters Ma thi Che and Ma thi Bau, in a house at the [village] school
located at some distance from the village [center]. The rebels forced him
to follow them. Che was also led away when she attempted to catch up
with the group and to give her husband some clothes to take along.
The following morning Che was found dead on the dike near Son-Luu,
her chest pierced by a pistol bullet. Kinh was seriously wounded with
scimitar strikes at the wrist, on the shoulder, and on the face. He could
not name the attackers. In striking him, they only said: "We have just
assassinated the district chief. Now it is your turn." . . . Kinh had
been affiliated with the VNP. It is probable that the Hung-Hoa group
wanted him to join them for the attack, but they killed him when he
refused. (French Sûreté report of March 1, 1930, AOM-P-NF, 323-2626)

Having earlier done propaganda work among the native guards of the Hung-Hoa post, the VNP attack contingent had expected the guards' cooperation. Unknown to the attack force, however, the French had sent a fifty-troop reinforcement to the post the day before on the basis of an anonymous tip from a local source about a possible attack. As a major VNP leader in Son-Duong village and a participant in the Hung-Hoa attack, the school teacher Bang recounted the unfolding of events differently from the official French report:

[After we forced our entry into the yard in our assault on the Hung-Hoa post] from the second floor of the blockhouse, the enemy counterattacked. A rain of bullets began falling all around us. Donning a beige khaki uniform, a cap, a pair of sandals, and a banner across my shoulder saying "Revolutionary Armed Forces: Every Sacrifice for the Liberation of the Fatherland and the Vietnamese People," I rushed to the house of the commanding French officer with my scimitar. Breaking in the door, I saw only a frightened French woman in her pajamas. She cried and begged for her life. "Don't be afraid," I told her. "We are revolutionary soldiers. We are looking for your husband, the commanding officer; we respect the lives of women and children." The three of us, myself and two comrades, frantically and thoroughly searched the entire house for the officer. When we rushed across the yard to the two-story blockhouse to continue our search, we heard an order in French from the second floor to open more fire. There was the French second lieutenant, the post commander!

Bullets heavily rained down in the darkness around us, and we found no comrades at all in the area. I sensed immediately that something had gone wrong. We rushed toward the back and escaped through the gate at the corner of the vegetable garden. I knew by heart the nooks and crannies of the town of Hung-Hoa, having attended school there a number of years earlier. We rushed through the deserted streets in the darkness of the night and ran back to the river. It was indeed a miracle that none of us got hurt! Perhaps the Vietnamese soldiers, among whom we had done a lot of propaganda work, simply fired into the air as a warning to us.

Arriving at the river bank well past three o'clock, we found Xu Nhu and other comrades anxiously waiting there for the sampans to take them back across the river. . . . Upon seeing Xu Nhu, I raised my voice in anger: "Comrade Commander, why weren't we informed of your retreat order? The three of us were left behind! We would have been captured on the spot had it not been for our knowledge of the escape route!" Realizing his fault, Xu Nhu responded with momentary silence and changed the subject: "There are bright lights from the direction of Son-Tay. Our comrades are probably attacking the Chua-Thong outpost there." [It turned out not to be true.]

Reaching the other side of the river, we were informed of our next battle plan: we were all to move to the Lam-Thao district seat to reinforce our troops there and then all together on to the Phu-Tho provincial capital, where we would wait for our fighters to arrive on the afternoon train from Yen-Bay before launching the attack on the Phu-Tho military barracks. After the takeover of the Phu-Tho post, we would advance toward Son-Tay and the rest of the provinces in the Red River delta. . . . In the darkness of the night, as we passed through the village of Kinh-Ke on a shortcut route to Lam-Thao, *Xu* Nhu asked us: "Does the French hunting dog teacher Kinh live in this village?" Upon my nod, he gave the French-trained Syria veteran in our ranks the pistol and the execution order. . . . We left behind Kinh's body and the wailing cries of his wife and children, and it was almost dawn when we reached the fields of Son-Duong village. I was ordered to remain behind to mobilize the inhabitants to join the uprising.

Bang's narrative and the French reports may not fully reflect reality. The former VNP member, Kinh, may have simply been left for dead by the anticolonial forces. And the French woman whom Bang reported to have encountered may not have been the wife of the commanding officer of the Hung-Hoa post. But it is significant that Bang's narrative highlights his humanitarian voice in this encounter during the attack on the Hung-Hoa barrack, while ignoring the assassination of the former VNP member's wife reported in the French Sûreté account. Bang's selective discursive emphasis, like that in the French report, constitutes a part of the larger ideological struggle couched in the idiom of humanitarianism. However, the assassination of the former VNP member's wife is shadowed by the larger chain of events as Bang narrated them:

A few hours later [after the return to Son-Duong from Hung-Hoa], on the morning of the tenth, I received the first news of our victory at Lam-Thao. The revolutionary fighters had taken the district seat and captured the weapons of administrative guards, despite the escape of the district chief. I was told that thanks to the propaganda efforts of my young brother Tang and his friends, peasant women had happily brought to our fighters rice, meat, cakes, and soup; and the inhabitants of the surrounding villages had been coming to the district seat in large number to volunteer to join our ranks, shouting en route the slogan "long live the success of the Vietnamese revolution!" On learning the news, although exhausted by the lack of any sleep for several consecutive nights, I felt an intense euphoria. I rushed to all the corners of the village, calling for my fellow villagers to join our forces at Lam-Thao.

However, the good news did not last long. Within half an hour I was stunned when a young pupil rushed back to inform us that a company of Vietnamese and French soldiers led by the deputy résident and a French captain had counterattacked and that our fighters, after a valiant defense for over an hour with small arms, had had to retreat and disperse because they were outnumbered and outgunned. I was also told that the veteran of Syria in our ranks had been wounded in the leg and that our soldiers were then trying to regroup to move on to the provincial capital.

The news that Bang had received of the development in the Lam-Thao district seat was essentially correct. The attack troops had not only captured arms from the administrative guards, but they had also set fire to the residence of the hated and corrupt district chief and raised their own flag on the main gate of the district administration building. It was Bang's adolescent brother who had read the revolutionary army's proclamation of victory in the district seat. However, the victory was short-lived. Under the daylight counterattack by a detachment of twenty native guards led by the Phu-Tho deputy *résident* (the de facto deputy province chief), the VNP forces had to make a full retreat. *Xu* Nhu was seriously wounded and reportedly attempted suicide several times, succeeding only on his third attempt (Co-Nhi-Tan 1969:103–104; Hoang-Pham-Tran 1949:96–97).

Bang continued recounting his agony as the events unfolded:

It was an endless and agonizing period of waiting for further news. . . . During the day [February 10, 1930], a villager returned from Yen-Bay to ask for further instructions: "Our revolutionary fighters have overrun the base of the Yen-Bay battalion of colonial infantry and captured all the weapons. [The front commander] has sent me back to report and to ask for further instructions from *Xu* Nhu for the next moves. . . ." I cut him short: "[The front commanders] know in advance all our battle plans. They also have the full authority to proceed in response to local developments. Why did they need to send you back for further instructions?" I was dumbfounded by his request and became highly suspicious of him. . . . It took me more than a few moments to decide what to do under the circumstances, as *Xu* Nhu had not returned from Lam-Thao. The situation, however, was too critical for me not to reveal to him the insurrection plan that had been approved at the last party strategy meeting.

(1) All party members, soldiers, and volunteers from the civilian population would gather to hear the key points of the revolutionary program from the front leaders and to receive instructions on the immediate steps to be undertaken; (2) they would organize a military command comprising both officers and political commissars; and (3) the revolutionary forces would be divided into three groups, each of which would be at least of company size (250 fighters). The first group would advance toward Lao-Kay and the Vietnam-China frontier to seize all the outposts and open the way for the return of revolutionaries currently taking refuge in south China. The second company would proceed to Phu-Tho and from there to the provinces farther south in the delta. The third would defend Yen-Bay. One platoon would be assigned to patrol and maintain order in the town [of Yen-Bay] and the surrounding areas. The defenders of Yen-Bay must occupy the railway station, dig trenches along the rail line in order to block and eliminate the counterattacking French forces, and establish anti-aircraft gun positions on the surrounding hills. A propaganda team would be attached to each company in order to mobilize the populace for the uprising.

As the messenger and fellow villager indicated the desire to return to Yen-Bay right away with the instructions, I hastily noted down the details for him, gave him several piasters for travel expenses, and told him to hurry away. Glimmers of light and hope disappeared as night fell. My young brother Tang and other villagers had not returned. Bad news began to arrive from neighboring villages: many of their members in the unit attacking Lam-Thao had been arrested and taken to Hung-Hoa. Xu Nhu had been wounded and taken away with them. I could hardly sleep that seemingly endless night.

The major uprising in Yen-Bay had not unfolded smoothly either, despite the active cooperation of many Vietnamese soldiers in the colonial infantry battalion. The anticolonial forces did succeed initially in seizing the arms warehouse, and they caused the French numerous casualties among their twenty-nine officers and warrant officers. That night they proclaimed victory. The yellow-and-red pennants of their revolutionary army waved over the barracks, while white-and-red revolutionary flags were raised at the district seat. The leaders of the insurrection also sent a patrol into the town to invite the populace to join them in the uprising, claiming that all the French officers and warrant officers had been killed. The colonial armed forces in Yen-Bay, however, were far from united in their support for the insurrection. In contrast to the colonial infantry, the native guards did not join the uprising. The latter even gathered to defend French civilians and the main

administrative building in the provincial capital. Having failed to gain
the support of native guards, the revolutionary fighters did not proceed
to seize the train station and other major provincial buildings as previously planned (AOM-P-NF, 323-2626). Toward daybreak a small number of colonial infantry soldiers managed to report to their French commanders in the still French-controlled upper barracks, claiming earlier
coercion by the revolutionary forces. As the revolutionary forces had
forgotten to cut the telegraph line, a reconnaissance plane was sent in
from Hanoi in response to reports from Yen-Bay, and the French counterattack began at daybreak. Once firing began from a French airplane,
according to one revolutionary participant from Phu-Tho (Nguyen-
Hai-Ham 1970), the revolutionary forces quickly retreated. The French
reports also mention that the fighters fled after only two shots from the
counterattacking forces (Wintrebert report, AOM-P-NF, 323-2626;
cf. Sûreté report 2967/s, AOM-AP-I, 7F-57). The most important
attack in the VNP insurrection scheme quickly turned into a rout.
Although the uprising had been prepared with some care, the Vietnamese Nationalist Party leadership had apparently not planned for unexpected developments.

It is not surprising that the VNP armed movement in the rest of the
Red River delta fizzled out in the face of subsequent tight French security measures throughout Tonkin (North Vietnam), particularly in the
provinces along the route to Hanoi from the Chinese province of Yunnan. A curfew was imposed in Hanoi for twelve days. The isolated
bombing incidents in Hanoi on February 10, 1930, did not succeed in
preventing the colonial authorities from sending French troop rein-
forcements to Phu-Tho and the neighboring provinces of Yen-Bay,
Son-Tay, and Tuyen-Quang. French and legionnaire troops were also
sent to the previously all-Vietnamese garrisons at Sept-Pagodes, Phu-
Lang-Thuong, as well as to the potentially troublesome provinces of
Hai-Duong, Nam-Dinh, and Kien-An (Robin report 1930, 14–16,
AOM-P-NF, 323-2626). Many VNP suspects, both within and outside
the colonial armed forces, were arrested in the provinces of Hai-Duong
and Bac-Ninh.

These moves by the colonial government notwithstanding, six days
after the Yen-Bay and Phu-Tho incidents, the VNP leadership mounted
a last-ditch challenge to the French in two districts on the boundaries
of Hai-Duong and Thai-Binh provinces. In Thai-Binh a hundred-

strong VNP force led by a village school teacher and a deputy canton chief attacked the district seat of Phu-Duc. Many fighters disguised themselves in the uniforms of the colonial infantry. The local administrative guards were taken in by the ruse, and the revolutionary forces subsequently destroyed the Phu-Duc post, wounded three guards and one of the district chief's daughters, and captured the district guards' rifles. A similar attack took place in the neighboring district of Vinh-Bao (Hai-Duong province) on the same night. After killing the district chief, the VNP forces occupied Vinh-Bao for one day before being dislodged to Co-Am, a village well known for its strong tradition of Confucian scholarship and civil service. The village was subsequently bombed at the order of the French Résident supérieur for Tonkin (Robin report 1930, 20, and police report, AOM-P-NF, 323-2626). As a warning to the rest of the Vietnamese population, the French Résident supérieur ordered French provincial chiefs to give maximum publicity to the Co-Am bombing (ibid., 20). A two-hundred-man native guard column was sent in for a mopping-up operation, moving gradually from the Phu-Duc–Vinh-Bao region to the provinces of Kien-An, Bac-Ninh, Son-Tay, and Yen-Bay (Robin 1930, 21–22, AOM-P-NF, 323-2626). By 21 February all the VNP front commanders had been arrested, including party president Nguyen Thai Hoc himself.

The village of Son-Duong was not spared the French punitive measures in the aftermath of the VNP insurrection. Damages were reported in the village president's letter to the newspaper *Le petit parisien*. The letter was fully couched in the colonialist rhetorical discourse to invoke the sympathy of readers among the colonial masters:

> Dear Sir:
>     I hope that for the sake of all of us and of our unfortunate families, you will represent France and respond to my request as the president of the village of Son-Duong, Lam-Thao district, province of Phu-Tho (Tonkin), in order to conduct an investigation [into the French burning of Son-Duong houses]. Of the sixty-nine homeowners [in Son-Duong] whose properties were burnt down in a punitive measure [by the colonial government], only five deserved the punishment for having participated in the revolt. . . . Dau, Toai, Tin, Sy, Tin. The rest were innocent victims who [unfortunately] lost their homes. . . . Please imagine our misfortune when, instead of finding our houses, we found

only embers and ashes. . . . The fire destroyed everything we had: not only our houses, but also all our belongings, cereals, objects, clothes, and even our sacred ancestral altars. We could not save anything because, before the disaster bell tolled, we had to line up two by two, men and women, the young and the elderly, at the end of the village under the command of armed soldiers. We had to face two machine guns that forced us to remain silent. . . . But that was not the end. Despite our misery and our pain, and besides the two-hundred-piaster penalty, we were required to carry our bamboo to the district seat and to reconstruct the buildings destroyed by the revolutionaries as well as to deliver bamboo to the provincial capital at a distance of sixteen kilometers. The magnitude of our misfortune could hardly be greater, because our poor village lost considerably with this cruel punishment, more than Xuan-Lung, Cao-Mai, Kinh-Ke, Phung-Nguyen, La-Hao, Vong-La.

Not knowing how to make the mother country understand all our misfortunes at [such a great] distance, we trust and beg you, Sir, to kindly help the weak like ourselves see the light of French justice. . . .

May these lines prove to the Mother Country our loyalty, of which the living proof is our more than twenty foreign-war veterans [Vietnamese fighting for France in Europe during World War I] who nonetheless lost their houses for no understandable reasons.

May our grievances lead to your assistance and to redress for the unjustly big losses imposed upon us without any pity, losses similar to those that the Chinese pirates caused to our ancestors in a still memorable past era. May our poor peasants with their pitiful earnings benefit from the kindness of the noble maternal France, which undoubtedly did not order the imposition of those terrible punishments [upon us]. . . .

President of the village of Son-Duong

I could not ascertain from oral historical or archival sources whether Son-Duong had as many as twenty foreign-war veterans, if any at all, returning from World War I in Europe. However, the village president clearly hoped that the adoption of the dominant discursive practice of a "noble maternal France" would signify the acceptance of the colonial masters' ideological hegemony and invoke their sympathy for the submissive colonized subjects. The letter was enclosed with a receipt from the French Résident in Phu-Tho for two hundred piasters as a "contribution to the expenses incurred by the rebellion in which certain members of the village have participated" (Viollis 1935:204–206).

It was not entirely unpredictable that the Yen-Bay insurrection would fail, although the magnitude of the revolt did catch the French by surprise. In contrast to the first wave of Vietnamese anticolonial resistance against the French at the end of the nineteenth century and the Communist-led armed movements in both 1930–1931 and 1946–1975 (to be discussed in depth), the VNP leadership relied on a quick-strike strategy for seizing urban centers. Facing an enemy with overwhelmingly superior arms, the VNP leadership neither prepared for protracted guerilla warfare in the countryside nor systematically cultivated strong rural support among the indigenous masses as a precondition for such a strategy.

Moreover, the colonial government had received signals of a coordinated armed uprising in Tonkin. They ranged from the reports from a high-ranking VNP informer in late 1929 to numerous and large discoveries of tracts, bombs, and other weapons from October 1929 to January 1930 in different Tonkinese locations. The invaluable informer was in fact the head of military affairs on the VNP central committee.[5] Questions had been raised about the loyalty of native troops in the colonial forces in Hanoi and Nam-Dinh and the possibility of breaking up Vietnamese units or transferring them to more remote regions of North Vietnam had been discussed (Robin report 1930, 46–55, 66–67, AOM-P-NF, 323-2626). A number of Vietnamese warrant officers in the Tonkinese colonial forces had been arrested or transferred in 1929, and such moves within the colonial infantry had weakened the party structure in the armed forces. Arrests of other VNP members in 1929 had also shattered the VNP infrastructure in many Tonkin provinces.[6] With the active participation of the same high-ranking informer on the VNP central committee, the colonial authorities had come close to arresting the entire top VNP leadership at a December 25, 1929, meeting in the Phu-Tho village of Vong-La, not too far from Son-Duong. Although the informer's collaboration with the French had been exposed by this arrest attempt, the colonial authorities still received sufficient information in two northern provinces about an insurrection plan around Vietnamese New Year (early February 1930). They had ordered provincial chiefs and military commanders to be on the alert throughout the New Year period and emphasized the need for close collaboration between military and civilian authorities in order to suppress revolutionary propaganda among the troops.[7] In the province of Phu-Tho, tipped off by a written warning of an impending attack on the town of Hung-Hoa, colonial authorities had responded with a troop reinforcement in the town. Unknown to the local VNP command, fifty additional native guards had been ordered to the Hung-Hoa post on the eve of the uprising (Sûreté report of March 1, 1930, AOM-P-NF, 323-2626).

The French crackdown and precautionary measures on the eve of the Yen-Bay uprising disrupted the VNP leadership's insurrection plan. The party president's order to postpone the uprising by five days arrived in the village of Son-Duong only after the departure of many villagers for Yen-Bay. In the end, the colonial government regained control of Yen-Bay in less than half a day.

From a historical perspective, however, the significance of the Yen-Bay insurrection transcends the series of events in February 1930. The uprising and the local popular support for it in the fertile agricultural district of Lam-Thao and in Phu-Tho in general were far from isolated developments. For most of the period since the official establishment of French colonial power in the north and the center (Tonkin and Annam) in 1883, anticolonial resistance had simmered in this long-settled area of northern Vietnam. The "pax colonia" and the history of Western capitalist expansion in this part of the country were punctuated by eruptions of armed unrest—the first wave in 1884–1893; the second, a relatively minor one during World War I; the third under VNP leadership in 1930; and finally, the most serious one, from 1941 until the violent end of French colonialism in 1954.

The first anticolonial movement in the Phu-Tho area followed the fall of the Son-Tay citadel in December 1883, a fall which seems to have left the populace with a bitter taste of the Western encounter and to have consequently strengthened their resolve of resistance. The French attack on Son-Tay took place in the aftermath of the Harmand convention of August 1883, which ceded Tonkin to the French as a protectorate and effectively gave the colonial regime access to the vast Chinese market from the south (see Truong-Buu-Lam 1968:16–23). This treaty notwithstanding, Tonkin was far from secure, and French control was limited to a number of areas in the Red River delta.

The province of Son-Tay, which at this time included the district of

Lam-Thao and the village of Son-Duong, had long served as a base for Black Flag troops to harass and attack French forces near Hanoi (Marr 1971:41–43). Black Flag soldiers came from the ranks of the troops in the Taiping movement who had sought refuge in north Vietnam following the defeat of the movement in China in 1865. They maintained a de facto control of the region along the Sino-Vietnamese border. Enlisting their services, the Hue court appointed the Black Flag leader ranking military commander of the provinces of Son-Tay, Hung-Hoa, and Tuyen-Quang in 1880. In addition to the Black Flag troops, since late 1881 regular Chinese government troops had been crossing the border into Vietnam in response to the Western threat to a country under Chinese suzerainty.

In December 1883, in order to reduce the military threat to French forces in the Hanoi area, the French mobilized 5500 troops for the assault on the Vaunbanesque Son-Tay citadel. Although Black Flag forces mounted a valiant defense of the citadel, suffering an estimated 1000 casualties and inflicting 403 casualties on the French-commanded troops during the course of the armed conflict, the citadel fell on the third day to the technologically superior invading troops (McAleavy 1968:26–27; Tran-Trong-Kim 1964:537; Scott 1885:86). The French victory terrorized the Vietnamese population, as reported by a British journalist in Tonkin at the time:

> That was a terrible night in Sontay. The Turcos [in the French foreign legionnaire troops] had entered, with comparatively little opposition, by the eastern gate, and they admittedly killed men, women, and children—every living thing they came across. The French troops were not so bad, but the butchery of Chinamen and cropped-headed Annamese [under the Vietnamese governor general's command] . . . was sickening. . . .
>
> Even so late as May 1884 . . . most of the houses remained gutted and empty. . . . Liu Jung-fu [or Luu-Vinh-Phuc, Black Flag troop commander] carried off all the inhabitants, so say the French, but the Chinese say the French killed them all. Women are very scarce in Sontay still, and that can be said of no other post where the French are in Tongking. The sacking of the place was a terrible affliction, which the Tongkinese will not forget readily.                    (Scott 1885:85–86)

With the fall of the Son-Tay citadel, Black Flag troops temporarily withdrew to the citadel of Hung-Hoa, across the river from the village of Son-Duong. In direct violation of orders from the conciliatory and resigning Hue court, a ranking Son-Tay official, Treasury Director Nguyen van Giap, like quite a few other Vietnamese mandarins, retreated to the district of Lam-Thao, where he set up two major anticolonial guerilla bases in Thanh-Mai and Thach-Son. Both villages neighbor on the Lam-Thao district seat and are situated at a distance of five kilometers from the village of Son-Duong (Le-Tuong and Vu-Kim-Bien 1981:113–114). An anti-French mandarin appealed to the populace:

> The provincial citadel [of Son-Tay] has been lost, and it becomes increasingly painful for us to receive the orders,
> The garrisons have been withdrawn and the imperial edicts reach us in bitterness.
> The French plots are indeed fearful. They are like silkworms gnawing at the mulberry leaves.
> Luong van Dat [a petty officer] was a God-cursed traitor who acted like a worm in one's bones. He delivered the citadel to the enemy.
> Because of that, the situation now is almost desperate and the country disintegrates.
> Because the court's officials were cowards and excessively anxious to save their lives, they hurriedly surrendered to the enemy.
> Given that advantage, the enemy now moves freely and kills our people with impunity,
> But people like us must try to preserve the country in which we live. Shall we just stare at our decay? . . .
> Since we are determined not to live with the enemy, we shall not be deterred by their overwhelmingly superior forces,
> Since we believe that success rests upon the people's will, we shall not fret over our futile efforts.  (translated in Truong-Buu-Lam 1967:113–115)

Despite the small odds for success, anticolonial support among the population seems to have been partly sustained by the native sociocultural logic that places greater emphasis on effort than on short-term consequences, as seen in the last phrase of the appeal. The achievements of native actors were measured in terms of the moral nobility of their acts as much as on the basis of concrete results.

After seizing the Bac-Ninh citadel in March 1884, the French turned their attention to Hung-Hoa and began a campaign to consolidate control of mountainous regions close to the Sino-Vietnamese border. On April 5, 1884, eight thousand troops advanced toward Hung-Hoa.

Although they encountered some resistance at the conjuncture of the Red and Black rivers, the French troops moved steadily upstream with few casualties. The Vietnamese governor of Hung-Hoa (Nguyen Quang Bich) and Black Flag commanders seem to have ordered the harassment of French troops only in order to buy time for the organization of their retreat: the citadel was burnt and abandoned on April 12 with practically no resistance (Scott 1885:176–185; McAleavy 1968: 231–232; cf. Le-Tuong and Vu-Kim-Bien 1981:114). The surrounding countryside, including the other side of the river where Son-Duong is located, was virtually depopulated, possibly because the retreating troops had drafted able-bodied men to carry weapons from the citadel but most probably because the reported Son-Tay massacre had frightened the peasant population in this part of the country (McAleavy 1968; cf. Scott 1885:185). Part of the Black Flag force withdrew toward Lam-Thao. Bich moved to the hilly area on the other side of the Red River, near the boundaries of Cam-Khe, Ha-Hoa, and Yen-Lap districts, to lead the guerilla resistance in coordination with Giap in Lam-Thao.

The village of Son-Duong was located precisely on the route of attack and counterattack between the French-controlled town of Hung-Hoa and the major guerila base of Thanh-Mai in Lam-Thao (see Kieu-Huu-Hy et al. 1961:9; Dang-Huy-Van 1967:48–49). As the French attempted to seize control of the rest of Tonkin and Chinese troops and Vietnamese guerillas counterattacked the invading forces, this area of northern Vietnam to the Vietnam-China border became a major battle zone. In November 1884, for example, Chinese government and Black Flag troops began moving from northern Phu-Tho and Yen-Bay to encircle the French-controlled Tuyen-Quang citadel for a three-and-a-half-month siege. The more mountainous districts of Hung-Hoa (Tran-Yen, Van-Chan, Yen-Lap) and Son-Tay (Ha-Hoa and Thanh-Ba) fell back under the control of anti-French forces (Dang-Huy-Van 1967:48). In March 1885, as Chinese troops from Kwangsi defeated a French force 35,000-strong in Lang-Son, Black Flag troops and Vietnamese guerillas also intensified their attacks in the Lam-Thao area and four other agriculturally fertile districts of Son-Tay province (Dang-Huy-Van 1967:48–49).[8]

It was at this juncture in early April 1885 (the twenty-fifth day of the second lunar month) that, according to oral historical sources in

Son-Duong, three hundred villagers were massacred. The disaster became a part of the village's collective memory, and a ceremony to commemorate the deaths of villagers' ancestors was added to the village's annual ritual calendar. The exact circumstances of this major disaster to Son-Duong, however, remain shrouded in mystery. Village oral history speaks of an attack by Chinese Black Flag troops whom a major anti-French leader in Lam-Thao district, *Lanh* Mai, had successfully enlisted to eliminate the Son-Duong guerilla leader, *Doi* Bon, supposedly a follower of yet another anti-French leader, *De* Kieu. *Doi* Bon was reportedly killed in this 1885 Chinese attack (Son-Duong 1987:12). However, a different historical source lists *Doi* Bon as a local guerilla leader during the second period of anti-French activity into the early 1890s (Le-Tuong and Vu-Kim-Bien 1981:119–120). In any case, Son-Duong was clearly under the control of the anticolonial resistance when the entire district of Lam-Thao fell into Vietnamese and Chinese (Black Flag) hands in May 1885. From this base and from the other side of the Red River, guerilla forces intensified their attacks on other districts, seizing the strategically located town of Viet-Tri and the districts of Bat-Bat and Quang-Oai, and destroying the French military post in Hung-Hoa in May and June of the same year (Dang-Huy-Van 1967:49).

The anticolonial resistance in the Lam-Thao area in particular and in northern Vietnam in general took a major turn in the summer of 1885. In July 1885 King Ham-Nghi fled the capital at Hue and issued an anticolonial "Aid-the-King" edict to his subjects.[9] As the historian Truong-Buu-Lam has remarked, "The edict . . . was warmly received by the population and immediately set in motion the strongest resistance the French had encountered since they first set foot on Vietnamese soil." (Truong-Buu-Lam 1968:25). In terms of the relationship between the court and the population, the royal edict lent legitimacy to the resistance movement: "Royal sanction was thus squarely behind popular resistance—too late for any temporal success, but still of great importance in sustaining resistance through its most barren years. With the flight of the monarch, indignation could no longer turn against him and therefore focused increasingly on the French" (Marr 1971:51). One month earlier Chinese government troops had begun withdrawing from Vietnam following the Franco-Chinese Tientsin agreement, according to which China recognized Vietnam as a French colony and protectorate in exchange for an end to French attacks on Taiwan and other points along the Chinese coast. The Vietnamese anti-colonial movement thus became strongly rooted in the indigenous soil, relying primarily on the local population for support. Its leadership was provided primarily by Confucian literati: of the thirty-four prominent leaders whose biographical data were available, twenty-two were former mandarins, and eight others were Confucian degree holders (Tran-Huy-Lieu, Van-Tao, and Nguyen-Khac-Dam 1957:70–82).

At this point in 1885 the Hung-Hoa area became the liaison center for the anticolonial movement in the north, as the fugitive monarch bestowed on the Hung-Hoa-region guerilla commander, former governor Nguyen Quang Bich, the titles of minister of rite (including foreign affairs), marquis, and deputy troop commander of Tonkin.[10] The countryside in which the village of Son-Duong is located thus constituted a major northern base in the first wave of Vietnamese anticolonialism (1883–1896), with links to the Aid-the-King headquarters in Thanh-Hoa province through the hilly Muong country of Hoa-Binh.[11]

It is not surprising, then, that the area around Son-Duong became a point of concentration for French military power. In October 1885 the French mobilized six thousand troops armed with cannons to attack the guerilla base at nearby Thanh Mai (Le-Tuong and Vu-Kim-Bien 1981:116). Clearly overwhelmed in number and firearms, the guerillas had to retreat to the other side of the Red River and farther upland. Military posts were set up by the French in many locations. However, taking advantage of the difficult but familiar terrain and the strong support of the local population, the guerilla forces selectively attacked administrative seats and military posts throughout the province and temporarily dispersed into the surrounding hills whenever they encountered overwhelming enemy forces. The anticolonial resistance made maximal use of a strategy of guerilla warfare in which they relied on their own mobility in the midland hills as well as the peasants' food supply and intelligence for tactical advantages. At the same time guerilla forces arrested and even executed certain French-collaborating mandarins and local officials (ibid.:117–119). Some district chiefs sought refuge in the military posts. It was a classic guerilla war that prefigured the strategy of the Communist-led armed movement against the French and American forces from 1930 to 1975.

At the end of 1888 a newly emerging commander from the ranks of

Giap's staff, *Doc* Ngu (General Ngu), and other guerilla commanders
began a successful strategy of bolder attacks on French forces in the
Hung-Hoa area. The Lam-Thao district seat was sacked on December
30 and 31, 1888. Son-Duong was reported to be one of the three main
anticolonial bases in the district, the other two being the neighboring
village of Ngu-Xa and the traditional base of Thanh-Mai (ibid.:120).
Approximately one year later, in late 1889, all of the administrative and
military staff members in the Lam-Thao district seat joined the anticolonial movement and took their arms to a guerilla base in Thanh-Ba district (ibid.:119). According to a French Catholic priest, in 1889 "the
rebels became stronger and more numerous [in Hung-Hoa and Son-
Tay]. In the districts of Quang-Oai, Lam-Thao, Bat-Bat, Tam-Nong,
An-Lac, Cam-Khe, Son-Vi, Ha-Hoa, and Thanh-Ba, rebel groups
roamed freely at night and occasionally even during the day. . . . I
would say that in these districts, the rebels have more control than the
protectorate government forces do. The authority of the protectorate
government is more formal than real" (Puginier, quoted in Dang-Huy-
Van 1967:49–50). Another observer remarked that "in all the villages
there exist two mayors, one with real power and collecting taxes for
the rebels; the other a puppet mayor, an official working for the French
government and lying to the latter from dawn to dusk" (Girod,
quoted in ibid.:50). A French native guard commander in the Hung-
Hoa area remarked: "Everywhere that we have passed, and no matter
how much good will our own chiefs have, we have actually left regrettable traces of our passage. A house destroyed? A buffalo disappearing?
As soon as we have left, *De* Kieu [the major guerilla commander mentioned earlier] has sent the peasant a buffalo or money equivalent to the
price of the house" (Pouvourville 1892:10). *De* Kieu reportedly also
maintained strict discipline among his troops and meted out harsh punishments, including execution, to troops pillaging the property of non-
hostile populations (ibid.:14).

By mid-1890 conditions had deteriorated for the French in Lam-
Thao district. French military posts were set up only along the rivers,
and there existed no civil guard posts in the central part of the district
(April 30, 1890, report of the French Résident in Hung-Hoa, AOM-
AP-RST, 27-656). Many villages were reportedly abandoned with land
having lain fallow for up to three years, although the exact reasons for
this abandonment were not clear (May 5, and July 31, 1890 reports of

the French résident AOM-AP-RST, 27-656). Guerilla troops in the district were estimated at three to four hundred. The French chief administrator for Son-Tay province commented specifically on Lam-Thao district in a report to Hanoi: "I am convinced that many canton chiefs and village mayors are accomplices to the pirates [guerillas]. I suspect [the complicity of] even certain higher-ranked Vietnamese authorities. I have ordered the surveillance of many" (April 1890 report, AOM-AP-RST, 27-656). After a temporary calm in July 1890, guerilla activities intensified again in the fall. The same administrator described guerilla troops as numerous, well organized, well disciplined, and roaming the area with impunity (Oct. 14, 1890, report, AOM-AP-RST, 27-656). At one point numbering as many as twelve hundred in the Hung-Hoa and Lam-Thao area, the guerilla force was armed with modern weapons and hundreds of thousands of bullets, either purchased in China or seized from French forces (Pouvourville 1892:72–73; Pouvourville 1923:317). In October 1890 they even successfully attacked the major Son-Tay citadel and released a large number of their imprisoned comrades (Dang-Huy-Van 1967:53; Le-Tuong and Vu-Kim-Bien 1981:121). Three months later they attacked the provincial capital of Hoa-Binh and seized a large amount of ammunition (Le-Tuong and Vu-Kim-Bien 1981:121). Defeats of French forces along the Red and Black rivers in this period from 1889 to 1893 were numerous and substantial (Dang-Huy-Van 1967:51–55; Le-Tuong and Vu-Kim-Bien 1981:119–124). The resistance movement reportedly gained the collaboration of certain high-ranking Vietnamese mandarins, such as the district chief of Cam-Khe and the second-ranked official in Son-Tay province (Dang-Huy-Van 1967:50). To "pacify" the country the colonial regime had to station a regiment of native guards in the town of Viet-Tri in 1890 and one company of the elite marine forces in nearby Doan-Hung district from 1891 onward (Le-Tuong and Vu-Kim-Bien 1981:124).

In order to force guerilla leaders to surrender and to pressure their villages into delivering them to the colonial authorities, the French ordered the arrest of their families, the seizure of their property, the removal of the sacred bones of their ancestors from ancestral graves, and the arrest of key notables (Oct. 28, 1890, report, AOM-AP-RST, 27-656). They also attempted to divide anticolonial forces along ethnic lines, pitting ethnic Muong against Vietnamese, and to gain the alliance of local officials. However, it was not until the 1893 assassination of *Doc* Ngu and the surrender that same year of *De* Kieu, the guerilla leader and a big landlord in Cam-Khe district on the other side of the Red River, that the French regained control of the area of the future province of Phu-Tho (Le-Tuong 1967:54).

The end of the guerilla movement in Phu-Tho in 1893 marked the virtual completion of the French pacification campaign in Tonkin. It brought to a close the nineteenth-century spontaneous resistance to the French invasion in north Vietnam—a resistance that grew out of patriotism, monarchical loyalty, and attachment to tradition. The remaining incidents of resistance involved the *De* Tham movement, which, until 1913, militarily harassed the French all the way from the hilly Yen-The area to the neighboring provinces of Phuc-Yen and Vinh-Yen (later merged with Phu-Tho into Vinh-Phu). This movement combined elements of patriotism and defense of tradition with a Robin Hood–type redress of social grievances (Truong-Buu-Lam 1967:27–28; Marr 1971:73–75; Le-Tuong and Vu-Kim-Bien 1981:141–144). However, it was not of such a magnitude as to prevent the colonial regime from turning its attention to the consolidation of political control and the development of capitalism in the land.

The French Indochinese Union was formed in 1887, including Tonkin (North Vietnam), Annam (Central Vietnam), Cochinchina (South Vietnam), and Cambodia, to which Laos was added in 1899. Cochinchina was a direct French colony headed by a French governor. In the four other parts of the union, nominally French protectorates, the French appointed *résidents supérieurs.* For easier military and political control of the largely mountainous and strongly resistant Hung-Hoa province, the colonial regime divided the territory west of the Red River into smaller provinces: Hoa-Binh (ethnic Muong province, 1886), Son-La (1895 [1886]), Yen-Bay (1900), Lao-Cay (1907 [1886]), and Lai-Chau (1909) (Vu-van-Tinh 1970b:60–63; Vu-van-Tinh 1970a: 44).[12] The new province of Hung-Hoa was formed from the remaining provincial territory together with Lam-Thao district of Son-Tay province (merged in September 1891) and most of Doan-Hung district of Tuyen-Quang (merged in 1895). Its capital was moved in 1903 to the town of Phu-Tho, situated over sixty miles from Hanoi on the strategic Hanoi-Yunnan railway, which the French had constructed to facilitate the movement of goods onto the southern Chinese market and the movement of troops into the northwestern frontiers of North Vietnam. The province itself was also renamed Phu-Tho in 1904. Like other northern provinces, it was headed by a French *résident* and supported by a French provincial staff, French commanders of the native guards, and Vietnamese mandarins, including a nominal governor, a provincial native court judge, and district chiefs. Sustained partly by alternating the myth of the French civilizing mission and that of French-Vietnamese coexistence (*huyen thoai khai hoa* and *huyen thoai Phap Viet de hue;* see Nguyen-van-Trung 1963), the colonial system was also maintained by the use of a combination of naked coercive power and rewards to the collaborators who constituted the majority of the native intelligentsia.

Parallel to the consolidation of political control was the development of a colonial economic policy that created conditions favorable to the capitalist exploitation of land, labor, and other natural resources, and that compounded the problems faced by peasants in maintaining their livelihoods. Specific colonial measures in Indochina included the introduction of direct and indirect taxation and the conversion of tax payments from kind to cash in order to facilitate capitalist growth, the concession of indigenous land to colonial settlers for the development of major cash crops, the appropriation of labor through a corvée system, and the introduction of repressive labor laws to hold down labor costs for capitalist agromineral ventures.

In the province of Phu-Tho the capitalist sector of the economy consisted primarily of French tea and paint plantations in the hilly parts of the province, a tea-processing plant in Phu-Ho, and a small pulp mill in Viet-Tri. The plantations were set up on land conceded to French settlers and Vietnamese collaborators—concessions amounting to 10,969 hectares, or approximately 22 percent of the province's cultivable land in the 1930s (Pham-Xuan-Do 1939:62–63; Henry 1932:23). In the late 1930s, Phu-Tho annually exported 1,100 tonnes of paint to China and Japan (Pham–Xuan-Do 1939:69). The province also exported 900 tonnes of dried tea a year to France, North Africa, and the New World (ibid.). By 1931 the concessions of indigenous land in Vietnam to European settlers alone amounted to 890,000 hectares—approximately 19 percent of cultivable acreage at the time (see table 1).

The land concessions for capitalist agricultural development involved a labor-intensive capital accumulation with a most limited capital rein-

**Table 1. European land concessions in colonial Vietnam (in thousands of hectares)**

|  | CULTIVABLE LAND | LAND OCCUPIED BY CONCESSIONS | PART OF CONCESSION LAND ACTUALLY CULTIVATED |
|---|---|---|---|
| Tonkin | 1200 | 120 (10%) | 30 |
| Annam | 1000 | 170 (17%) | 25 |
| Cochinchina | 2400 | 600 (25%) | 300 |
| Total | 4600 | 890 (19%) | 355 |

*Source:* J. Chesneaux, reprinted in Murray 1980:66.

vestment in the local economy. In Phu-Tho, for example, despite the importance of tea as an export commodity, tea pressing and drying machines were not introduced until 1938 (Le-Tuong and Vu-Kim-Bien 1981:131). Although land in the village of Son-Duong, unlike many other villages in the province and in the midland region of North Vietnam, was not appropriated for colonial exploitation, the colonial system did adversely affect the lives of many poor villagers through the French requirement of tax payments in cash and a significant increase in both direct and indirect taxes.[13]

With respect to direct taxes, within the three decades from the end of the nineteenth century to the mid-1920s, poll taxes quintupled to 2.5 piasters for both property owners (de jure) and landless male laborers (de facto). However, the price of first-class rice increased only 200 to 300 percent in this period (August 1898 and August 1900 reports of Hung-Hoa Résident, AOM-AP-RST, 27-664; *Bulletin économique de l'Indochine*). More significantly, the precolonial tax exemption and reduction in cases of natural calamity were no longer granted. Additional charges were imposed to finance cantonal schools and public works. Even in the province of Phu-Tho, where skilled agricultural laborers commanded wages four times higher than in overpopulated Thai-Binh province of the lower delta, the poll tax inflicted serious hardships on many poor families in periods of crop losses or low rice prices. Its adverse impact on the lives of the village poor is probably best highlighted by the case of a Son-Duong villager, the old lady Thanh, whose labor her father had to mortgage for five piasters to make the poll tax payment in 1918:

My family conditions were very difficult in those days [in my youth], especially during the tax season. The poll tax for a man, starting at the age of eighteen, amounted to three piasters, equivalent to the purchase price of a thatch hut—an amount we could not count on our relatives for much help with. It was because of the need for money to pay my father's poll tax that my parents had to mortgage my labor for five piasters to a wealthy relative, the owner of eleven *mau* of rice fields. I ended up working for this relative for twelve years.

Although many major direct tax increases had been introduced by 1910, between 1911 and 1930 the colonial state's direct tax revenues in Tonkin still increased by 109 percent, in comparison with 115 percent and 130 percent respectively for Annam and Cochinchina.

The colonial government also introduced indirect taxes through its opium, alcohol, and salt monopolies in order to increase its revenue. Monthly and quarterly reports from the French Résident in Phu-Tho in the first decade of the century meticulously discussed the quantities of opium and alcohol sold through the government monopolies. The fines imposed on villages for any discovery of moonshine on their territories were at one point so stiff that, short of cash, they had to deliver oxen and buffalo to provincial offices (November 1899 report from the Résident of Hung-Hoa, AOM-AP-RST, 27-664). In the early days of the colonial establishment, the overwhelming majority of local court cases involved moonshining and opium smuggling: eighty-four of the ninety-eight court verdicts in 1905, for example, involved infringements on government monopolies (1905 report from the Résident of Hung-Hoa, AOM-AP-RST, 27-664). In 1907, after a 25 percent decline over the previous year in the sale of monopolized alcohol, the provincial administration actually considered instituting a forced consumption measure based on the number of adult male villagers. The French Résident in Phu-Tho discussed in great depth, in October 1910, his efforts to promote the sale of monopoly alcohol:

> In my meetings with district and canton chiefs and with village authorities, I have attempted to make the populace understand its own advantages from the new sale regime that is to be rigorously put into effect next January. I have repeated numerous times [to the native population] that they have an interest in not stopping through smuggling the flow of this indispensable revenue source to the protectorate [government]—the [very] revenue that has allowed the government to

undertake large hydraulic projects to enrich the country. However, one cannot hide the reality that smugglers will continue to be active so long as the moonshine is sold to consumers at a price lower than that offered by the monopoly and so long as consumers seem to prefer the taste of the moonshine to that of the alcohol on sale by the administration. . . .

I reproduce in their entirety the instructions that I gave to the provincial authorities on March 25, 1909, soon after I assumed this office:

> The Compagnie générale [government monopoly] has informed me that the alcohol sale figure in Phu-Tho leaves much to be desired. Smuggling is quite active. The instructions that I have recently received from the Résident supérieur [of Tonkin] on this subject are precise. Smuggling is an act that disturbs public order, for which, with the support of all the indigenous authorities, I am responsible. I would therefore like to ask . . . you, all the district chiefs, to exert maximum effort in order to discover clandestine distilleries. Despite accusations, I do not believe that the mandarin chiefs of the six districts willingly close their eyes to the clandestine production houses known to them. The support that I expect and demand from the district chiefs does not consist only of the occasional arrest of a coolie or a destitute woman carrying a bottle of moonshine. Such a repressive method is ineffective and disturbing to the populace because the penalties are out of proportion to the reported misdemeanor. I would like the district chiefs, upon receiving these instructions, to secretly find through their informers the moonshine producing houses. . . . I would like to inform you, the chiefs of districts, that I will pay the closest attention to the manner in which these instructions are followed and that I will take seriously into account your achievements in this respect when I make promotion recommendations.                                    (AOM-AP-RST, 27-665)

By the first quarter of 1911, as a result of district officials' sale pressures and a new retailing system in which well-off villagers were recruited to manage the sale of government alcohol within their communal boundaries, sales by the government monopoly had increased by 50 percent from 1906 (Reports of the Résident of Phu-Tho in the fourth quarter of 1910 and on March 31, 1911, AOM-AP-RST, 27-665). Due to a price reduction in 1913, sales doubled over the previous level. The colonial government also used its monopoly in order to set the price of salt at five to ten times higher than the price obtained by producers. The general colonial budget, approximately 70 percent of which was derived from indirect taxation through the government monopolies on alcohol, salt, and opium, increased from twenty million piasters in 1899 to sixty-five million in 1924 (Murray 1980:68–81).

The revenue increase financed the expansion of the administrative apparatus, the provision of new medical and educational services, and the construction of a modern communication system. The annual mortality rate in Phu-Tho declined from 4 percent in 1900 to 2.2 percent in 1929, although as late as 1943 there still existed only three hospitals in the province and one doctor for 77,000 natives (Le-Tuong and Vu-Kim-Bien 1981:129). Access to modern education beyond third grade was limited mainly to the children of the upper indigenous social stratum because of the considerable direct and indirect expenses of an education beyond this level. By 1933 in the entire province of Phu-Tho (est. pop. 270,000) there were only four primary schools (through the sixth grade). Most families that sent their children to primary school would be deprived of the children's labor. The monthly tuition, room, and board for a boarding student in Hanoi might cost up to ten piasters. Yet, even in the midland region of Phu-Tho, where the income of an annually hired agricultural worker was on average four times higher than in the lower Red River delta of North Vietnam, it amounted to only thirty-six to forty piasters a year.

By the mid-1930s the modern communication system included 73 kilometers of rail line, 140 kilometers of paved roads, and 396 kilometers of unpaved roads in the province of Phu-Tho (Pham-Xuan-Do 1939:72–73) and 2000 kilometers of rail line and 28,000 kilometers of paved and generally passable unpaved roads in all of Indochina (Murray 1980:172, 177). Constructed mainly through the use of compulsory labor (thirty to forty-eight days a year) in the first few decades of the colonial order, this transportation infrastructure served primarily the government's military purposes and the interests of capitalist agromineral ventures. In the province of Phu-Tho it was no coincidence that by 1940, aside from the national and interprovincial highways with their clear strategic and commercial value, one of the three other year-round passable provincial roads ran through the major tea plantation area (called the Tea Road, or *Duong Che*)—an area with an export-oriented economy (Pham-Xuan-Do 1939:76). On the colonial landscape were thus juxtaposed a new export-oriented system of roads and barefoot peasants too poor to afford modern transportation walking up to eighty kilometers a day to gain their livelihood. Plans for a water control project for the Lam-Thao–Hac-Tri plain of Phu-Tho were never realized in the colonial period. As suggested by the French scholar Paul Mus (1949:269), peasants' livelihoods were sustained within a subsistence-oriented framework, but their taxes were calculated on the terms of the capitalist world economy.

Despite the ideologies of *mission civilisatrice* and Franco-Vietnamese association as well as the material and status rewards to the collaborators among the native intelligentsia, in the twilight of the Confucian era a minority of the Confucian-educated elite could never come to terms with French colonialism. Realizing the futility of blind, uncoordinated resistance to the technologically superior French forces, in the first quarter of the twentieth century some advocated popular social reforms as the means to progress, turned a critical eye to tradition, and mounted a thinly veiled attack on old institutions, including the monarchy and the mandarinate. Others, still considering violence as a means to terminate the French colonial system, actively recruited young students for modern technological and military training in China and Japan and readily solicited the aid of any foreign power to achieve that goal. In Tonkin the reformist trend was actualized in 1907 in the Dong Kinh Nghia Thuc (Tonkin Free School). As characterized by the historian David Marr, it was "in the narrow sense a private school in Hanoi for four hundred to five hundred students, but in the broadest sense a popular educational and cultural movement of real significance to subsequent Vietnamese history" (Marr 1971:164). The school attacked traditional Confucian literary studies, used the modern Vietnamese script *(quoc ngu)*, introduced rudimentary Western science and philosophy, and emphasized both the development of native commerce and industry, and the heroic defense of the country against Chinese and Mongol invaders in previous centuries. The movement put the collaborationist establishment on the defensive (Marr 1971: chap. 7). It spread quickly to the surrounding provinces. In Phu-Tho the movement took root strongly in the village of Kinh-Ke, neighboring on Son-Duong, and in Nguyen Dac Bang's maternal ancestral village of Xuan-Lung, both of which later lent strong support to the VNP uprising in Phu-Tho and Yen-Bay (Le-Tuong and Vu-Kim-Bien 1981:145). Bang's father reportedly came into brief contact with the movement in the neighboring village of Kinh-Ke. However, before he could become further involved, the free school was closed down and many leaders of the movement imprisoned.

The efforts to better prepare for armed violence against the colonial regime did not fare well either. The soul of this movement was the Confucian examination laureate Phan Boi Chau, who left the country in 1904. He subsequently came into contact with major exiled Chinese leaders like Sun Yat-sen and Liang Ch'i-ch'ao, contributed to fundraising campaigns at home with his widely distributed literary indictments of French colonialism, and helped to place a total of two hundred Vietnamese students in Japanese schools. However, the training of future revolutionary leaders in the land of the rising Asian power came to an end in 1908 under French pressures on the Japanese government. After a period of exile in Thailand, Phan Boi Chau returned to China in the aftermath of the success of the Chinese revolution in 1911 and began laying the groundwork for a "Restoration Army" (Quang Phuc Quan). Caught in the dilemma of a negatively reinforcing cycle of limited foreign support and uncoordinated domestic anticolonial resistance, from 1913 onward Phan Boi Chau authorized a series of isolated strikes, including assassination attempts (Marr 1971: chaps. 6, 9). In Phu-Tho province Phan Boi Chau's "Vietnam Restoration Society" attracted followers in certain villages, especially in Lam-Thao district.[14] On the night of January 7, 1915, anticolonial forces attacked the provincial capital of Phu-Tho. Their primitive weapons were no match for French superior firearms. This abortive uprising led to harsh reprisals by the French and the execution of twenty-eight anticolonialists in Phu-Tho three months later. A resurrected anti-French association was also quickly suppressed the following year (Le-Tuong and Vu-Kim-Bien 1981:145–147; Billes 1916, AOM-AP-I, 7F-49). The isolated attacks on French border posts in the 1915–1918 period encountered a similar fate. Phan Boi Chau was eventually arrested and given a life sentence in Hanoi in 1925. Phan Chu Trinh, the soul of the reformist movement, passed away the following year in Saigon.

However, like the guerilla movement of the late nineteenth century, the anticolonial movements of the early twentieth century did not constitute complete failures. As Marr argues, "They succeeded in creating and recreating resistance symbols and ideals for subsequent generations. Without this, who can say that the men who came after them would

have the sense of continuity and historical purpose to act as they did?"
(Marr 1971:275). The power of the symbols of resistance and the
mythical ideals of the late nineteenth and early twentieth centuries can
hardly be overestimated. In the village of Son-Duong, for example, one
century after the defeat of the Aid-the-King movement, the tomb of
the anticolonial guerilla leader remained a village landmark. It was far
from insignificant that his daughter continued his idealism with financial contributions to the anticolonial cause, both to the Yen-Bay uprising and the Marxist-led Vietminh movement, until the violent end of
French colonialism in 1954. And no matter how shrouded in mystery
were the circumstances of the April 1885 massacre in Son-Duong, it
was no coincidence that the village mayor in 1930 and many following
generations blamed the massacre on a foreign presence, i.e., on Chinese
troops. Symbols and myths of resistance as well as the experience of
foreign brutalities nurtured the following generation of French-educated anticolonial leaders—a generation that had also to reconcile its
newly learned French ideals of liberty, fraternity, and equality with the
stark reality of the colonial order. Their role in the unfolding of historical events after 1925 and the continuity and discontinuity in the six
decades to follow can only be understood in relation to the undercurrents of social formation in colonial Vietnam, which emerged in the
context of the encounter between the indigenous tradition and Western capitalist imperialism.

CHAPTER 2

•

# Village Structure in Revolutionary Processes, 1925–1930

In Hanoi on November 23, 1925, Phan Boi Chau, the soul of anticolonial activism, was sentenced to life imprisonment with hard labor. On March 24, 1926, Phan Chu Trinh, the other much admired anticolonialist and the primary spokesman for the reformist school, died in Saigon shortly after his return to Vietnam from a fourteen-year exile in France. The trial of Phan Boi Chau in Hanoi provoked nationwide agitation for his pardon. In Saigon sixty thousand mourners attended Phan Chu Trinh's funeral processsion. His passing was also observed in at least sixteen other localities throughout the country (Marr 1981:15–23).

These tumultuous events marked a major turning point in the history of Vietnamese anticolonialism: with them came the end of the era of leadership of the anticolonial movement by Confucian literati. The younger, French-educated intelligentsia began in large numbers to engage in acts of passive resistance to the colonial regime. For the next three decades the middle and top ranks of anticolonial parties, both Marxist and non-Marxist, were filled largely by young men from this sector of the indigenous society. They played a key role in mediating the relationship between French colonialism and the noncapitalist rural communities, where the most successful anticolonial movements were nurtured by an intricate and extensive social network and within the context of a dialectical ideological tension between collectivism and male-centered hierarchy. These movements arose during the post–

World War I phase of capitalism in colonial Vietnam, after the infrastructure for capitalist development had been well laid during the previous decades of colonial rule. It was a period which witnessed both a dramatic expansion of metropolitan capital in the productive sphere and a significant increase in the size of the indigenous industrial, mining, and plantation proletariat—a fourfold increase in the European-employed labor force to at least 221,000 by 1929 (Murray 1980: 96–162, 211–254). Although labor unrest amongst this growing proletariat constituted an important factor in the Vietnamese revolution, active support by the nonindustrial rural masses and prominent leadership by the more progressive elements among the indigenous intelligentsia were at least as critical for revolutionary success. The Vietnamese Nationalist Party insurrection of February 1930, for example, was launched with the support of the rural population in Son-Duong and many other communities. A 1930 analysis after the fact by the French Résident supérieur in Tonkin concluded: "The facts have recently demonstrated that numerous cantonal and village authorities share the ideas of the rebels and provide the latter with effective support. It has also become certain that the peasants were not as unreceptive to revolutionary propaganda as we had thought" (AOM-P-NF, 323-2626, 64).

A full understanding of Vietnamese revolutionary dynamics requires an in-depth analysis of the structure of the colonial social formation. The dynamics of the Vietnamese revolution, in other words, are deeply rooted in the inequality and contradiction within the capitalist imperialist system, on the one hand, and in the indigenous sociocultural framework, on the other. Within the structure of French imperialism the racial diarchy of the colony stood in stark contrast to the discourse of "liberty, equality, and fraternity" of the metropolis. At least in the perception of many native leaders, this inequality extended beyond the colonial context to the political and economic relations between metropolis and colony, which were structured to benefit metropolitan capital. The inequality became particularly apparent to members of the French-educated elite that mediated between the colonial masters and the indigenous masses, and it was from that elite that the revolutionary leadership largely sprung.

Local tradition in northern and central Vietnam proved a fertile soil for indigenous resistance to French colonialism. Despite the dialectical tension between the collectivist ideology and the class-structured, male-centered hierarchy, local tradition nurtured the symbols of inter-class solidarity and anticolonial resistance. It also provided the organizational resources for the revolutionary leadership through an intricate intra- and intercommunal network based on both kinship and nonkinship principles. In the following microscopic description of the structure of Son-Duong village, the ethnographic details on the interplay of kinship, class, and community structures provide an indispensable background not only for the understanding of revolutionary dynamics, but also for an analysis of structural continuity and discontinuity in the socialist era.

## HIERARCHY AND COLLECTIVISM IN VILLAGE STRUCTURE

On the eve of the anticolonial uprising in February 1930, the community of Son-Duong included three different villages: Son-Duong itself (known as Muong in the vernacular language), Dung-Hien, and Thuy-Son. The three villages possessed a total of 1009 *mau* of rice fields: Son-Duong had approximately 600 *mau* for a population of 1464; Dung-Hien had 250 *mau* for 240; and Thuy-Son, a single-lineage village, had 150 *mau* for 70 people (land data from Son-Duong 1987; 1927 demographic data from Ngo-vi-Lien 1928:134, 323, 351).[1] The cultivated surface per inhabitant averaged 2030 square meters for the three villages as a whole and 1470 square meters in the original village of Son-Duong. The latter figure approximates the average both for the province of Phu-Tho (1460 square meters) and for North Vietnam in general (1470 square meters) (Henry 1932:23).

Throughout the colonial period Son-Duong relied on agriculture for its livelihood and on women's marketing activities as a secondary source of income. In the fields of Son-Duong, only one rice crop could grow each year. In the low-lying fields, rice seedlings were transplanted in either the twelfth or the first lunar month for a harvest four months later *(lua chiem)*. Inundated in the summer and serving as the village fishing ground during this period, these fields yielded only one crop a year. In the high-lying fields, the transplanting was done in the fifth or sixth lunar month, and rice *(lua mua)* was harvested in the tenth or the eleventh month (see also Ta-Long 1976:83). The fields were then plowed for the growing of melons and vegetables (onions, leeks, peas, gourds, and pumpkins). Of the agricultural tasks, plowing was normally assigned to men, transplanting to women, and weeding and harvesting to both; in Phu-Tho women at times took charge of plowing and most other tasks (Pham-Xuan-Do 1939:38). Female villagers, regardless of class backgrounds, often engaged in marketing activities to supplement family incomes, moving from one rural market to another. Most markets were held periodically, usually for six days a month. For example, the Son-Duong market met on the third and the eighth day of each ten-day cycle; the neighboring Ngu-Xa market, on the second and seventh days; the Cao-Mai market in the district seat, on the fourth and ninth days; and the Phu-Tho provincial market, on the fifth and tenth days (ibid.:70). Some women even traveled as far as the neighboring provincial capital of Yen-Bay, a distance of eighty kilometers, on foot. Son-Duong did not have any handicrafts. The textile handicraft of neighboring Ngu-Xa village did not spread to Son-Duong until the very end of the colonial period in the 1940s.

Both in the nineteenth century and throughout the French colonial period, Son-Duong, Dung-Hien, and Thuy-Son were linked together administratively, ritually, historically, economically, and sociopolitically. Administratively, the original Son-Duong was the head village in a canton of the same name that, besides Dung-Hien and Thuy-Son, included four other villages (pops. 871, 719, 504, 74) and was administered by a canton chief and a deputy chief. From 1921 onward each village was ruled by a village executive council, called the "lineage representative council" *(hoi dong toc bieu)*. Headed by a president and a vice-president (respectively, *chanh huong hoi* and *pho huong hoi*), the council included a directly elected mayor and deputy mayor as well as council-appointed officials (such as secretary, treasurer, and village guard chief, among others; see also Tran-Tu 1984:60–81).[2] Ritually, Son-Duong, Dung-Hien, and Thuy-Son worshiped the same tutelary deities, albeit at three different communal houses. At a major area festival on the third day of the third lunar month, the members of the three villages, male and female, and young and old, allied in a ritual fight against the residents of Ngu-Xa in the neighboring canton of Vinh-Lai. Historically, according to a local Communist Party historian, it was not until the early nineteenth century that the Kieu lineage seceded from Son-Duong to form the tiny village of Thuy-Son and that Dung-Hien followed suit.[3] Economically, the three villages shared the same periodic rural market, which was located by the gate of Son-Duong village, in front of its pagoda. The market met six times each lunar month, on the third, eighth, thirteenth, eighteenth, twenty-third, and twenty-eighth days. Sociopolitically, the elites of at least Son-Duong and Dung-Hien, if not of all three, were closely linked through both extensive school ties and class-based marital alliances. As the head village, the village of Son-Duong had the only elementary school (up to the third grade) in the canton. At the time of the 1930 uprising, students from throughout the canton attended the elementary school in Son-Duong. The elite of Son-Duong village was thus linked by extensive school ties with the young members of the intelligentsia in the local area. The bonds were further reinforced by marital alliances, overriding the local preference for village endogamy. Beneath the structure of all three villages lay an ideological tension between collectivism, on the one hand, and a class-structured, kinship-centered, and male-oriented hierarchy, on the other.

### Collectivism and the Village Network

Within the bamboo hedge of a rural community like Son-Duong, members related to one another within the framework of a corporate peasant village. They were considerably differentiated in wealth and status yet linked together by extensive social ties within a communal framework. Although the sense of communal unity and collectivism in Son-Duong may seem attenuated in the context of a weaker communal land tradition than in a number of northern villages, villagers still shared the annual cycle of communal deity worship, a sharp distinction between insiders *(noi tich)* and outsiders *(ngoai tich)*, and the corporate fiscal and nonfiscal responsibilities (corvée and draft quota) toward both the precolonial and the colonial state. It was in the village rituals and the communal land institutions that the collectivist ideology was clearly manifested.

At the large communal house Son-Duong villagers worshiped as their tutelary deities General Quy Minh of the Hung dynasty (to the third century B.C.) and General Lan Ho of the Tran dynasty (thirteenth century). In light of the considerable anticolonial activities in Son-Duong over the past century, it is significant that both of its tutelary deities were heroes who fought against foreign invaders. General Quy Minh was believed to have played a major role in defending the Hung dynasty against foreign troops (Le-Tuong and Nguyen-Khac-Xuong 1987:69–70).[4] Similarly, General Lan Ho, who died from a serious battle wound in 1287 in Ngu-Xa village, was a major hero against the Mongols (Le-Tuong and Vu-Kim-Bien 1981:89–90).[5] Besides tutelary deity worship, villagers participated in many other annual rituals, some of which marked the temporal transition in the annual village calendar and enhanced their solidarity vis-à-vis outsiders, whereas others functioned to alleviate the anxiety of daily livelihood. For example, during the New Year celebration, work, loud speech, and demands for the repayment of debts, among other things, were taboo. These taboos officially ended only after village literati and officials had made an offering to the tutelary deities at the communal house. On the fifteenth day of the first month, villagers planted reeds in paddy baskets, which they offered to the deities, symbolizing the growth of paddy even from reeds (Ta-Long 1976:79). On the first day of the sixth month, they participated in the ritual of (paddy) field descent *(le ha dien)* on a communal field to mark the beginning of the rice cultivation season and to wish for good crop growth. And on the third day of the third lunar month, they joined together in a ritual fight against the villagers of Ngu-Xa.

The annual rituals and certain other institutions in Son-Duong were partly sustained by communal land. The communal ownership of the three villages together amounted to sixty *mau,* or 6 percent of the cultivated area, in comparison to the average of 9.1 percent in the province of Phu-Tho and 21 percent in Tonkin (Henry 1932:23, 109). Of the forty *mau* under communal ownership in the smaller Son-Duong village, three were reserved for an educational fund *(hoc dien)* that defrayed the expenses of one or more free village schools. A small acreage supplemented soldiers' incomes *(binh dien).* In the original village of Son-Duong at least, the remaining communal land was divided among neighborhood groups *(giap),* which in turn used the proceeds from the land to fulfill their responsibilities for the expenses of village feasts. *Giap* membership and village insider status *(noi tich)* were granted only after one's family had settled in the village for a few generations. The conceptual categories of insiders and outsiders involved a rigid distinction of community membership, both reflected in and reinforced by an extraordinarily high level of village endogamy. Although precise figures for the rate of village endogamy in colonial Son-Duong are not available, in the pre-1945 northern rural communities for which data were available, it reached at least 80 percent (see Luong 1984:298). The distinction between village insiders and outsiders constituted a part of the general and persistent conceptual distinction between the members and nonmembers of a social unit, be it kinship, communal, or ethnic, that underlay the northern tradition of great formality in interaction with outsiders.

Beyond communal linkages, villagers in Son-Duong related to one another extensively through territorial and voluntary association ties as well as through genealogical and fictive kinship. The village of Son-Duong was divided into five hamlets *(khu)*, each of which was further divided into patrilineage-dominated neighborhood groups *(giap* or *phe)* for a total of thirteen groups. Each hamlet or neighborhood group comprised households of different patrilineages, although due to territorial clustering of relatives within a smaller unit, each neighborhood group was normally dominated by one patrilineal group. At birth, each boy would have to be registered with a *giap,* a patrilineage *(ho),* and a *khu* to prepare for fuller participation in public activities within the kinship and communal frameworks later on. In a household with two sons, the first son belonged to the same *giap* as his father, with whom he normally resided. Although also residing with his father, the second son shared *giap* membership with his mother's father, who usually resided in another hamlet, because most marriages involved villagers from different hamlets and because women moved into their husbands' parents' households upon marriage (patrilocal residence). As a result, although the nucleus of a *giap* membership resided within the same territorial unit, the *giap* always had many male members from other hamlets in the village. In general, *giap* membership was considerably more significant than *khu* membership because communal land was divided among the *giap* for cultivation. In return, each *giap* was obligated to contribute to public expenses as well as to provide food (e.g., glutinous rice, pork, and chicken) for the worship of communal tutelary deities and for communal house feasts on festival and New Year occasions *(ngay cau;* cf. Tran-Tu 1984:46–60). On the third day of the first lunar month, the entire *giap* also participated in a pig husbandry competition at the communal house. In order to meet its communal obligations, each *giap* contracted with its own members who had achieved a certain seniority to receive the land for the year and to prepare for the feasts from the yield of the earth. The fact that two brothers who resided in the same household and shared the same patrilineage membership belonged to different *giap* in different hamlets increased the cross-cutting ties within the community.

Villagers of the same socioeconomic standing also formed voluntary associations to meet their various needs. Most notable were two villagewide associations, the exclusively male literati association *(hoi van than)* and the elderly women's Buddhist association *(hoi chu ba)*. The former included both Confucian teachers and, as a reflection of the colonial transformation, the holders of the Franco-Vietnamese *certificat d'études élémentaires* (for the successful completion of the third grade examination). It organized the annual worship of Confucius at the literary shrine *(van chi)*.[6] In the colonial period the literati association was still assigned the honored task of delivering formal speeches at communal deity worship rituals at the communal house *(dinh)*. The elderly women's Buddhist association, in contrast, met at the village pagoda, constructed around 1810, for the worship of Buddha on the first and the fifteenth day of each lunar month. Other voluntary associations included the female-controlled rotating credit associations *(ho)* and the household-centered ceremony assistance associations. Members of these associations came mainly from within a hamlet. The five to twenty members of a typical *ho* took turns obtaining the periodic contributions necessary to meet their own financial needs. Members in need made bids to obtain credit with offers of discount for other members' periodic contributions. Only members who had not yet obtained credit received this discount. In other words, for a ten-member association with an originally agreed on contribution of one hundred kilograms of paddy each harvest season, if the first member in need of credit made a successful bid with a 20 percent discount, other members had to contribute only eighty kilograms. Since the last member did not need to bid, she would receive the contributions from others with no discount. Many associations also gave the organizer the right to be the first to receive credit without having to give other members a discount for their contributions. The elderly lady Thanh, whose labor was mortgaged at the age of seven for her father's tax payment, discussed how her family was able to purchase 1.2 *mau* of rice fields in the 1930s to become a middle-peasant household:

People wondered how I obtained the money to purchase the rice field. But I bought the field without any help from relatives. I did it by saving pennies and by joining a small credit association in the village. I repaid the loan obtained for the purchase of the rice field over two and a half years, one hundred kilograms of rice from each crop and twice a year.

The ceremony assistance associations were formed for mutual assistance among members on the occasions of weddings, examination success, rituals honoring the elderly, and funerals within members' households. They were called *ho tien, ho gao,* or *ho co,* depending on whether the assistance took the form of cash, rice, or labor contributions at the time of a ceremony. Most village households participated in at least one of these mutual assistance associations. Bang's narrative on the funerals of his father and his father's senior mother (that is, his grandfather's first wife) illustrates the role of these mutual assistance associations in village life:

My father died in 1928 of a gastrointestinal disease. My grandfather's first wife died in early 1929 in her old age. These two funerals were the two major ones in my life. At the funeral for my father, visitors came from all over Lam-Thao district since he had had many pupils and because he had been president of the village council. Buddhist nuns also came in large numbers for prayer sessions. Relatives and acquaintances from elsewhere came to pay their respects. Visitors squeezed into the courtyard, bringing with them cash, rice, meat, and boiled chicken as funeral offerings and contributions. They kowtowed and, as the sons of the deceased, we had to reciprocate. We wore special mourning dresses made of coarse white fabric and donned banana-leaf hats and belts. We had to walk stooped over with canes both in the house and during the funeral procession. My knees became bruised from all the kowtowing during the three days of funeral ceremony. My brothers and I were joined by [our cousin] Mai [a son of Bang's father's junior half-brother, raised by Bang's father] in kowtowing to visitors in reciprocation for their kowtows to my deceased father. He wore the filial funeral dress for the occasion [i.e., he ritually assumed the role of a son]. We had to welcome and provide a feast for a lot of people. As a result, many pigs were sacrificed during the funeral.

The entire village had to contribute to my father's and grandmother's burials because my parents had been members of feast associations. Association membership ranged from nine to eighteen individuals who came mostly from the same neighborhood. A member of a rice association usually contributed a basket of rice [twenty liters]. A member of a cash association might contribute six or seven piasters to the ceremony. The members of feast-preparing associations contributed their labor to prepare the feast to feed visitors from within and from outside the village. When my father died, the members of the associations with which he had been affiliated had to pay their dues.

Beyond territorial and voluntary association ties, as in other northern villages, the intracommunal social network in Son-Duong was rendered more intricate by extensive kinship ties, both fictive and nonfictive. In an agricultural environment with high infant mortality, many well-off families without sons or with few (surviving) offspring adopted children, either actually or nominally, both within the local community and beyond. In addition to contributing to the household labor force, the prevalence of adoption also involved native beliefs in the necessity of patriline continuity only through sons and in the role of adoption in warding off the decimation of one's own offspring by evil supernatural forces. Bang's narrative highlights the frequent adoption process in his household:

It was partly out of a belief in supernatural causes of deaths that many adoptions, real or nominal, took place in my youth. My paternal grandfather adopted a daughter, who in turn had two daughters. I had to address these two women as *chi* (elder sister). Because my grandfather's adopted daughter did not have any sons, her husband and she in turn had to adopt a nephew as the heir to their wealth—someone who could continue their line and worship them after death. . . .

My senior mother also adopted a daughter after failing to raise any of her first seven children. This eldest sister of mine was adopted during a big flood in the region of Nam-Dinh and Phu-Ly in the lower delta, when her real mother had taken her along to the midland region and begged for food at the Cao-Mai market [in the Lam-Thao district seat]. That was how my sister had the nickname Mon [picking the leftovers]. After this adoption and after my birth, my senior mother succeeded in raising two sons. My parents also gave me up for nominal adoption by the employer of my first love, Lu. The practice of nominal adoption was prevalent in the old days, especially among those whose children were few or whose many children died young.

I myself also adopted three sons altogether. One of the three, Dan, came from my village. Dan was actually a distant relative of mine, although not in my patrilineage. Because he seemed a bright kid, I asked his father why he was not sent to school. His father mentioned the poverty of the family. I told the father that I would be willing to adopt Dan and take care of his schooling, given his apparent intelligence. His father agreed. My wife and I raised Dan together with our first son even when my father was still alive [before 1928]. After my father's death, I adopted two other sons among my pupils, one from Huu-Bo village and the other a son of a Chinese medicine practitioner in my native Lam-Thao district. Both came from poor families. As the former's father had also died, his widowed mother could not support his schooling after a while. My senior mother was kind to them, raising them like her grandsons and encouraging their schooling. My wife and I had two sons. But my first son died quite early because we did not have a maternity clinic in those days. We had to rely on old village women using unhygienic instruments during delivery. That was why my son's health was poor. If he had survived, he would be over fifty years old now.

The kinship network within the village was formally organized into a number of patrilineages *(ho)* whose membership was passed from father to son. In Son-Duong as well as in other northern rural communities, the different patrilineages in a village were linked by extensive affinal ties—an extensive network that resulted from the strong preference for village endogamy. The affinal ties were by no means insignificant because a married-out woman continued to maintain ritual obligations toward the members of her natal patriline or local patrilineage. She was expected to bring her children to her parents' home to attend the important death anniversaries in her family of birth. At the wedding of any of her children, ancestral offerings were made not only to her husband's ancestors (including offerings at the houses of her husband's patrilineage chief and lineage branch chief), but also to the ancestors of her own father and mother. The extensive social ties reduced the possibility of permanent cleavages within the corporate community, a community also bounded by tutelary deity worship and other annual rituals, corporate responsibilities (corvée, taxes, and military draft) to the state, and the institution of communal land.

## Class, Gender, and Hierarchy

Despite a degree of communal solidarity among villagers, the structure of Son-Duong and other northern villages in the colonial period was clearly dominated by a considerable class cleavage and a class-structured, kinship-centered, and male-oriented hierarchy. This class- and gender-based hierarchical framework dominated village institutions from the household to the communal levels. The hierarchy was male-oriented despite the significant labor contribution of women, regardless of their class backgrounds.

Village households were considerably differentiated in wealth and status, with numerous cases of class mobility even within the same generation. Even by the time of the Marxist-organized 1954 land reform, when large landholders with a sense of the political wind had partially dispersed their holdings, the twelve Son-Duong households classified as landlords and rich peasants (2.6 percent of the households and 4.5 percent of the population) still owned 23 percent of the rice fields in the village (230 *mau*). The wealthiest villager still retained 110 *mau* or 11 percent of the cultivable land. At the other end of the spectrum were landless and poor peasant households, which, at the time of the 1954 land reform, made up 70 percent of the village households. The process of socioeconomic differentiation seems to have proceeded slightly further in Son-Duong and in the district of Lam-Thao than in the rest of the province of Phu-Tho because the percentage of landless and poor peasant households in Phu-Tho in 1954–1955 was only 54.16 percent (White 1981:423). The data on land distribution in the native population also suggest a slightly greater socioeconomic differentiation in Lam-Thao district in the late 1920s (see table 2).

As a result of the greater socioeconomic differentiation and an unfavorable people-to-land ratio in Son-Duong, many poor villagers found work in other villages in the area. Although probably reflecting to some extent the discourse of the Marxist-led class struggle of the 1950s, Bang's cousin Te's narrative remains quite informative on the working conditions of a hired laborer in the 1930s—conditions that

**Table 2. Distribution of cultivable rice fields under native ownership in Lam-Thao and Phu-Tho (percent)**

|                | LAM-THAO DISTRICT | PROVINCE OF PHU-THO |
|----------------|-------------------|---------------------|
| 0–1 *mau*      | 62.5              | 59.1                |
| 1–5 *mau*      | 29.6              | 34.6                |
| 5–10 *mau*     | 6.1               | 5.2                 |
| 10–50 *mau*    | 1.7               | 1.0                 |
| 50–100 *mau*   | 0.03              | 0.02                |
| Over 100 *mau* |                   | 0.002 (1 landowner) |

*Source:*   Henry 1932:92–93.

seem to have remained essentially the same throughout the colonial period:

I was born into a well-to-do family. My paternal grandparents had bequeathed my father and his two brothers more than thirty *mau* of rice fields. My senior uncle occupied the position of a deputy canton chief in the area. However, my father had treated my mother very poorly in favor of his second wife. My mother and I left the household to work for other people when I was only five. When my father fell seriously ill around 1930, he called me back. But my father's second wife beat me heavily and fed me little. I left again to join my mother.

Late in 1931 my father died in poverty, since a large part of the ancestral land had been sold in the aftermath of the VNP uprising to secure the release of my senior uncle. As a result of their frustration and depression after this abortive uprising, whatever remained was lost through their gambling and opium smoking. Even the family pond and half of the three *sao* of ancestral residential land were sold. Few people came to our house in my father's final hours, partly because of our poverty and partly because of the rumor that he had contracted the contagious disease of tuberculosis. I still remember vividly his final moments: a chicken was tied to the foot of the bed, a piece of paper was placed over his mouth to check his breath, and I silently sat in a corner of the house on the floor. He was buried on the same day by eight pall bearers.

When my father's junior wife left to remarry, my mother and I returned to the pitiful house, a two-room hut with a termite-bored bunk bed. Yet, at the approach of the lunar new year, we had to hide away from the house to avoid our creditors. We returned only on New Year's Day, since it was a taboo to demand debt payments on the first few days of the new year. We cooked our rice cake in an earthen pot. We had no copper one.

Feeling bad about the family's poverty and my mother's hardships, I began working again at the age of twelve, this time as a babysitter. I worked for an aunt and then for another household. I was paid four piasters a year plus sufficient food for myself. In the colonial period children could pursue education beyond the second or third grade only if their families were wealthy.

At the suggestion of my acquaintances, I soon gave up babysitting in order to apprentice as a plowman for Mayor Huu in the village of Vinh-Lai. I remember that on the first day he beat me left and right with a bamboo rod in the field as I tried the plow. The following morning, weeping and holding the plow but determined to master the technique, I succeeded at the task. I became an accomplished plowman at the age of fourteen or fifteen. The work schedule was heavy. At the first cock crow of the day, I would get up to gather three to four baskets of water lentils and to pound them in the mortar so that the wife of my employer could just pick them up for sale in the morning in the market. The food was seldom sufficient to fill my stomach. I usually had just about three hundred grams of leftover rice for breakfast, two bowls for lunch, and the same for dinner. At lunch and dinner time I had some banana broth to add a taste to the rice. I had to go into the field rain or shine. When it rained, I had to check the condition of the banks of my employer's field in order to ensure their strength to contain rain water. When the sun was scorching, I had to catch field crabs and tend the buffalo. The work was demanding, as the employer tried to make the most of the salary that I received from him. I did whatever he ordered: plowing, transplanting, weeding. He simply supervised. I always went to work hungry. Even at their family celebrations, I ate the leftovers when I returned from the field. My annual salary was thirty piasters, two pairs of brown coarse cotton pajamas, a belt, and, in those days, a turban. If we bargained well, we might obtain a brown coarse cloth formal dress instead of two pairs of pajamas. I was allowed to go home for major death anniversaries and for the New Year celebration only upon my mother's request to the employer. It was a heavily exploitative system.

I worked for six years as a live-in plowman and jack-of-all-trades in Vinh-Lai, where many of my fellow Son-Duong villagers also found work. We did not work in Son-Duong because our village was more densely populated and because we were not fed as well as in Vinh-Lai. For all those years, my mother remained a hired laborer in Son-Duong.

Fortunately, I did not run into any difficulty with the local officials regarding the payment of taxes. Any failure to pay in time would lead to the arrest and minor torture of one's brother or adult family member in the communal house courtyard. No matter whether one could afford it or not, under the circumstances, one had no choice but to contribute a few dimes toward a close relative's tax obligations. I paid only two and a half to three piasters a year for poll tax and less than a dime on the piece of residential land. I managed all right.

Opportunities for upward mobility through educational achievements and other means were not as limited as Te suggests. Bang's favorite student and later the president of the Son-Duong Communist Party branch, Mr. Le van Tiem, obtained a *certificat d'études primaires* and became a village teacher despite the economic hardships of his family:

I owed a lot to Mr. Bang, who, finding me quite intelligent among his thirty to forty students, cared a great deal about my educational success. My family was so poor at the time that I had only rice soup, as occasionally we did not even have enough rice to cook steamed rice. We did not own any land because my father was addicted to opium. It was my mother who supported the family as a seasonal seedling transplanter. Despite our poverty, my parents made the sacrifice for my education, and our relatives lent us some money and rice whenever necessary, because Mr. Bang and everybody else had said that I was quite intelligent. We were so poor that [unable to pay for room and board] I had to ask for a free sampan ride across the river daily to attend the provincial school in Hung-Hoa. Working quite hard, I passed the examination for the *certificat d'études primaires* quite early, on my first try. It took other students four or five tries before they succeeded. In 1931, at the age of eighteen, I became a private tutor in the house of a landlord in the neighboring village of Phung-Nguyen. My salary amounted to a few piasters a month.

The elderly lady Thanh (born 1912) recounted at length her experiences as a poor villager and her family's upward mobility in the 1920s and 1930s:

I worked very hard [as a laborer] after marriage [at the age of nineteen] because my husband and I were so poor that we had to live initially on the land of his uncle. Even when tending buffalo for somebody else, I managed to dig and collect two baskets of tubers such as potatoes and manioc in fields that the owners seemed to have harvested cleanly. I sold them in the market. We purchased rice for our meals on a day-to-day basis. Still, we managed to pay our taxes in order not to get into trouble with the government. Five years later we purchased a small thatch hut for three piasters. We purchased the land for the hut the following year and 1.2 *mau* of rice fields (0.432 hectare) the year after for twenty-seven piasters. I also began raising this younger brother of mine [pointing to a younger brother], since my parents had died.

In those days, without a draft animal to plow the land, I had to loosen the earth with a hoe in preparation for planting. I hoed one and a half *sao* of land [0.12 acre] a day. [I did all the farmwork because] at the time my husband and his two brothers jointly owned a sewing machine and worked on the other side of the river, around the town of Hung-Hoa. During the slack season my adolescent brother helped to cook for them. For the rest of the year he assisted me with minor agricultural tasks. After each harvest he and I also picked the fallen grains and leftover potatoes. Furthermore, even while transplanting for the spring crop in the middle of the winter, I always managed to catch at least a basket of fish before going home. The water was so cold at that time that the fish became sluggish and were unable to swim. Every few days I would go to the district seat market in Cao-Mai [approximately six kilometers away] to sell my fish. At night, my sleep was less than sound as I worried about getting up by two o'clock in the morning in order to have an early start at the working day. When not working the land, I walked eighty kilometers a day to a market near the capital of the neighboring province, Yen-Bay. I left the house at six o'clock in the morning and reached there after nightfall. I sold onions and bought dried fish, which I exchanged for manioc and rice. Later, we managed to obtain the coownership of an ox. I worked so hard that I could not bear any children myself.

Despite such examples of upward mobility, downward mobility was not insignificant, as illustrated in the case of Te's family; and the poor in Son-Duong labored under difficult conditions. Poor villagers who chose sharecropping did not fare considerably better than laborers: landlords reportedly took one-half to two-thirds of the harvest, depending on whether they were to pay for the seeds and land taxes or not.

In contrast, most sons of elite families in Son-Duong engaged in a long and arduous educational process in preparation for rather leisurely lives, at times in positions as teachers and village officials. Bang, the French-educated teacher, described in detail the division of labor in his family, which, with twenty to thirty *mau* of rice fields, ranked among the wealthiest 2 percent of village households:

I was born into a family that had been well-off for generations, although it did not own a large amount of land. We had twenty to thirty *mau* of rice fields, a few buffaloes, at least two live-in workers-cum-plowmen, and share-croppers. My family ranked fifth or sixth in the village in terms of wealth. During the transplanting and harvesting seasons we hired, in addition, several seasonal laborers to work on the land that we cultivated directly. We also received half of the crop from the sharecropped land. My family also had a brick factory when I was a small kid. As a result, our pigsty, buffalo stable, and entire courtyard were constructed with bricks. It was one of approximately one dozen brick houses in the village. All the rest were made of bamboo, wood, and thatch.

My father had studied Sino-Vietnamese and Confucian classics. Qualified to take the regional Confucian examination, he passed the first two tests to get into the third of the four rounds. He did it a few times but was not able to advance into the final round. Frustrated, he stopped taking the examinations. After a short stint as a teacher of Sino-Vietnamese in the village, he became the mayor of Son-Duong and then moved up to the position of president *(chanh huong hoi)* of the lineage representative council [village executive council]. While a village chief, he also ran for the position of canton chief.

However, he lost to a poorer candidate because he offended people with an arrogant statement. Nevertheless, he achieved more than my paternal grandfather, who reached only the position of mayor and did not master Confucian classics to become a candidate at the regional examinations. My father was called *Chanh* Ty after his highest title and after my original name *Ty*, Nguyen Doan Ty. He was called after me because I was his first son, although I have two older sisters and although my mother was only his third-ranked wife.

[My mother died of a supernaturally induced illness when I was only five.] I was raised by my senior mother, who was very kind to me. At the age of six, I entered a village school where modern Vietnamese, Chinese characters, and Confucian morality were taught. . . . Three years later, I began attending a Vietnamese public school in the village. Finding me intelligent, the village school teacher suggested to my father that he allow me to continue with primary education at a provincial school. . . . With the concurrence of my senior mother, my father followed [my teacher's] suggestion. He was progressive, because older women in the village had discouraged people from learning the modern Vietnamese script. They cited the strange-looking and unsacred nature of modern writing. In those days villagers even used the paper from modern Vietnamese books as paper towels or toilet tissue. Nobody dared to trash Sino-Vietnamese books.

I was already in my teenage years—it was around 1916—when I took the entrance exam for the provincial Franco-Vietnamese school in Viet-Tri. Because there was an age limit, we had to make a new birth certificate in order to lower my official age by four years. My name was also consequently changed from Nguyen Doan Ty to Nguyen Dac Bang. . . . I stayed in Viet-Tri for over a month. Then I moved to the provincial capital of Phu-Tho, where I entered the second grade and lived for over a year. As my future good friend Lap of neighboring Kinh-Ke village and a few of my cousins went to the Hung-Hoa school, I was sent along with them to Hung-Hoa. Later, my brothers Tang and Gia followed me there. I was in the third grade when I moved to Hung-Hoa. I also got married at this point. I still remember that after the wedding, my wife carried 30 *dau* of rice every month to Hung-Hoa in order to pay for my room and board. I usually returned home on Saturday and left early on Monday for school.

Although I was the best student in my class in Hung-Hoa and received the honors prize, I twice failed the examination for the *certificat d'études primaires.* Candidates had to pass all five written tests (two math, one drawing, one essay, and one dictation test) before they could be admitted to the last round of oral examinations. I had problems primarily with the dictation test because my French teachers were all Vietnamese and the dictation examiner was French. I eventually obtained the *certificat d'études primaires* on the third try. It was thanks to my father's progressive attitude, my senior mother's kindness, and my intelligence inherited from my mother's father, a mandarin and a doctorate degree holder *(pho bang).*[7]

After obtaining the *certificat d'études primaires,* I studied for two years at the private teacher-training school Tri-Tri in Hanoi. It cost a little less than ten piasters a month in those days. My parents paid five or six piasters for room and board at a boarding house on the outskirt of Hanoi. After graduating with the *Brevet élémentaire, mention pédagogique,* I returned to my native village in early 1927, started private elementary classes, and began my career as a school teacher. Such an education was the privilege of the sons of relatively well-off families. Scholarships were not available then as they are now.

[Throughout all those years of schooling] my brothers and I were not allowed to get involved much in manual labor. During my earlier years of Sino-Vietnamese education in the village, I usually tended buffalo in the afternoon after my return from school—not because I had to but because I liked to get a chance to play games with other buffalo tenders from different villages. The buffalo were simply permitted to roam in the fields near the wood. It was so much fun that I had to compete with household members to be allowed to take the buffalo to the fields. I occasionally also watered the trees and plants in the yard. After I started learning French, my father prohibited me from getting involved in those tasks and required me to study after school. My brothers Tang and Gia never got involved in those tasks, even when they were young.

Bang's father's prohibition of menial labor represented the rigid distinction between mental and menial labor and the Confucian emphasis on the role of educated *men* in providing moral leadership for society at large. Because of this Confucian ideal, the sons of elite families went through a long educational process, while their mothers, sisters, wives, and daughters made a significant contribution to the household and village economy. The labor contribution of women from elite families is elaborated in Bang's continuing narrative:

*Given the amount of land owned by your family, did the members of your family work on the land at all? Do I assume correctly that laborers were hired to work all the land?*

My family members did contribute their labor. My elder sister, my older female cousin, my wife, and the wives of my two brothers Tang and Gia all worked and worked very hard. Waking up before dawn, they divided the various tasks among themselves, including pounding the rice paddy, boiling water, cooking rice, and feeding the pigs and chickens. During the peak agricultural seasons, not only did they cook for a lot of day laborers, but they also had to help with transplanting and harvesting. In the evening, they had the same tasks to perform: pounding paddy, cooking rice, and feeding the pigs and chickens. They could not go to bed until midnight. Meals had to be cooked five times a day in my family during these seasons. In my youth, for example, in the early morning while my brothers, my father, and I were still sleeping, my elder sisters and female cousin had to cook for my paternal grandmother, my father's wives, and the workers leaving early for the field. We men did not wake up until about halfway through the morning, that means, around eight o'clock. My father then had a porridge of rice, peas, and eggs. Each of us boys got one bowl and then we left for school. My brothers and I came back around eleven o'clock for lunch. The workers were also fed around that time. In the afternoon, after the workers had left, we had dinner around five o'clock. We had two main meals a day besides breakfast; those working in the field had three main meals a day. It was the same when I became a teacher in my village. During other seasons the young female members of my family grew vegetables and melons. It was always one crop or the other on my family's land. My wife, cousin, and sisters-in-law had to retail the secondary crops in periodic rural markets. They occasionally had to walk sixteen kilometers each way to the Phu-Tho provincial market. The market in Son-Duong was held only six times a month. So was the only other market in the neighboring villages, located in Ngu-Xa, held on alternate days. Produce peddlers had to move from one market to another to sell their produce. During my school days in the provincial capital of Phu-Tho, the women from my native village would already have arrived there on foot when I was responding to nature's call in the yard early in the morning.

The narrative of Bang, the school teacher, on the division of labor in his household not only revealed in sharp detail the significant labor contribution of women in elite families, but also confirmed his cousin Te's account of the conditions of the poor:

Our live-in workers took charge of heavier work, such as plowing. Usually coming from poor families outside my patrilineage, they were paid thirty-six to forty piasters a year and two pairs of pajamas. They were given three days of vacation as well as rice, meat, wine, and cash gifts at New Year's. The work in the fields was supervised by my cousin Mai, the grandson of my paternal grandfather by his mistress. Mai lived in the same house with us and woke up at around four o'clock in the morning like my wife and sisters-in-law.

The conditions of our live-in workers might not be great, but workers who could not till the land received little more than food for themselves, the poll tax payment, and two pairs of pajamas for a year of work. Many women also worked as migrant laborers, moving from one village to another as part-time seedling transplanters. Working from dawn till dusk, each normally received two working meals of a mixture of rice and other cereals, and one *dau* of rice to take home. In my youth a lot of villagers were poor, working for a few land-holding families in Son-Duong and elsewhere. The landless people were in particularly dire circumstances in those days in our country. In a very poor family, the migrant-laborer mother could only take care of her children in the evening, usually breast-feeding a baby and then cooking for others the rice that she had been paid at the end of the day. Although the village had over a dozen *mau* of communal land, it was not sufficient to distribute among the poor. . . . The poor did not benefit much from communal land in Son-Duong. . . . Life was not easy for either the seasonal and live-in workers or the young female members of the land-owning families, especially during the transplanting and harvesting seasons.

The gender-based division of labor derived from the exclusive reserve of public power and societal leadership roles for men. In the Confucian view widely accepted by the indigenous population at the time, educated men in particular played a vital role in the moral leadership and ideological formation of society. In order to fulfill this mission, the educated had to transcend their financial self-interest and maintain exemplary behavior. For example, Bang's salary payment as a private school teacher had to be handled by a committee of pupils' parents and not directly by Bang himself. When Bang became heavily engaged in gambling for entertainment at one point in his teaching career, his senior mother successfully intervened to end his gambling activities with the argument that as a teacher, he had to set a moral example for his students and other villagers.

In the communal life of Son-Duong, both the role of educated men and socioeconomic differences were ritualized through communal house feasts from which women and the very poor *(bach dinh)* were excluded and at which any violation of the codified seating order and food distribution arrangements could lead to litigation. At the lowest level sat honorary occupants of general village positions *(xa tien)* who purchased their titles from the colonial government for half of a laborer's annual income and who could provide a celebration feast for villagers in accordance with a long-existing tradition. At the next level were former holders of lower-level village offices and honorary deputy mayors who obtained their titles for the equivalent of a landless laborer's full annual income. On the first-class mats were all the current and other former village office occupants, holders of at least the honorary mayor title, and, as a reflection of the well-entrenched Confucian emphasis on scholarship, the members of the literati association *(hoi van than)*, which included both Confucian scholars and holders of the Franco-Vietnamese *certificat d'études elementaires.*

The male-oriented and class-centered model of social hierarchy played an equally prominent role in structuring relations within the household and the patrilineage. It was a hierarchical model in which descent was traced through men, residence was patrilocal, and authority, both domestic and public, rested primarily with wealthy and educated men not engaged directly in manual labor, the prominent role of women in household production processes notwithstanding.

In early 1928 Bang's household was a classic polygynous, patrilineally extended family that, both in terms of household formation and gender relations, was firmly rooted in the Vietnamese male-oriented model of Vietnamese kinship. The household formation approached the Confucian ideal of *ngu dai dong duong* (a family with members of five consecutive generations together under the same roof). Bang's household had sixteen members belonging to four consecutive generations, including all the surviving male descendants of the three wives of the household founder (i.e., Bang's paternal grandfather). As seen in figure 1, it comprised Bang's paternal grandfather's (A1) first wife and her granddaughter (C1, temporarily separated from husband); the three-member nuclear family of Bang's grandfather's grandson (C7) by the grandfather's third wife; Bang's father (B2, born of Bang's grandfather's second wife) and the father's two surviving wives; Bang (ego, C6), his wife, a son, and an adopted son; as well as Bang's two senior brothers Tang and Gia (C3 and C4) and their two respective wives. The formation did not merely highlight the patrilineal linkage to the household founder (ego's paternal grandfather) at the expense of matrilateral ones (the founder's three wives). It also strictly followed the rule of patrilocal residence. Bang's married half-sister (C5) and his father's adopted daughter (C2) had moved to their husbands' households. By the same principle, Bang's wife and his half-brothers' wives, all of whom had married their husbands when the latter were only thirteen or fourteen years old, resided with their husbands' large extended family.

Bang's early-1928 household exemplifies well the male- and elite-ori-

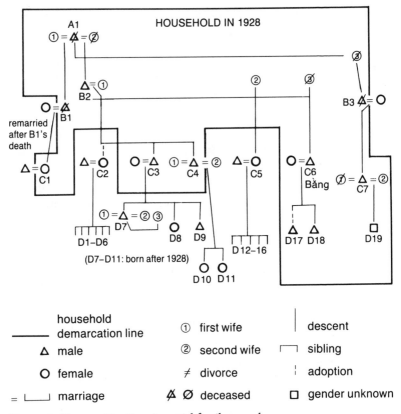

FIGURE 1. Nguyen Dac Bang's partial family genealogy

ented model in Vietnamese kinship—a model clearly dominant among the precolonial and colonial elite. Centering on a male-female hierarchy and its isomorphic relation to other conceptual dichotomies such as center versus periphery and spatially bound versus spatially unbound, the male-oriented model emphasized the rule of patrilocal residence (male/female :: center/periphery :: spatially bound/spatially unbound), a formal separation of the sexes, the domestic-centered role of women in patrilineally extended families, and the public-domain orientation of male household members. In this model, even when the wife actively participated in the labor market, as she did in Son-Duong in the precapitalist and colonial eras, ideally it did not replace her domestic-centered role but merely increased the financial resources of the unit for which she was responsible. A woman's financial contribution was made without any necessary increase in her authority. Formal education as an avenue to public status was not available to women in Son-Duong until Bang started teaching in 1927. In terms of domestic authority, despite the presence of Bang's grandfather's first wife in the household at the time, it was Bang's father (B2, born ca. 1865–1870) who officially headed the household. The main room of the house was a male domain where important guests were received and where the ancestral altar was located. Not only were junior female members of the household such as Bang's wife unable to enter this main room in the presence of guests, but they reportedly had to cover their faces with conical hats when passing in front of it in the presence of male guests. Male and female household members were separated to the extent that married male members continued to sleep in the main room of the house apart from their spouses. When questioned about the consummation of his marriage at the age of fourteen, Bang responded:

It took quite a while for the marriage to be consummated. After the wedding, I still slept with my brothers and my cousin Mai in the living room, where the ancestral altar was located. My wife slept with my senior female cousin. For intimate moments with my wife, I had to wait until everybody fell asleep. We had to spend time together discreetly in a corner of the house.

The male-oriented model also, and obviously so, emphasized male-centered continuity of the kinship unit. In terms of the internal logic of this male-oriented model, polygyny ensured the quintessential male-centered continuity of the kinship system. Beyond its internal logic, in the polygynous households of the elite, wives also constituted an important labor source, given their significant role in the domestic economy. Bang's grandfather and father each had three wives. The wealthiest Son-Duong villager, whose second wife was a sister of Bang's father's second wife, had seven wives altogether. The second wealthiest man, who also occupied the position of village mayor (ly truong), had at least four wives, albeit with no children. The rank of children in polygynous families depended primarily on their mothers' seniority. In other words, a younger son born of the first wife is senior to and addressed as anh (elder brother) by his older half-siblings.

In Son-Duong the sons of the elite got married through parental arrangements at an early age, usually before the age of fifteen. Because of the need for female labor, the daughters-in-law were slightly older women who could contribute their labor to the household production processes. Only the daughters of the wealthiest families might be able to stay on with their natal kin groups in order to help their parents for a short period after marriage. In this context of parental arrangements, the young couple did not always fully understand the significance of the marital bond. Bang related his naive reaction to his marriage at the age of fourteen:

Despite the big wedding, I was still too young then to understand that my wife, Mrs. Lan, had moved into my family after the ceremony. I asked her after three days why she still remained in my house, not yet returning to her home. My elder sisters had to tell me: "She is your wife." . . . You see, when my half-sister got married, thanks to her mother's wealth and power, she could remain at home for almost one year before moving to her husband's household.

In the male-oriented model, resources were allocated in favor of sons and other patrilineal relatives. Rice fields were divided among the sons. Because of his ritual obligations toward his parents after their deaths and to other patrilineal ancestors, the most senior son was entitled to inherit the parents' house and possibly a larger share of the parents' land than the others. Other sons might also receive branch houses, as in the case of Bang's father (B2). In Bang's family, branch houses were bequeathed according to a strict inheritance rule. When Bang's father returned to the main house of the family as the surviving senior male member of his generation after the death of a senior half-brother, the branch house was passed on to his junior half-brother's married son (C7), the most junior and married member of the C generation. When C7 moved into the main house, the branch house was given to Bang, the most junior son, after Bang's marriage. In the male-oriented model, daughters might also receive some property in the form of a dowry.

As a reflection of the strength of the male-oriented model in the village of Son-Duong, among Bang's relatives the distinction between patrilineal and matrilineal kin was emphasized to the extent that D1 referred to his mother's siblings' sons (D7 and D12) not as *chu* (father's younger brothers and junior male cousins) but as *cau* (nonpatrilineal male relatives of one's parents' generation). The distinction between patrilineal and nonpatrilineal relatives corresponded to the formal organization of the local kinship network into patrilineages, the larger of which had their own ancestral halls and were divided into lineage branches *(chi)*. Male lineage (branch) members attended the annual rituals of worshiping the founding couple—a ceremony that the lineage (branch) authorities prepared with the assistance of other members and their spouses.

The male-oriented and class-structured model of the kinship system exerted its influence beyond the male elite to affect many women of lower socioeconomic strata. The elderly lady Thanh related with pride her critical role in raising the children of her husband's junior wife:

[Because] I worked so hard that I could not bear any children, I managed to persuade my husband's junior wife to have six children, four sons and two daughters. Altogether, I directly raised eight children, my younger brother, six children by my junior cowife, and my husband's brother's son [who, as the secretary of the Communist Party in the village in 1987, occupied the most powerful position in Son-Duong].

In colonial and precolonial Son-Duong the kinship system was also partly structured by the class dimension through a process of class-based marital alliances that occasionally overrode the preference for village endogamy. The class-based marital alliances among the elite are partially illuminated in Son-Duong school teacher Bang's narrative on his and his siblings' marriages:

I got married at the age of fourteen, when I still attended school in Hung-Hoa. My marriage was arranged between two families of the same status, between the son of the presiding official of one village and the granddaughter of his counterpart in another [Dung-Hien]. The marriage was arranged with concern about the social standing of the two families as the primary consideration.

The girls whom I had truly loved and who wanted to marry me I could not marry: Lu, Duyen, and Tho. Lu was such a beautiful lady. However, her parents were poor. Her father had joined the native guard; her uncle lived at the pagoda. She herself tended buffalo for my godfather. She wanted to marry me. . . . I had known Lu while attending the village school at the communal meeting house, that is, before my schooling in Viet-Tri at the age of twelve. She frequently teased me in those days. I ended up engaging in sex with her and deflowering her with reluctance. . . . On the occasion of my half-sister's marriage to Ho, later a village mayor, a classical opera *(cheo)* was performed for days as a part of the wedding celebration. It was the wedding of the daughter of my father and his second wife to the son of another wealthy family. As the bride's brother, I had the honor of sitting on a raised platform in the courtyard during the opera performance. Lu happened to sit on the floor by my side, and she whispered to me: "Would you let me know when you want to go home? I would like to leave together with you." At one point during the performance I stood up, but only to go outside to urinate. Lu joined me and kept me from returning to the courtyard. I did not know much of anything about sex then. I did it with great reluctance. . . . My senior sisters helped to communicate to my parents my preference to marry Lu, as I did not dare to speak too often to my father let alone to state my desire to marry Lu. In our system it was the parents who expressed opinions and made the decisions. As soon as my father learned of my preference to marry Lu, he called me in immediately. He said that it was a matter of matching wealth and status. He asked me: "How could you dare to think of a marriage to a buffalo tender whose father works as a lowly soldier in the native guard and whose uncle is so poor as to live at the pagoda?" I stood quite embarrassed and silent like a stone. . . .

My two [half-] brothers, Gia and Tang, got married at an even earlier age, that is, at the age of thirteen. Just as my wife was sixteen, two years older than I was, at the time of our wedding, they married slightly older women so that the latter could help with household chores. Mrs. Gia's father, elder brother, and elder brother's son all held the title of deputy mayor at one point or another, although they owned only a few *mau* of land. Tang's first wife also came from a land-owning family with a few *mau* of land. The man whom my eldest sister, an adopted daughter of my parents, married was a son of the president of the neighboring village Dung-Hien and a brother to a canton chief. Her husband was actually my father-in-law's younger brother. . . . All of us were married through parental arrangement with utmost concern for the social standing of the involved families.

However, even among the elite of colonial Son-Duong, the male-oriented model was to some extent countered by a non-male-oriented system. Bang's four-generation, patrilineally extended family had reached the culminating point of its remarkable formation by 1928 through somewhat fortuitous circumstances. Around the turn of the century Bang's grandfather's first two wives established two separate households in the same village.[8] The grandfather's patrilineally extended household had split into at least two units. The first household included the grandfather (A1), his first wife, their son (B1), their daughter-in-law, and their granddaughter (C1). The grandfather's second wife (Bang's father's mother) resided in a separate house with her son (B2) and the son's family. It was only through a fortuitous combination of circumstances that Bang's father (B2) moved to the main house as the senior male descendant of his generation (ca. 1905–1910). Those circumstances included the death of the senior male descendant (B1) around the turn of the century, the lack of male descendants in the senior branch of the family, and the death of Bang's father's mother (his grandfather's second wife). Bang's junior cousin did not move into the main house until shortly before 1928. In the predominantly patrilineal system of northern Vietnam, with its partible inheritance rule, the process of household fission, as exemplified by the half-brothers in the second generation of Bang's family, points toward the significance of matrilateral linkages to the founder's different wives and to the operation of an alternative kinship principle long observed by analysts of patrilineal systems (Wolf 1972; Kelly 1977). In colonial Son-Duong the non-male-oriented kinship principle was weakly manifested in the tradition of establishing the second son's ceremonial membership not in his father's *giap* but in his mother's father's *giap*. This non-male-oriented kinship model, incorporating the bilateral descent principle, also underlay the wedding offerings not only to the bride's and groom's patrilineal ancestors, but also to their respective maternal grandfathers' and grandmothers' ancestors (see also Luong 1989). Among the poorest village households the non-male-oriented model was also manifested in the relatively egalitarian labor contribution of both men and women. In these households both men and women directly engaged in manual labor. Because of poverty the men married late and most remained monogamous for the rest of their lives. For example, Bang's cousin Te (born in 1921) did not marry until the age of twenty-seven because of the dramatic downward mobility in his family in the aftermath of the Yen-Bay uprising. In general, the non-male-oriented model was overshadowed by its male-oriented counterpart in the colonial period, the attenuated impact of the latter among the poorer households notwithstanding. I suggest that both the division of labor within Bang's household and the limited visibility of Son-Duong women in the local revolution in general relate to the dominance of a kinship-centered, male-oriented, and class-structured model in the local universe of the colonial social formation.

On the eve of the Yen-Bay uprising, the structure of Son-Duong village involved a tension between such a model of hierarchical relations, on the one hand, and a heightened consciousness of the village as a collectivity bonded by extensive kinship, communal, and ethnic ties within a corporate framework, on the other. In this context, the ideology of equality in the French metropolis notwithstanding, French colonialism both reinforced the hierarchical model within the microcosm of Son-Duong village and reconstructed the hierarchy of the colonial social formation in the form of a racial diarchy (Woodside 1976).

Under the colonial social formation the model of hierarchical relations in rural communities was partly reinforced by the formation of the lineage representative council in the 1921 French administrative reform whereby the council of notables was replaced. This reform heightened the role of the patrilineage in village structure. More important, status within the community became more commoditized than ever as male villagers could directly purchase honorary titles from the colonial government for a fixed price: fifteen piasters for an honorary hamlet title *(xa tien)*, thirty-five piasters for the deputy mayor title *(pho ly tien)*, and fifty piasters for the honorary mayor title *(ly quyen)*.[9] Upon hosting a banquet for other title holders, relatives, and neighbors, the new honorary office holders were exempted from corvée labor and could participate in the village feasting system—the system for which most of the communal land was reserved. Villagers *(bach dinh)* who could not afford honorary titles were both excluded from the feasting system and obligated to provide the state-imposed corvée labor. They had constantly to refer to both honorary and actual office holders as well as their spouses with the names of these notables' offices (e.g., *ong Chanh* Con, grandfather Canton Chief/Village President [father of] Con). Among relatives, the commoditized titles had to be added to the kinship terms of both the title holders and their wives to mark the addressor's due respect (e.g., *bac Ly* Mai, senior uncle/aunt Mayor [father of] Mai). Even in referring to title holders and their spouses in their absence, poor villagers had to avoid personal pronouns, because in the dominant discursive practices of the native universe, these linguistic forms presupposed and implied a lack of respect for the referents. In contrast, the poorer villagers were addressed either in terms of their kinship positions or more contemptuously with personal pronouns. Unlike many other northern communities where elderly men could participate in the communal house feasts on the basis of their age, the elderly poor of Son-Duong remained excluded from formal public events to the very end of their lives. Although they could participate in lineage ceremonies on the basis of their age and kinship status, it was the village title holders who, regardless of their kinship ranks, became the lineage spokesmen. Formal public rank became an obsession among villagers with some land ownership: after achieving middle-peasant status through the purchase of land and the coownership of an ox, the elderly lady Thanh saved and borrowed enough money to purchase titles for both her husband and his brothers and to give banquets for relatives, neighbors, and other title holders on the occasions on which these titles were conferred. In the encounter between the local universe and French capitalism, commoditized status took precedence over all other criteria of rank with the exception of academic achievement. In Son-Duong and numerous other northern villages, the importance of academic achievement in the local status hierarchy reflected the widely accepted Confucian view that education essentially involved moral cultivation and that educated men played a vital role in societal leadership. However, in general, commoditized status pervaded the entire structure of social life in the village of Son-Duong.

## The Rise of Modern Anticolonial Movements

Beyond the microcosm of the village, the colonial social formation was structured by a racial diarchy of colonial masters and colonized indigenous masses (Woodside 1976:17). At the top were approximately ten thousand Frenchmen who filled important positions in the government, in professions, and in industrial, commercial, and agricultural enterprises. Within the governmental structure the French managed to absorb 60 percent of the general personnel budget, although they held only 20 percent of all positions (Marr 1981:24). They ruled over the indigenous masses, most of whom lived in agricultural communities and whose livelihoods were sustained within a subsistence-oriented framework. The racial diarchy of colonial Vietnam is described particularly well in the French-educated novelist Nhat-Linh's account of his journey to France:

The farther the ship got from Vietnam and the closer it got to France, to the same degree the more decently the people aboard the ship treated me. In the China Sea they did not care to look at me. By the Gulf of Siam they were looking at me with scornful apprehension, the way they would look at a mosquito carrying malaria germs to Europe. When we entered the Indian Ocean, their eyes began to become infected with expressions of gentleness and compassion . . . and when we crossed the Mediterranean, suddenly they viewed me as being civilized like themselves, and began to entertain ideas of respecting me. At that time I was very elated. But I still worried about the time when I was going to return home!   (translated in Woodside 1976:4)

Mediating between the colonial masters and the indigenous masses was the emerging Western-educated native intelligentsia that, even with the minimalist criterion of three years of French education, made up at most 0.8 percent (150,000) of the native population by the late 1930s. With the termination of the Confucian examination system in Tonkin in 1915, this French-educated native elite was trained to fill low- and middle-ranking positions in the colonial public and private sectors (as clerks, interpreters, and elementary school teachers, among other positions). Among this Western-exposed elite the conceptual distinction between insiders and outsiders, nurtured in the native communal framework, combined with the French ideals of equality and liberty to sharply heighten the consciousness of racial inequality (see also Emerson 1960:54–57). This emerging French-educated elite saw themselves as the vanguard of the new era and as the new leaders of the native masses. Their aspirations rose higher than ever when, during World War I, the French promised the indigenous elite a more active role in colonial affairs and when a socialist governor general (Varenne) arrived in Hanoi in 1925. Many were subsequently disappointed by the considerable persistence of a colonial order rooted in the reality of racial inequality dressed in the discourse of benevolent association. As repeatedly remarked by both French colonial analysts and leading scholars of twentieth-century Vietnam, from 1925 onward many of these French-educated members of the intelligentsia, who had been nurtured by the symbols of anticolonial activism in the preceding four decades, filled the ranks of new anticolonial parties, both Marxist and non-Marxist (GGI-DAP, 1930–1933). Nguyen Dac Bang spoke of the reasons for his political activism:

[During my school years in Hanoi in the mid-1920s] I was strongly inspired by discussions with [the future VNP leader Pho Duc] Chinh and other progressive students on the many injustices perpetuated by the French colonizers against the colonized, some of which I had witnessed myself. For example, on one occasion a Japanese friend of mine and I took a train from my home district to Hanoi. Reading French books on the train, we talked to each other about them in French. A French train conductor made a contemptuous comment to the effect that Vietnamese like us could not—I no longer remember the exact comment, but it was contemptuous regarding the Vietnamese race. The Japanese told him to shut up and simultaneously slapped the racially arrogant conductor. The conductor pulled out his pistol. "He is Japanese," I had to shout to the French agent. The French obviously did not dare to bully a Japanese. Told to leave by my Japanese acquaintance, the Frenchman simply left. The Japanese dared to slap the French conductor in response to the insult because of the emergence of Japan as a power after her victory over Russia in 1905. The French had to treat the Japanese with some respect. As a Vietnamese, I was boiling with anger at being insulted and not being able to respond at all. What could a Vietnamese do, given the power of the French conquerors? I felt deeply humiliated.

That incident was only one example of the injustice imposed by naked power. In my Hanoi school days, Chinh, Lap [my friend from Kinh-Ke village], other progressive students, and I often commiserated about the powerlessness of a conquered race and about the contemptuous treatment of Vietnamese by the French on a daily basis. I was also inspired by French books regarding the noble ideals of liberty—Rousseau—democracy, and civil rights—Montesquieu. The flame of patriotism in my heart was kept alive through my participation in the tumultuous student demonstration in Hanoi against the life imprisonment sentence of Phan Boi Chau, a leading anticolonial activist in the first quarter of the century, and the memorial service on the shore of West Lake for Phan Chu Trinh, a reformist and well-known patriot of the same era. These events kindled and nurtured the patriotism of Vietnamese youth. French injustices had destroyed the basis for any peaceful coexistence.

The new French-educated political activists became conscious not only of the racial diarchy of colonial Vietnam but also of the impact of French capitalism on the indigenous social formation, as indicated in the following manifesto of the Vietnamese Nationalist Party on the eve of the Yen-Bay uprising.

Proclamation to the people of the nation:

Compatriots! Countrymen!

A duty it is to demand back a conquered country; an obligation it is to take collective vengeance against a common enemy. A calling it is to help one's countrymen in misfortune and to rescue one's own race from danger. They are all responsibilities of human beings.

For over sixty years, the French have called themselves a protector in order to appropriate our country and oppress our people. Their intention is to eliminate our race. In face of this common knowledge, how can we sit still? We all know without saying how barbarous and disreputable their policy is in this country. Power they monopolize, treating our people like animals. Schemes they devise, in order to imprison our patriots. This is to silence our countrymen in the face of oppression and injustice. Monarchy they extol, corrupt officials they tolerate, and lackeys they protect. This is to encourage brothers and sisters and fellow countrymen to kill one another off. Education they limit, free speech they prohibit, association they constrain, and mobility they restrict. Our fellow countrymen cannot learn albeit possessing brains, cannot speak although having mouths, cannot hear despite their ears, cannot move in spite of their legs, and cannot plan to work together, even among brothers and sisters. They increase taxes, exploit the mines, destroy the forests, build factories, open plantations, and use a thousand other means to carry off the wealth of our people. Our fellow countrymen are deprived of food and shelter, suffering the misery of hunger and cold. They distill poisonous alcohol and open opium shops to sell to our fellow countrymen. The health of our people declines steadily; diseases spread gradually. They deceive our fellow countrymen into leaving for New Caledonia and places with unhealthy climates so that our race is weakened. In a word, it is impossible to enumerate all the brutal acts of the French and the visible threats to the survival of our people.

Alas! In view of the wild ambition of the French and the present conditions of our country, unless we carry out a revolution soon, our race may not survive the elimination process at work. Unless we eliminate the French [from this land], they will annihilate us. In accordance with heaven's will and the people's wish, on the basis of justice and humanity, for the sake of the country of Vietnam, eighteen million compatriots, and the Hong-Lac [Viet] race, our party makes the first sacrifice, takes the initial step forward in order to lead the revolution and to capture towns and destroy citadels. We are determined to expel the French to France, to demand Vietnam back for the Vietnamese, and to found a democracy so that the people can escape miseries and live in happiness. We hope that all our compatriots will understand our obligations, will share the sacrifice, will work together with us to eradicate the French pirates in order to wash away the shame from our land and rescue our race. Dear compatriots! Dear countrymen! The opportunity has arrived. The movement has started. Our revolutionary forces have risen up. The success of the revolution depends on the contributions of our compatriots and countrymen. Let us stand up and risk our lives in order to eliminate the enemy. As you make sacrifices for the country, please shout "Long Live Vietnam! May the Vietnamese Revolution Succeed!"

Central Committee of the Vietnamese Nationalist Party

The proclamation of the Vietnamese Nationalist Party (AOM-AP-I, 7F-4) sought to increase the solidarity among the native population through a heightened collective consciousness of the French threat to the Vietnamese race and nation. In this respect it bore a remarkable thematic resemblance to the nineteenth-century anti-French exhortation to the indigenous population that was discussed in chapter 1.

> Because the court's officials were cowards and excessively anxious to save their lives, they hurriedly surrendered to the enemy.
> Given that advantage, the enemy now moves freely and kills our people with impunity.
> But people like us must try to preserve the country in which we live.
> Shall we just stare at our decay?
> Since we are determined not to live with the enemy, we shall not be deterred by their overwhelmingly superior forces,
> Since we believe that success rests upon the people's will, we shall not fret over our futile efforts . . .
>
> (translated in Truong-Buu-Lam 1967:113–115)

That proclamation by the VNP built on the powerful and evocative symbols of the precolonial native tradition that had served to unite most of the indigenous population in the earlier decade-long anti-French resistance. It echoed a recurrent theme in the life of Son-Duong village—a theme manifested in the annual ceremonies honoring the two tutelary deities who had played important roles defending the country against foreign intruders. Perhaps as a sign of the times, the VNP proclamation reflected a heightened sense of nationhood, i.e., through the appeal to all the indigenous ethnic groups in the eighteen-million population with a specific reference to the Hong-Lac race, within the boundaries of a country. Beyond the foremost objective of national independence, the VNP program combined a Western discourse on justice and civil liberties (freedom of speech, association, and mobility) with a socialist vision of political economy. Bang elaborated in his discussion of the three principles of the party:

The first principle is nationalism. Vietnam is to be liberated from foreign domination. All Vietnamese people, including all ethnic minorities, are to become citizens of an independent and sovereign Vietnam. The second principle is democracy. Every citizen is entitled to four fundamental rights: the right to vote, the right to impeach elected officials, and the rights to ratify and to abolish laws. The third principle involves the livelihood of the people. It would entail imposing severe limitations on capitalism through the nationalization of industries, the improvement of workers' working conditions, and an egalitarian distribution of land to the peasantry. It aims at increasing productivity and at reducing the gap between the rich and the poor to guarantee the livelihood of each citizen.

Bang's recollective interpretation of the third principle was not necessarily influenced by his later exposure to Marxism and the rise of Marxist power in Vietnam. He reported intense debate as early as the late 1920s between party ideologues favoring communism and collective ownership and those defending the principle of private property. The debate indirectly echoed the potentially discordant voices of village institutions: those rooted in the long-standing collectivist tradition of communal land and communal tutelary deity worship, and those rooted in the class-structured hierarchy of village social life. In many northern and central villages, communal land was distributed to all adult male villagers, reinforcing a strong sense of collectivity. The collectivist vision of communal life was not restricted to the communal rites of passage: in the nineteenth century, on two separate occasions, Nguyen emperors actually ordered the appropriation of private land in certain parts of the country in order to increase the amount of communal land available for distribution (Nguyen-The-Anh 1971:111–112; Nguyen-Thieu-Lau 1951). With clear precedents in Vietnamese history, the official VNP position on people's livelihood (the third principle) envisioned an active use of state power to guarantee the welfare of the working masses.

In order to achieve the dual objectives of national independence and socioeconomic welfare, the VNP leadership sought to combine both the activist and reformist traditions of the first quarter of the twentieth century. They hoped not only to overthrow the colonial state but, like most other members of the French-educated native intelligentsia, also to strengthen the Vietnamese system through systematic reforms. Although the official VNP program did not strongly emphasize socio-economic reforms, the VNP leadership actively pushed for them at the local level, as Bang discovered in the preparation for the funeral of his father's senior mother in Son-Duong in 1929:

According to custom, relatives both within and outside the patrilineage met for the entire night to discuss the funeral arrangements and to prepare for the funeral. Since I had joined the Vietnamese Nationalist Party by then, [the deputy VNP leader] Chinh suggested that I cancel the big [wasteful] funeral feast. Following this suggestion, at the gathering to prepare for the funeral, I took the position that on the date of burial, villagers should simply accompany the deceased to the burying field and that they simply be offered drinks and native cigarettes. No more than that. When the idea of skipping the funeral feast was proposed, my paternal aunts strongly opposed it. They said: "If there is no funeral for the old lady, how will you have your wife claim the [feast association] debts afterwards? How will you get the rice and other contributions that the members of those associations owe us? We can only claim the debts on the right occasions." Only a senior relative [Te's father's elder brother] had a sufficient sense of the modern era to support my idea. My brothers Tang and Gia had also seen the new light on the issue by then. But all other male relatives supported the old ladies, forcing the organization of a funeral feast. Chinh expressed a great deal of displeasure with me about this funeral. He complained about the waste of money for the funeral.

In the context of post-1925 colonial Vietnam, the Vietnamese Nationalist Party proclamation could have been made by either of the two other anticolonial parties of this period in northern Vietnam—the virtually moribund New Vietnam Revolutionary Party (Tan Viet Cach Mang Dang) and the rapidly ascendant communist movement. Despite the differences in their vision of a postcolonial societal order as well as in revolutionary tactics and organizational bases, all three parties were formed in the political ferment of the 1925–1927 period. They all attracted members of the modern-educated intelligentsia, and they shared both the perception of French "brutalities" and the objective of national independence. They also had in common the search for a synthesis of the activist and reformist traditions.

Formed in 1925 and unable to transcend either an elitist network or regional ties, the New Vietnam Revolutionary Party (Tan Viet) recruited most actively among students and the low-ranking civil servants in northern central Annam.[10] It was in this part of the country that thirty of the forty-two party cells were located in 1928.[11] In the province of Phu-Tho by the end of 1928, the New Vietnam Revolutionary Party had formed only one cell, in the town of Hung-Hoa (Cao-Tien-Phung et al. 1985:34). The New Vietnam Revolutionary Party was gradually absorbed by the Vietnamese Revolutionary Youth League (Viet Nam Thanh Nien Cach Mang Dong Chi Hoi), which was formed by Ho Chi Minh in Canton in 1925 and which had a considerably wider regional and class organizational basis.

Like the two other anticolonial parties of the post-1925 period, the Vietnamese Revolutionary Youth League recruited 90 percent of its original membership among the educated "petite bourgeoisie" in which the intelligentsia played a dominant revolutionary role in relation to small shopkeepers and capitalists (Nguyen-Cong-Binh et al. 1985:224). However, in accordance with Marxist-Leninist doctrine, the Vietnamese Revolutionary Youth League emphasized the revolutionary potential of the industrial proletariat and launched a successful "proletarianization" campaign among its better educated members to strengthen its roots among the emerging working class. The percentage of bourgeois revolutionaries consequently declined over time, although they were still well represented in the Communist Party membership, as partially reflected in the membership data for the provinces of Nam-Dinh and Ha-Nam, presently merged into Nam-Ha (see table 3).

The proportion of Communist Party membership from the bourgeoisie in Nam-Ha in 1927–1931 was considerably higher than the percentage of bourgeois in the native population (3 percent) in the late

**Table 3. Backgrounds of Communist Party members in the provinces of Nam-Dinh and Ha-Nam**

|           | WORKERS | PEASANTS | "BOURGEOIS" | LANDLORDS | OTHER | TOTAL |
|-----------|---------|----------|-------------|-----------|-------|-------|
| 1927–1929 | 39      | 30       | 77          | 12        | 3     | 161   |
|           | (24%)   | (19%)    | (48%)       | (7%)      | (2%)  |       |
| 1929–1931 | 91      | 80       | 45          | 9         | 4     | 229   |
|           | (40%)   | (35%)    | (20%)       | (4%)      | (2%)  |       |

*Source:*  Quoc-Anh 1975:46.

1930s (Marr 1981:31). Furthermore, the percentage of "bourgeois" Communist Party members in northern Vietnam may be underrepresented by the data from Nam-Ha. The percentage of Communist Party members from the working class in Nam-Ha probably exceeded that in most other northern provinces, because Nam-Ha included one of the three major industrial centers in the north. Even at 20 percent, party members from the bourgeoisie played an unusually important role within the ranks of anticolonial party leadership. The overwhelming majority of the party leaders came from the Western-educated intelligentsia that, even by the minimalist criterion of a three-year formal education, made up only 0.8 percent (150,000) of the population by the late 1930s.

Communist Party membership, although still strongest in northern central Vietnam, was widespread throughout the country. By 1930, despite its temporary split in Ho's absence into three regional parties, the Communist Party had emerged as a powerful alternative to the Vietnamese Nationalist Party even within the latter's stronghold in North Vietnam where, within slightly over one year of its formation in December 1927, the VNP had built up a network of 120 cells and 1500 activists (GGI-DAP 2:12).

National independence constituted the first and foremost objective of the Vietnamese Nationalist Party, which derived its ideological inspiration directly from the Chinese revolutionary leader Sun Yat-sen's Three People's Principles (nationalism, people's welfare, and human rights) and indirectly from both Western democratic ideology and the indigenous collectivistic tradition.[12] The VNP was led by Nguyen Thai Hoc (born 1901), a graduate of the Ecole Normale and a native of Vinh-Yen province. As a student at the Advanced School of Commerce in Hanoi at the time of Phan Boi Chau's trial and Phan Chu Trinh's death, Hoc was swept up in the tidal wave of student activism of the period. Initially, Hoc had hopes for the possibility of reforms within the colonial system under the principle of French-Vietnamese association: in 1926 he submitted proposals for reforms in Vietnamese industries, commerce, and agriculture to the new French governor general, who came from the ranks of the French Socialist Party. But he received no response. When his subsequent application to publish a monthly magazine to promote practical education was denied, his last hope for reform within the colonial framework was also extinguished. Hoc and numerous friends embarked on the path of revolutionary militancy and linked up with other groups in the provinces of Bac-Giang, Bac-Ninh, and Thanh-Hoa to form the Vietnamese Nationalist Party.

The primary objective of nationalism in combination with a Confucian-based elitism shaped both the VNP recruitment methods and the course of its development at this major juncture in Vietnamese history. The VNP leadership recruited members mainly among the nationalist and activist elements of the native elite: the modern-educated young intelligentsia, the traditionally oriented rural notables, and, for tactical purposes, the warrant officers in the colonial armed forces (cf. GGI-DAP 2:12). The party leadership in the Son-Duong area was no exception in this regard: it included the Confucian teacher Toai and the French-educated Nguyen Dac Bang. The VNP regional committee was chaired by an elderly notable, the mayor of Son-Duong's neighboring Duc-My village. Of the 223 Vietnamese Nationalist Party members convicted at the 1929 criminal tribunal in Hanoi, 40 percent (91) came from the Western-educated intelligentsia (GGI-DAP 2:13). With few exceptions, other members of the native society (e.g., women, soldiers, students, workers, and peasants) were organized simply into party-affiliated associations (ibid.: appendix 2; Hoang-Pham-Tran 1949:87).[13]

The Vietnamese Nationalist Party briefly and unsuccessfully explored the possibility of a political merger with the other two parties in order to strengthen the cause of national independence and the base of Vietnamese anticolonialism (Hoang-van-Dao 1970:41–43; Hoang-Pham-Tran 1949:39–43).[14] In the town of Hung-Hoa it succeeded in absorbing the only New Vietnam Revolutionary Party cell in the province (Cao-Tien-Phung et al. 1985:34).

The momentum of the party, however, screeched to a halt in February 1929, when local party activists assassinated Bazin, a chief labor recruiter for the plantation coolie trade, on the occasion of the new year. The French arrested over two hundred party members, initiating a phase of strong repression.[15] The assassination reportedly was attempted with the hope of demonstrating VNP activities and power among commercial and industrial workers in the face of an active and competing recruitment drive by the Marxist Vietnamese Revolutionary Youth League (Hoang-van-Dao 1970:54–58). Certain party members' betrayals in the face of French manipulations compounded the

VNP's problems in its long-term planning for the uprising (Hoang-Pham-Tran 1949:73–80). Deeply concerned about the further erosion of VNP strength by French repression, the party leadership decided, after a turbulent debate in mid-1929, to expedite the insurrection time table, to intensify the recruitment of new members and the mobilization of local populations, and to actively prepare for an uprising. They realized the small odds of success but won over the objections of a moderate minority with a well-known phrase predicated upon the native cultural logic: "Even if victory were not achieved, we would fully mature as human beings with our [heroic] efforts" *(Khong thanh cong cung thanh nhan)*. It is a logic that evaluates human achievements at least as much on the basis of moral nobility as in terms of concrete results.

Within the village of Son-Duong, as the preparation for the insurrection intensified, local leaders who came from the ranks of the native elite made extensive use of the hierarchical structure of the village as well as kinship and communal ties in order to mobilize other villagers. Nguyen Dac Bang discussed the process of political mobilization within the communal framework and the responses of Son-Duong villagers:

Revolutionary tasks required a lot of energy and a heightened activism. Starting in November 1929, I received instructions from the party to look after many fugitive comrades who came to my village to help with the production of bombs and hand grenades. I arranged for their food and shelter at my relatives' homes in the daytime. In late December 1929, when the party traitor Duong brought secret service agents to a leadership meeting in Vong-La village to arrest the party president Hoc and ended up wounding [his deputy] Chinh, I had to organize the transportation of Chinh to my village by sampan on the Red River. Chinh stayed in my village, actually at the Confucian teacher Toai's house next to mine, to recover from the wound. As a result of Chinh's rehabilitation in my village and the concomitant shift of the regional party headquarters to Son-Duong, party activities in Son-Duong further intensified from that point onward.

*Why did everybody move to your village?*

They came to my village because the Confucian teacher Toai and I provided an active local leadership. Some villagers joined as party members and party-affiliated association members. The mayor and the administration in my village simply turned their eyes away from our activities. They understood.

Their relatives were party members. On the eve of the uprising the village looked like a festival day. Village administrators like Deputy Mayor Kiem and Acting Mayor Di took the oath of loyalty to the movement at my house in a ceremony administered by teacher Hop, a relative of mine from Xuan-Lung. The mayor and his people had high regard for us. They respected me personally for my education. Furthermore, my family, although not a big-landlord family, was well-off. My father had been involved in the anti-French Tonkin Free School movement. It was thanks to my standing and relations with village officials that they connived at our activities and alerted us to any potential problem.

The local party membership amounted only to five, but we had approximately ten activists in a party-led association, and villagers were quite sympathetic. The Sino-Vietnamese teacher Toai and I were leaders in the local party organization. No party member [in Son-Duong] came from the local notable ranks. We also organized an association with approximately ten members. In contrast to party members, the latter came from the manual-labor class and therefore did not provide leadership.

*Were you related to many of the party and association members?*

The Confucian teacher Toai and I were related. His mother, my mother-in-law, my paternal grandfather's first wife, and the mother of another party member, the deputy mayor Thanh, were all sisters. A fourth member of the party, Tin Quay, was related to the Confucian teacher Toai. His younger brother was a pupil of mine. Another party member, Tap, was a distant relative of mine. His mother was a native member of my patrilineage. . . . Within my patrilineage, a few uncles and other relatives of mine actively assisted us on the eve of the uprising. Even my brothers Tang and Gia joined in the preparation for the uprising without any mobilization efforts on my part. . . . The teacher Toai had persuaded Gia to participate. Tang joined the Student Association through his own network, asking his friends to join him in the propaganda talks to other young people and in the distribution of leaflets in many places. It was through Tang's organizational efforts that I, as the propaganda commissioner on the regional committee, went to Hung-Hoa for a talk with prospective young party supporters. We discussed, for example, the patriotic movements of Japan and other countries, as well as the Three People's Principles of the Chinese revolutionary leader Sun Yat-sen. I discussed this doctrine because I knew nothing about Marxism and because it was impossible to find any book on Marxism then. The discussion aimed at inspiring in these young participants patriotism and progressive political attitudes.

*How did other wealthy families in the village respond to the movement?*

It was mainly my relatives and relatives of the teacher Toai who got actively involved at the beginning. But financial contributions were provided by quite a few wealthy families in the village, especially those with literati backgrounds and with some connections to the Tonkin Free School movement. The wife of the wealthiest villager, the late canton chief Chi, contributed a few hundred piasters to the party fund for the purchase of pistols and other weapons. The second wealthiest Son-Duong villager, called Mrs. Village Mayor An [wife of the late village mayor An], and other well-off families also patriotically responded to our requests for assistance. The father of the wife of the late mayor An, Mr. *Doi* Bon [Squad Leader the Fourth], had joined the anticolonial movement earlier, in the late nineteenth century. A matrilineal relative of the teacher Toai, she [Mrs. Village Mayor An] was the most devoted matron of the anticolonial movement in Son-Duong.

The local party membership was small. However, thanks to the sympathy of village officials and other villagers, bombs and leaflets were produced with little difficulty in Son-Duong every night for over a month in early 1930. As school was still in session, I had to neglect my teaching from time to time. During the intense preparation for the uprising, although leaflets and bombs were produced mainly at night, the school was even closed down at times in the daytime.

Indeed, the VNP activities in Son-Duong could not have taken place at all within a close-knit rural community without at least the passive support of village authorities and other villagers. Because of the virtually impenetrable bamboo hedge that surrounds each village, fugitive political activists had to enter Son-Duong through the village gate under the watchful eyes of many villagers. A secret report to higher authorities would have led to the arrest of many anticolonial activists. The bomb manufacturing team included approximately twenty people working under the supervision of fugitive VNP members and with the sympathy, if not the support, of certain elderly members from the elite families of Son-Duong. As narrated by Bang:

In my capacity as propaganda head of the Phu-Tho–Yen-Bay local committee, I assisted Chinh in writing, printing, and distributing leaflets to French, legionnaire, and Vietnamese soldiers, as well as to the Vietnamese populace at large. Chinh and I also took charge, starting in late 1929, of the production of hand grenades in preparation for the uprising. The well-educated party members such as Hoc and Chinh had learned the bomb production techniques from books. We produced two kinds of bombs. One had a cast-iron shell that was manufactured in the neighboring province of Vinh-Yen and transported by sampan at night to my village. The other kind of shell was adapted from cement opium containers that were bought openly on the market. The purchased gun powder was simply added to these shells.

It was actually in my housing compound, in an uninhabited cottage reserved for me and my wife, that the bombs were produced. It was the branch house occupied first by my father and then by my cousin "Uncle" Mai before he moved in with my father. It was moved onto our land for me, but I never lived in it.

*Did your family learn in advance about the production of bombs in your own house?*

After the French break-up of our regional revolutionary center at Vong-La village on the other side of the Red River, the teacher Toai cleverly found a way to obtain my senior mother's approval to turn my house into a bomb manufacturing center. She was the senior person in the house, because my father had died of a gastrointestinal disease in 1928 and because my grandmother had died of old age in early 1929. The teacher Toai worked through Ngan, a fugitive female comrade who had been the obstetrical nurse at the Hung-Hoa hospital and who occasionally came to meetings with Nhu at the teacher Toai's house during the intense preparation period. Earlier on, when my brother Gia had been hospitalized in Hung-Hoa, my senior mother had taken care of Gia there and got to know Ngan. The teacher Toai asked Miss Ngan, also called Miss Secretary, to make a visit to my mother on behalf of the party. So glad to see an old acquaintance, my mother invited the visitor to stay overnight. Needless to say, Miss Ngan accepted the invitation in order to talk to my mother at length about the need to gain independence from the French. That was how my mother became sympathetic to progressive causes. And that was how bombs could be produced in my house. Every day when bombs or leaflets were produced, my mother plus one or two additional household members had to serve meals to about twenty people.

*Did your senior brothers participate?*

My brother Gia did, but without enthusiasm. My other younger brother, Tang, a sixteen-year-old student at the Franco-Vietnamese school in Hung-Hoa at the time, was a member of the Youth Association.

*Did your wife and your brothers' wives object to it?*

They did not dare to object to it, as my senior mother supported our activities. Nobody in the household dared to raise any objection under the circumstances. For our wives, the Confucian maxim applied: "When at home, obey your father; after marriage, obey your husband; after the death of your husband, obey your sons."

During the bomb production period, Bang was summoned by the French Résident, Colas, to the provincial capital of Phu-Tho. Colas advised Bang that Bang's name had been put on the secret police blacklist of revolutionary suspects and that he should not engage in underground activities. Bang reported on a subsequent meeting with the Vietnamese chief of Lam-Thao district:

On my way home from the provincial capital, I also stopped at the office of the Lam-Thao district chief to submit my monthly school activity report. This district chief told me that the leaders of the party, Hoc, Nhu, and Chinh, were reported to be hiding in the district. He told me: "If you can help the government to find them, you and I will be well rewarded. The Vietnamese, having no capacity and resources for modern warfare, will never succeed in opposing the French government, a great Western power, with its modern weaponry and its military might." He obviously knew neither of my party membership nor of the presence of two of these top party leaders in Son-Duong. I simply smiled and nodded my head in reply. But I told myself: "This idiotic bastard knows little of Vietnamese history. We will simply capture French weapons to kill the French themselves. A day of independence will arrive, enabling us to put behind us the shame of losing our country. If everybody thought in the same cowardly way as he does, the Vietnamese would remain forever enslaved, and independence would be a completely lost cause."

Bang's and the Lam-Thao district chief's perspectives on the colonial system represented the two opposite positions in the resistance-collaboration continuum among the native intelligentsia. Although only a minority of the native elite embarked on the path of active resistance owing to its high cost and small probability of success, many others were not reluctant to lend it at least passive support, as they did in the village of Son-Duong during the preparations for the uprising.

The uprising in Phu-Tho and Yen-Bay took place on February 10, 1930, as Hoc's order to postpone the armed insurrection for five days arrived only after the departure of Phu-Tho civilians and the transportation of additional arms to Yen-Bay. Because of a lack of VNP coordination and the previous repressive moves of the French, the movement fizzled. With the subsequent destruction of VNP infrastructures in North Vietnam, the Vietnamese Nationalist Party ceased to play a significant role in Vietnamese anticolonial politics. The failure of the Yen-

Bay uprising reinforced the prominence of the competing Indochinese Communist Party, unified by Ho Chi Minh in February 1930, in the making of modern Vietnam.

The failure of the Yen-Bay uprising notwithstanding, the rise of the Vietnamese Nationalist Party and other modern anticolonial movements from 1925 onward was deeply rooted in the structure of the colonial encounter, that is, in the disjuncture between the metropolitan discourse of liberty, equality, and fraternity and the racial diarchy of the colonial periphery as well as between the capitalist imperialist system and the indigenous precolonial framework. The colonial masters' formidable coercive power, their selective rewards to native collaborators, and their rhetoric of civilizing mission and benevolent Franco-Vietnamese association brought an end to the active resistance by the majority of the indigenous population if not an exploratory accommodation of French colonialism, in the first quarter of the twentieth century (see also Emerson 1960:10–11). However, in this process of exploratory accommodation many Vietnamese both within and outside the French-educated intelligentsia became acutely aware of the contradictions of French capitalistic colonialism in and of itself and in its relationship to the native sociocultural framework. To many revolutionary leaders after 1925, the contradictions became increasingly salient between the colonial racial diarchy and political economic transformation, on the one hand, and the official French discourse on the other.

In the period from 1925 onward many members of the French-educated intelligentsia, descended from the traditional elite, embarked on an active search for national independence. Through their exposure to the West, their world view was partly shaped by the Western ideological emphasis on liberty and civil rights, as seen in the VNP proclamation and as emphasized by Emerson (1960:212–237). However, in accordance with the local tradition, the ideas of equality and liberty were understood not in terms of individual benefits, but as *collective rights in the relations between the Vietnamese and their colonial masters.*

The influence of the indigenous tradition was also reflected in the considerable attention in the VNP proclamation to the capitalist exploitation of the indigenous socioeconomic formation as well as in the party's socialist vision of the political economic framework. Shaped by the doctrine of the Chinese revolutionary leader Sun Yat-sen, this collectivistic vision would not have formed strong roots in the Vietnamese landscape if the native soil had not proved fertile for its growth. In northern and central Vietnam, this vision was nurtured by the fairly strong institutions of communal land and communal tutelary deity worship, although the tradition of communal land was considerably weaker in Son-Duong than in many other villages and although the significance of both institutions was slowly being undermined by increasing class differentiation.

The precolonial northern tradition also intensified the negative reaction of many native actors to foreign domination in a racial diarchy through the sharp distinction between insiders and outsiders in the native conceptualization of kinship, communality, and ethnicity. On one level modern Vietnamese anticolonial movements capitalized heavily on this salient conceptual dichotomy between Vietnamese and non-Vietnamese "races" as well as on the symbols of active native resistance against foreign intruders in previous centuries. They also built extensively on the structure of particularistic relations within the native precapitalist framework. The Vietnamese Nationalist Party, for example, recruited members primarily through school bonds among the sons of the traditional elite—bonds formed in the new context of the colonial educational system. Reproducing the dominant male-oriented and elite-centered model in the local tradition, the VNP found its leadership among the male members of relatively privileged backgrounds. Within the bamboo hedges dotting the rural landscape, VNP leaders relied heavily on kinship and village-bound hierarchical ties in the mobilization process. In Son-Duong, for example, educated VNP members from the privileged social stratum made extensive use of the traditional respect for education and their rural kinship network. The rise of modern Vietnamese anticolonialism can be separated neither from the fundamental inequalities and contradictions within capitalist imperialism nor from the salient features of the native sociocultural framework.

# CHAPTER 3

•

# In the Name of "Liberty, Equality, and Fraternity"

IN THE AFTERMATH of the Vietnamese Nationalist Party uprising in February 1930, the French undertook quick and strong repressive measures. In Yen-Bay French troops maintained a careful check on the population. They prohibited the movement of wood rafts down the Red River from the highlands and hindered other normal economic activities, causing a loss of ten thousand piasters in revenue in March alone. As a collective punishment, the defensive bamboo hedges of Son-Duong and many other villages were leveled, exposing the internal landscape, "shamefully" in native perception, to the entire outside world. A large number of Son-Duong houses were burnt down. French planes also bombed the village of Co-Am in Hai-Duong province. In the province of Phu-Tho, by February 20, 1930, 200 persons had been arrested, among whom 60 were considered to have directly participated in the insurrection and 140 to have been accomplices. The number of arrests had increased to 340 by February 26 and reportedly remained in that range into and beyond March (*Trung-Bac-Tan-Van,* February 26 and March 30, 1930). Eighty-two political activists were subsequently sentenced to death. Other political prisoners were deported to less accessible parts of Vietnam and other corners of the French empire, where the colonial masters planned to use their labor to exploit the resources of the regions at the periphery of the world capitalist system.

On a personal level, the repression temporarily traumatized countless villagers and also further radicalized many political activists. On the national scale, the Vietnamese Nationalist Party was virtually destroyed within the country. The Indochinese Communist Party consequently emerged as an even more powerful anticolonial force and eventually led the indigenous northern population in a violent and successful resistance to colonialism in 1954.

On the theoretical level, the Millean approach to political action encounters an anomaly in the lack of a complete success by the French in extinguishing the flames of Vietnamese anticolonialism in spite of their generous cooptation rewards and the severe punishments imposed on anti-French activists. In the structural tension between French colonialism and the indigenous system, the impact of the dominant ideology of the capitalist core on the native elite of the periphery was amply reflected in the emphasis on liberty and equality in the discourse of Vietnamese anticolonialists in the aftermath of the Yen-Bay uprising (Emerson 1960). However, in the context of little direct exposure to Western Marxism, the collectivistic vision of the political economic framework advocated by many VNP members, not to say the Indochinese Communist Party, suggests that local tradition also played an important role in shaping revolutionary ideologies.

≫ ≫ ≫

Among the convicted political activists was the native son of Son-Duong village Nguyen Dac Bang, who received two death sentences for his role in the uprising. More fortunate than his comrades, he was eventually granted a commutation of both. He was sentenced instead to hard labor for life in another corner of the French empire halfway around the globe in South America, where his experiences radicalized his vision of the sociopolitical order and where he worked actively for Ho Chi Minh's cause of national independence after 1945.

Bang related at length his experiences in the aftermath of the VNP uprising:

[On the night of February 11, in the aftermath of French soldiers' encirclement of Son-Duong] I sneaked back home from neighboring Ngu-Xa village, where I had attended a teacher-honoring banquet hosted by the parents of my pupils. Upon seeing me, my elderly senior mother broke into tears: "Tang hasn't come back. Gia was arrested this morning. Your name, together with many others, was called. The district chief warned that if you or any of the absentees didn't report to him within two days, the absentee's house would be burnt to the ground!"

I stood there, speechless. Hundreds of depressing thoughts swept through my mind. I told myself: "Tang and Gia have been arrested. They will certainly be tortured. They will end up with prison terms because, unable to suffer through all the torture to the end, they will probably end up confessing their affiliation with the party. Who will take care of my elderly senior mother? She is not my blood mother. However, since my own mother's death when I was five, my senior mother has given me even more love and care than she has given to her own two sons, Tang and Gia. Whatever it is, clothes, books, tuition, or a bicycle, she has taken care of my needs first. And she even went out of her way to take care of the meals and the daily needs of those who came here to make bombs! She is a truly exemplary senior mother! What will happen to her now that my two brothers and I will be gone?" During that sleepless night, the more I thought of the country, the party, and my family, the more anguish I suffered. I was also extremely anxious for further news from Yen-Bay and other fronts.

The following morning, I finally learned that the French forces had reoccupied Yen-Bay and that a number of our fighters had been captured, while others had fled. Our major front of Yen-Bay turned out to be a total rout!

Bang's concern about the lack of filial care for his senior mother highlights the persistent conflict in the native system between the kinship duties defined within a male-oriented model and the obligations within a larger collectivistic framework.

At the urging of relatives, friends, and neighbors, Bang decided to report at district headquarters on February 12. However, unlike many Son-Duong villagers who were allowed to return to their village, Bang was arrested: a chief of the district native guard contingent had mistaken Bang for a comrade who had called upon the guards to surrender during the VNP's earlier attack on the district headquarters. Bang's retrospective account of his prison torture experiences highlights the contradiction between the dominant ideology of the capitalist core calling for "liberty, equality, and fraternity" and the political reality of the colony. Bang's prison experiences and death sentences under the French were particularly ironic because the Vietnamese Nationalist Party had adopted "equality, liberty, and fraternity" as a motto in its official program (GGI-DAP 2:47).

The following morning [February 13], I was brought outside the district headquarters and ordered to line up in the street with approximately thirty other prisoners, many of whom I had long known from the villages surrounding Son-Duong. We were all tied up in a line with a big rope, left standing in the sun for over an hour, and eventually ordered to walk to the provincial capital about thirteen kilometers away under the supervision of a native guard detachment. We were herded into a small hot and humid room at the police station, where we had to stand waiting for another hour for a clerk from the Résident's office to come for a basic identity investigation. We were then led to a big hall in the provincial prison, where at last we were at least untied and allowed to walk around. But even this big hall was gradually filled up the following day by newcomers, many of whom were my close comrades.

On the fifteenth I was removed from the group to an isolated cell where my legs were shackled in a wooden yoke. Somebody had provided additional information about me, because I was called not by my full name as earlier provided but as *Giao* [Teacher] Bang. In the early afternoon, in handcuffs, I was escorted by two European legionnaires armed with rifles and bayonets to the interrogation room about five hundred yards away. Two burly French interrogators had been waiting for me in this room full of torture equipment. The big one with a moustache signaled the guards to remove my handcuffs and then asked me in very good Vietnamese:

"You are *Giao* [Teacher] Bang, aren't you?"

"Yes."

"You are a member of the Vietnamese Nationalist Party, is that correct?"

"No."

"How did you get that blot?" He pointed to the small ink blot on my white trousers. I wore at the time not Western clothes but white Vietnamese mourning clothes.

"[As a teacher] I work in the classroom with ink. It happens not infrequently that ink spills on my clothes."

"That is not classroom ink. It is leaflet-printing ink. Now, tell me the truth! Who else was involved in this?"

The moustached investigator showed me a pile of leaflets in both French and Vietnamese on which I immediately recognized the handwriting of my pupils. We produced leaflets by first making a firm jelly and putting the original handwritten copy of the propaganda text on the firm jelly block—a text that I had asked students with beautiful handwriting to copy over at the school. Pieces of blank paper were then pressed against the original copy, one by one, in order to produce dozens of leaflets.

"I know nothing of the printing of leaflets," I replied.

A reeling blow from the moustached interrogator exploded in my face. Then punches and kicks rained down on my head, my back, and all over my body. "The evidence is that ink blot! If you do not admit it, I will beat you to death," roared the torturer. My blood began oozing out. I was almost unconscious, lying on the floor, when he stopped.

I did not know exactly how long it was before the other burly secret service inspector pulled me up and told me in French:

"You are a member of the Vietnamese Nationalist Party. You have printed all these leaflets. We have the evidence. You'd better admit it and tell us all the names of the party members in your cell and of those involved in the printing of the leaflets. You don't want us to torture you, do you?"

"Sir, I am not a member. And I know nothing of the printing of leaflets."

A blow immediately followed my reply, only to be followed by others. I was knocked down on the floor and totally lost consciousness this time.

It was still early in the afternoon when I regained my senses and was taken by two French soldiers back to the cell, where my legs were shackled again. This dark and windowless cell had only a small ventilation hole in the ceiling. There was no furniture except one hard wooden bed about one yard wide and a portable toilet bucket with no cover. Blood still oozed out from the swollen wounds all over my body. In deep pain and with hundreds of bed bugs crawling around me, I could not lie still in bed. I spent the rest of the day killing them with my fingers.

Bang reported being tortured three more times in the next four days for having steadfastly denied any involvement in and knowledge of the uprising in the local area.

In late February, together with three fellow political prisoners, Bang was escorted in chains by four French soldiers to Yen-Bay, the major site of the VNP uprising. Confronted with the testimonies of other fellow activists, Bang admitted his party membership, his authorization of the use of his house for grenade production, and his role in the printing of leaflets. However, in his narrative, he emphasized his success in hiding the names of his student assistants as well as in not admitting to all the transportation and communication tasks that he had carried out together with his comrades. He was also reportedly tortured for denying his participation in the VNP central committee meetings in Vong-La and La-Hao villages in Phu-Tho.

On March 23, 1930, the second formal trial of movement participants took place in Yen-Bay, following the first trial on February 27, 1930.[1] Defendants' responses during this two-day trial ranged from the acceptance of all responsibility, even for other uprising participants, to the essential acknowledgment of their roles but a denial of responsibility by emphasizing the authoritarian nature of the VNP chain of command or coercion and deception by party members, to the untruthful denial of their roles in the uprising and its preparation. The answers of the party president, Nguyen Thai Hoc, fell into the first category: he claimed to be a revolutionary by profession and assumed all responsibility for the uprising, even if certain tasks were not carried out directly under his orders. Some defendants, such as the Phu-Tho native Nguyen Nhu Lien, also valiantly emphasized that it was the duty of a citizen of a conquered country to liberate his fatherland by participating in the uprising. Within the Son-Duong party membership, Confucian teacher Toai's response fell into the first category, Bang's into the second, and *Pho* [Deputy Mayor] Thanh into the third (*Trung-Bac-Tan-Van* March 30, 1930; *L'Avenir du Tonkin,* March 28, 1930).

Bang recalled the court proceedings in greater detail:

One morning, a platoon of French soldiers came into the prison yard. Each of us was called out and handcuffed, and we were lined up in pairs. Walking in two lines along the road and escorted by the soldiers with rifles and bayonets, we were led to a long brick house on top of a hill. Our trials were to be conducted in barracks temporarily converted into a court house. . . . Approximately ten minutes after our arrival, there was a sudden loud command, and the soldiers stood at attention and raised their rifles in salute. The judges arrived. Total silence reigned over the court house. One defendant after another was called before the tribunal, handcuffs removed. Most memorable to this date were Nguyen Thai Hoc's answers:

"Are you the leader of the Vietnamese Nationalist Party?" the prosecutor asked.

"Yes, I am the leader of the Viet Nam Quoc Dan Dang," Hoc replied in Vietnamese. He forgot to say revolutionary *(cach mang)* party.

"What is the doctrine of your party?"

"We fight against the French colonialists for the independence of our country and for the freedom and the welfare of the people of Vietnam."

"You organized the uprising to kill the French, didn't you?"

"Yes. For years we followed a nonviolent policy, making petitions for our independence and freedom. But it was to no avail. To achieve our goals, we had no choice but to resort to violence. . . ."

Hoc went on and on speaking about the principles of freedom, equality, and so on, but the judge stopped him.

"This is not a place for your propaganda. You can answer only questions concerning the uprising."

"If this is not the place for us to talk about reason, justice, and freedom, I wish to say no more."

I was called before the judges in the afternoon, after a brief ceremonial proceeding and a cursory formal questioning of five other defendants:

"Are you a member of the Vietnamese Nationalist Party?"

"Yes. I just do the duty of a member of a conquered country."

"Did you organize the printing of leaflets?"

"Yes. I did so to mobilize my people into supporting our movement and our struggle to liberate the country."

"You allowed the production of grenades in your house, didn't you?"

"Yes. It was an obligation of every member in accordance with the oath of membership: 'I will sacrifice my own life and my own property, if required, and I will obey absolutely the instructions of the party.' The production of grenades in my house was thus the collective responsibility of the party and not my personal fault."

"Did you assign members to join the Yen-Bay attack and the murder of officers and warrant officers there?"

"I was only a low-ranking member. I had no authority to assign members to Yen-Bay. Only Xu Nhu, a member of the central committee, had this authority in my locality." With this statement, I was ordered to withdraw.

As a sign of the times, the discourse of many VNP activists reflects not merely an element of defiance derived from the legends of Vietnamese anticolonialism, but also the strong influence of French education on their thought process. For example, according to a Sûreté report (report 4213, AOM-AP, 7F-37), the teacher Nguyen thi Bac, a sister of party leader Hoc's fiancée, declared in the final round of statements that if she was not judged with justice, the statues of Joan of Arc in France might as well be destroyed. Nguyen Thai Hoc's testimony constantly referred to "equality" and "liberty," although in the context of racial diarchy and the dominant collectivist emphasis in the local tradition, the ideas of equality and liberty were understood not in terms of individual benefits, but as *collective rights.*

The following morning the French Criminal Commission sentenced thirty-nine political activists to death, thirty-three to hard labor for life, nine to twenty years of hard labor, four to life deportation, and one to five years of imprisonment. Among the death row convicts were six natives of Son-Duong village, including Bang and the teacher Toai (AOM-AP-I, 7F-37).

With the hope of saving the lives of many comrades, party president

Hoc first appealed the sentence to the Conseil de Protectorat and after its negative decision requested clemency. All the convicted political activists reportedly followed his lead, with the exception of his Deputy Chinh (AOM-AP-I, 7F-37; Hoang-van-Dao 1970:158), although Bang does not recall having either appealed or requested clemency himself.

The consideration of the clemency requests in Paris and the French measures in the aftermath of the uprising gave rise to diverse reactions and heated debates in colonial circles. With minor exceptions, French colonialists in Vietnam advocated strong punitive measures and broader power for French colonial authorities. The authorities in France defended the colonial government in Indochina although, not unsusceptible to liberal pressures, it tended toward a more moderate stand. Most Vietnamese officials took strong exception to the colonialists' view. After the metropolitan government commuted nine of the thirteen death sentences in the first Yen-Bay trial in early March, M. Borel, the delegate from North Vietnam to the High Council of Colonies in Paris, called a meeting of elected representatives in order to pressure the government into empowering local French officials to use all the measures necessary for the maintenance of the pax colonia. In a Vietnamese preparatory forum the native members of the Tonkin Chamber of Representatives unanimously agreed to make concerted efforts at the official meeting to protest both the bombing of Co-Am village in Hai-Duong and the decrees of the Criminal Commission. They argued that capital punishment must not be handed out to political prisoners. At the official meeting on March 11, they filibustered various resolutions, including one advocating the extension of the powers of the governor general and the provincial *résidents* in a modification of the 1927 decree. They refused to vote on a motion of confidence in the government's measures in the aftermath of the uprising. The native representatives also took the opportunity to air various grievances. They called for a greater role for Vietnamese soldiers in the colonial armed forces. They also suggested rescinding previous government orders that expelled participants in the 1926–1927 student strikes from school and barred them from the administrative apparatus of the colony (Sûreté report of March 14, 1930, AOM-AP-I, 7F-56). The only resolution that received the support of native representatives had to do with a "rational organization of the defense of Indochina along metropolitan lines" (i.e., the reinforcement of metropolitan troops in Indochina). The indigenous representatives subsequently boycotted the meeting en masse. In their absence the French voted for a resolution calling for an extension of the powers of the governor general, granting him the power to decide on capital punishment cases himself without having to obtain the opinion of the metropolitan goverment in Paris, in order to suppress the current movement quickly (AOM-P-NF, 323-2625). The resolution was subsequently sent to France, and received wide coverage in the French press in Indochina.

Bang elaborated further on the sympathy of many native authority figures with the VNP uprising as he recalled his investigation back in Phu-Tho after returning from the Yen-Bay prison:

Returning to the Phu-Tho prison from Yen-Bay, we were imprisoned, this time together, in a large empty hall with hardwood platforms built along the wall. I was questioned again about the assassination of the teacher Kinh in neighboring Kinh-Ke village. This investigation, however, was conducted by a sympathetic Vietnamese provincial judge, Bui Thien Can. After being served tea, I declared having no knowledge of the case, because we had returned from the Hung-Hoa post not by the village of Kinh-Ke but by the village of Ngu-Xa. The native judge whispered to me: "I do not think that much information is [i.e., should be] revealed during this investigation. . . . Your declaration does not need to be in depth. I also want to let you know that without my intervention, your house would have been burnt down under the orders of District Chief Ngoc." It turned out that the Lam-Thao district chief had learned through the complaints of Son-Duong villagers that my house had not been burnt down, whereas their houses had been unjustly burned, despite their lack of participation in the uprising.

*Why had your house been spared?*

My house had been spared thanks to Canton Chief Con, a nephew of my father's second wife, the husband of my senior mother's younger sister, and at one point my gambling partner. His son had also attended my school. He told my mother: "I am going to point to a neighbor's house and tell the French that it is Bang's house." What a disaster it would have been if they had burned my four- or five- room house! Initially, I was told, only the houses of the movement participants were burned, but the fire spread quickly because most houses were constructed of highly flammable thatch. Because of the complaints by villagers, the district chief subsequently ordered the native guards to burn down my house. Mr. Bui Thien Can reportedly scolded the district chief: "The French have burnt down two-thirds of the village. If you order the rest burned, where will people find shelter? You should realize your

luck in not being captured and killed the other day. No more such orders!"
My house remained intact thanks to this intervention. This judge, like the
highest-ranked Vietnamese administrator *(tuan phu)*, was sympathetic to our
cause. When Duong betrayed the party and opened fire, supposedly on Hoc
but actually hitting Chinh, he reported that Hoc had been killed. Mssr. Le
van Dinh [the head mandarin, *tuan phu*] and Bui Thien Can [the provincial
judge] scolded Duong: "You are a troublemaker. What is the evidence that
Hoc is dead? Where is his body?" Duong was very upset by this question
from these mandarins, both of whom knew French despite their Confucian
backgrounds. Only the Lam-Thao district chief was loyal to the French. Later
on, this district chief was relieved of his position and imprisoned for extorting
money from local families in the aftermath of the Yen-Bay uprising.

In France itself liberal organizations such as the Human Rights
League, leftist politicians, and a large number of Vietnamese residents
openly protested against the executions of movement participants and
the Co-Am bombing (AOM-P-NF, 323-2623; AOM-AP-I, 7F-57).
The government of metropolitan France responded to the peaceful May
22, 1930, demonstration in Paris by summarily deporting approximately twenty Vietnamese, mostly students, to Indochina, although a
Paris court had earlier dismissed the goverment's charges against them.
The deportation reinforced the strong critique of the government's
Indochina policy by socialist and communist National Assembly representatives in their tumultuous debate with cabinet members and conservative representatives on June 13, 1930 (Records of the Chambre des
deputés, AOM-P-NF, 267-2328). The government of metropolitan
France defended the Co-Am bombing by citing the historical precedents of 1912, 1917, and 1920 and its effectiveness in restoring order
with minimal cost to the colonial forces. The defense essentially reiterated an argument that the French Résident supérieur in Tonkin had
articulated with a degree of rhetorical excess:

> In the attack on armed rebels, did I have to risk the lives of our own
> men in order to avoid striking a population whose hostility to France
> had long been confirmed and that had aided the assassins at Vinh-Bao?
> Instead of an easy success, did I have to risk a failure that could provide
> encouragement to the rebels recently suffering losses—conditions that
> would allow them to drag the timid and undecisive masses into their
> revolt? . . .
> In my reasoning, it was important to inflict on the bandits and those

sheltering them a quick and exemplary lesson. I judged that only a punishment capable of terrifying those tempted to participate in the rebellion could totally reassure the sane and peaceful elements of the population regarding our will to defend French sovereignty in that land and to stop the movement cold. (Robin report, 1930:18–19, AOM-P-NF, 323-2626)

The moral effect of the Co-Am bombing was immense [according to all the province chiefs] and sufficient for us to straighten out the serious situation in which we found ourselves. (ibid.:21)

On the basis of the information available from its Hanoi section, the French Human Rights League critically raised the issue of the legality and wisdom of burning houses in Son-Duong village with the Ministry of Colonies. The league considered the legionnaires' act in Son-Duong unjustifiable, mentioning that the VNP destruction of the district administrative building a few weeks before the burning of Son-Duong houses had been, according to Son-Duong village authorities, undertaken by the residents of communities on the other side of the Red River. The league also emphasized that the burning of inhabited houses was punishable with capital punishment under both the Vietnamese and French legal codes. After repeated inquiries by the league, the Ministry of Colonies eventually responded in August 1932 that considerable seditious activities had taken place in the village of Son-Duong with the complicity of village notables, and—powerfully illuminating the inequality in the relations between the capitalist core and the colonies— that the Son-Duong punishment was just and even humane in a situation in which European conceptions of justice would have been misplaced. The letter of response concluded in the same spirit as the defense of the Co-Am bombing by the Résident supérieur in North Vietnam: "Any other method would have been considered a sign of weakness . . . it would have led us not to the destruction of a few thatch houses, but to the use of arms and the sacrifice of a much larger number of people under our protection who might have been drawn into that movement" (AOM-P-NF, 323-2623).

Within the village of Son-Duong, residents were shaken by the destruction of their homes and the rather indiscriminate arrests of their relatives by French forces. According to a favorite student of Bang's (Le van Tiem), who had helped copy the propaganda leaflet and who later became a president of the local Communist Party cell: "A small number of villagers, especially women, cursed the revolutionaries for inviting disaster on the village. The more knowledgeable people, however, understood that the loss of their houses meant little compared to the sacrifice of imprisoned and beheaded revolutionaries [from Son-Duong]." Bang also spoke of incrimination from the community:

Many local officials were arbitrarily or mistakenly arrested in those days, like my friend the canton chief Con. Although not initially imprisoned with other local officials, Canton Chief Con was later arrested because of the accusation of a distant patrilineal "uncle" of mine, the teacher Tham. My uncle taught in the neighboring province of Son-Tay, near the Phu-Tho town of Viet-Tri. Participating in the Lam-Thao attack, my uncle was wounded but initially not captured. After being arrested, my uncle, the teacher Tham, suspecting Canton Chief Con of being a French collaborator, maliciously denounced the canton chief as a party member to the French. The accusation was made purely out of vindictiveness. Canton Chief Con was imprisoned. He ended up with a deportation sentence and died in the Poulo Condore prison [off the coast of South Vietnam] later on.

On May 26, 1930, Bang and the Confucian teacher Toai were tried for the second time at the Phu-Tho session of the Criminal Commission. With the exceptions of Toai, Bang's brother Tang, and a few activists, most defendants attempted to deny some of their own acts or to shift responsibility by citing coercion and deception by others. According to a newspaper report at the time, at the Phu-Tho trial, Bang admitted his VNP membership, participation in bomb production, and the recruitment of a number of villagers for the Yen-Bay front at *Xu* Nhu's orders. However, Bang insisted that because of an eye problem, he had excused himself from the Hung-Hoa attack group after participating in the discussion at the teacher Toai's house (*Trung-Bac-Tan-Van,* May 28, 1930; Roubaud 1931:120ff.). This denial notwithstanding, the commission sentenced Bang, Toai, and eight other political activists to death, twenty-seven to hard labor for life, thirty-seven to life deportation, and ten to various sentences, from detention in reeducation centers to twenty years of deportation. Bang's brother Tang received a twenty-year deportation sentence for his assistance in the bomb production process and for distributing propaganda leaflets. Their brother Gia was sentenced to life deportation despite his minimal role in the movement. The lack of any substantiating evidence notwithstanding, Bang's friend, Canton Chief Con, received the same sentence for purportedly offering a gift of one hundred piasters to the teacher Toai, who reportedly refused the gift. The canton chief's cousin Quyen, the president of the Dung-Hien notable council, was also sentenced to life deportation on the basis of accusations by three other defendants that he had contributed two hundred piasters to the Vietnamese Nationalist Party. Although French authorities stated that they could not independently confirm his party membership, he still received the sentence for being a part of the plot to "destroy or change the government of Indochina and to incite inhabitants to arm themselves against authority" (AOM-AP-RST, 53-427). A total of eighteen villagers from Son-Duong and Dung-Hien were convicted by the French Criminal Commission. Six were sentenced to death, nine to hard labor from twenty years to life, and three to deportation. Many local officials were also given shorter sentences in the native court for failing in their duties.

Bang related his prison days after the Phu-Tho trial, including his reaction to the news of the nearly successful assassination attempt on the major party traitor Pham Thanh Duong on May 30, 1930, in Hanoi:

Returning from the Phu-Tho trial, those of us with death sentences were kept in solitary cells, with our legs shackled in wooden yokes. However, in those three weeks at Phu-Tho, we were treated much better than before. By that time, the provincial authorities had resumed the management of the prison that had earlier been under the control of the colonial armed forces. French Résident Colas allowed our relatives to make prison visits and to bring in clothes, food, paper, pens, and ink. My wife and other family members visited me quite a few times and brought me food, since the death row inmates in particular were allowed under Colas' orders to receive food from relatives and, under supervision, to see our close relatives. On the daily trip to the septic tank to empty my toilet bucket, I was also allowed by the prison warden (a fellow Lam-Thao district native) to chat briefly with some other inmates and to exchange food gifts—gifts that they had also received from their families.

Our main pastimes in those days were writing poetry and letters both to our relatives at home and to such progressive organizations in France as the Union of Vietnamese, the French-Vietnamese Friendship Association, the Secours Rouge Internationale, and the French Communist Party. Our letters strongly denounced the unjust, inhuman, and barbarous acts of the French colonialists in Vietnam. With suggestions from all of us, the inmates who were well versed in Sino-Vietnamese literature, especially the Confucian teachers Toai and Diec, wrote long poems describing the events of our uprising. Among our prison poetry was one poem that we planned to recite publicly just before the execution, our "Guillotine Poem," which I still remember very well to this day:

> Mot bau nhiet huyet bay lau nay
> To diem non song giot mau nay
> Ke khuat nguoi con xin cho ngai
> Kem thua hon duoc cung tu day
> No doi gach vac, dan sau dam
> Cong cuoc gian lao, buoc truoc chay
> Ket qua sau nay mong lam ta
> Suoi vang huong duoc tieng thom lay.

The flame [of patriotism] burns in my heart to the very end,
I am now going to shed blood beautifying the Fatherland,
Don't feel sorry that I must go and you remain,
This sacrifice is simply a test, distinguishing cowards from great men,
It is now yours, the sacred duty to liberate our beloved land,
Success or failure will be in your hands,
Your victory in the future is my hope and my dream,
I want to share it in the golden stream.[2]

The most memorable event of my days in Phu-Tho prison occurred when the interpreter of the chief of Tonkin Sûreté informed us one day that a major traitor of the party and a former member of our central committee, Squad Leader Duong, had been assassinated on Leather Street (Hang Da) in Hanoi. (He had been promoted to the position of Sûreté inspector for his betrayal of the party and active collaboration with the Secret Service.) He had attended the Hung-Hoa school at the same time I did, when his father worked as the Hung-Hoa school principal, although he was a few classes ahead of me then. When I attended school in Hanoi, I had even paid a visit to his teacher father, who resided in the Hong-Phuc neighborhood. The father was assassinated by party members [on January 22, 1930] before the son was [on May 30, 1930]. [In reality, the son was only seriously injured, but did not die.] Knowing without much difficulty who was behind the son's assassination, the French Sûreté chief and his interpreter came to Phu-Tho for an investigation among the imprisoned party members. We learned that Duong's guts were ripped apart by a bullet that went through his abdomen. We were delighted at the news. And in mock pity for him and his earlier-assassinated instructor father, we wrote satirical parallel sentences, supposedly to pay respect to them: "Pity with a Broken Heart, Oh, the Elderly Teacher in the neighborhood of Phuc, / In pain and Twisted Guts, Oh, the Mandarin Inspector on the street of Da."

The satirical word play involves the subject in the first part of each phrase: was it the writer or the assassinated victims who were, in the Vietnamese idiom, so heart-broken and in such pain.

During this prison period, as a teacher fluent in French, Bang had the opportunity to engage in a few brief conversations with Résident Colas, a sympathetic socialist administrator. Centering on the familiar idiom of a civilizing mission, the discursive encounters highlight the logic of the challenge to the French colonial myth by many members of the French-educated intelligentsia:

French Résident Colas visited the death row inmates [in the Phu-Tho prison] one day around five o'clock. Sitting in a small chair under the arjun tree in front of our building, he ordered the guards to unchain us and bring us out to a long bench facing him. My two well-educated comrades Councillor Vi and Doctor Dao, who were imprisoned in Phu-Tho at the time serving their 1928 sentences, suggested that I come forward for a discussion with Colas. It was to be a casual conversation to allow Colas to learn more about us:

"*Giao* Bang, you have repaid us with ingratitude. The protectorate government has built schools, hired teachers, and educated you in the French system. And yet, you have repaid us by participating in a movement that involved the murder of Frenchmen and attempted to overthrow the government," the French Résident said with a smile.

"Mr. Résident, I think that deep in your heart you know the truth despite what you have said," I replied. "It is the French who should be grateful to us Vietnamese. You couldn't govern this country without the help of the natives. It is for this reason that you have built the schools, hired the teachers, and trained the native people. And it is with our labor and hard-earned tax money, Mr. Résident, that schools are constructed and teachers are paid!"

"But look at your country before the arrival of the French: there were neither modern buildings, modern highways, nor modern means of transportation. Don't you agree that these achievements have been brought about by the French?"

"Sir, the most beautiful buildings are built not for the Vietnamese but for the French; the highways have been constructed for French cars; by the same token, all the modern means of transportation have been introduced because of your own administrative and military needs. The economic development has taken place for the benefit of the French, who adopt a policy of exploiting and enslaving the Vietnamese. In the light of developments in Japan, it is not farfetched to say that Vietnam would be much better off without French colonialism!"

Smiling and not replying, Colas just said good-bye. I enjoyed a rare free moment after his departure before we were led back to our building. I took a walk in the yard, approaching several nearby halls where seemingly hundreds of local officials, the mayors and deputy mayors of all the villages supportive of the movement (Xuan-Lung, Cao-Mai, Chu-Hoa, Son-Duong, Ngu-Xa, and others), had been jailed. After we briefly exchanged news about recent developments in the area, they asked me to make a release request on their behalf to Colas if I had a chance to see him again. They had been detained for about four months without trial for lack of evidence. The decisions regarding these detained local administrators had been left to the French Résident.

On June 17, Bang and his three fellow death row inmates in the Phu-Tho prison learned of the commutation of the capital punishment sentences they had received in Yen-Bay (Bang had been given a second death sentence in Phu-Tho, however, which was not commuted at this time). Early that morning thirteen death row inmates sentenced at the same tribunal, including party leader Nguyen Thai Hoc, were executed by guillotine in Yen-Bay. Later that day Hoc's fiancée and key liaison agent committed suicide in his native province.

Continuing the narrative of his interaction with Résident Colas, Bang focused on an episode on the day of his transfer to the central Hanoi prison—an episode that revealed exceptions to the dominant view among the French colonialists on the pax colonia and the *mission civilisatrice*:

One day around the end of May or in June [actually June 20], other Phu-Tho death row inmates and I were brought in chains to the Phu-Tho railway station to take the train to Hanoi. The day of our departure for Hanoi was also the day of departure for the French troops that had earlier been sent into Phu-Tho to "pacify" the area. All the high-ranking provincial officials, both French and Vietnamese, were present for the farewell ceremony. We were taken to a corner under heavy guard by French soldiers, every two of us in one set of handcuffs.

Colas saw us and walked over: "The school teacher of Son-Duong, would you like to go into the pagoda to pray for the intervention of God and for the commutation of your sentence?" I said no: "I am not superstitious. I do not believe in it." He was actually joking. Glancing at the crowd of Vietnamese officials, he continued:

"Do you see a bunch of thieves here?"

"Do we have thieves around here?" I looked around in surprise and asked.

"It is these corrupt native mandarins! They demand bribes and kickbacks, robbing their own people for personal gain and trying in every way to conceal their corruption from the protectorate government. Few of them have any integrity," Colas replied in low voice, looking in the direction of the Vietnamese officials.

That comment showed how progressive Colas was. I was really surprised that Colas was so frank. Of course, his French regime must have known about the corruption of their mandarin henchmen. But they also ignored the blatant corruption as a part of the divide-and-rule policy toward the Vietnamese. They wanted to create a privileged class living on the exploitation of their fellow countrymen and subservient to French colonialism. They wanted to impoverish and enslave Vietnamese labor! And it was in the context of this pernicious scheme of the French colonialists that we had to stand up and fight.

In Hanoi, Bang and the other death row inmates were initially confined to individual cells in the Hoa-Lo prison [later nicknamed the Hanoi Hilton by American prisoners-of-war]. However, within a few weeks, the prison ran out of death row cells as more and more political prisoners with death sentences were transferred from other provinces. Bang was transferred to a large prison hall, where he learned more about the internal party politics on the eve of the uprising. He was also a witness to the continuing debate among VNP ideologues concerning their vision of a postrevolutionary order, a debate that did not merely echo ideological conflicts in the West, but also reflected the tension between the hierarchical model and the collectivist framework in the indigenous communal system:

Probably in August, we were transferred to a nearby and similar hall, where we were joined by several other comrades who had just been sentenced to death at the Hanoi session of the Criminal Commission. All in all, there were about twenty-five of us, chained one by one along two wooden platforms on the two sides of the hall. Because conversation was a main pastime for all of us, I obtained information about many other comrades. I learned for the first time from the new death row inmates of the debate and conflict within the central committee regarding the armed uprising of early 1930. Chairman Nguyen Thai Hoc, *Xu* Nhu, and numerous others had wanted to organize the uprising immediately, even under difficult circumstances, out of fear that the continued repression and arrests by the French would eliminate the top leadership and destroy the entire party. A few party members had insisted that the uprising be planned only after a long intensive propaganda and recruiting campaign throughout the entire country had awakened the majority of the populace into supporting and participating in the revolution. In the meantime, according to the suggestion of the second faction, the party leaders who were actively hunted should limit their activities to advising other comrades and writing books and propaganda pamphlets in a safe hideout in the mountainous province of Hoa-Binh, where the head native mandarin, Mr. Quach Vy, was in considerable sympathy with the movement. I also learned from Do, a fugitive comrade arrested in China and transferred to the Hanoi prison, that Ho Chi Minh, upon learning of the planned uprising, had intended to meet Hoc in Vietnam to advise its postponement but was without success.

This intense debate within the party was not limited to the timing issue but also extended to the question of ideology and postrevolutionary program. During this period in the Hanoi prison, our discussion went on day and night. At times the debate became violent between those favoring communism and collective ownership and those defending nationalism and private enterprise. Nguyen van Lien of the former group, a Phu-Tho native, and Dang Tran Nghiep of the latter were the two adversaries most active in the debate. On several occasions their heated arguments were followed by an exchange of flying milk cans or clothing parcels. We had to separate the two and calm them down.

In late 1930 Bang eventually learned that his second death sentence had been commuted:

One fall night, past midnight, in the death row hall in the Hanoi prison, I heard distinctly the heavy pounding of the boots of soldiers coming into the prison courtyard. Suspecting that it was our time of execution, I wakened my comrades, who were sleeping shackled on the two sides of the hall. There were about twenty-five of us in this building. "It is the time of our execution," I shouted to my comrades. Given the large number of soldiers, what else could it be but the arrival of the guillotine hour? I was quite sure that my life was coming to an end, given my two death sentences. The light was turned on, the metal gate to the hall was opened, and the soldiers and prison guards came in with handcuffs and heavy chains. As I was located right by the gate, they had to pass by my place before getting to other inmates. Seeing the deputy warden Cagino, I looked him straight in the eye and pointed at myself in a questioning gesture: "Is it my turn?" He had come to talk to me now and then because of my speaking ability in French. He shook his head, moving on to pick other inmates to take to the guillotine. As my comrades passed by my place on the way to the guillotine, I was truly overcome by a feeling of ecstasy. I felt as if I had been in a dream, an incredible dream. I was choked with emotion. Tears were fast pouring down my face. I lay down on the floor, repeatedly talking to myself: "I am not beheaded. Two death sentences, and I am not beheaded." I then lapsed into a strange and short sleep. When I awoke, other comrades applauded noisily.

Rushing through my mind was my mother's earlier declaration that I would not die. It was such a powerful emotion! I had thought that my execution was certain. I did not believe my mother's statement, made even after my second death sentence, that I would escape capital punishment. I could not imagine a double clemency, given my two sentences for producing propaganda leaflets and for assisting in the production of bombs and participating in the attacks. I had written to bid my mother farewell.

After realizing my luck with the second clemency, I thought immediately of my senior mother's prescient statement that, despite the two death sentences, I would not be executed. After learning the news of my two death sentences, my senior mother had come to visit me at the Phu-Tho prison. Seeing me, she broke down in tears: "Don't be afraid. You will not be beheaded. Wherever you go, write me; whatever you need, tell me, and I will send it to you." When her statement was translated into French for the investigator Riner, he laughed: "An escape from death by a convict with two death sentences?" My senior mother emphasized that our family had accumulated a lot of merit through our compassionate Buddhist acts. It was touching for me to learn later that [after seeing me] my senior mother had submitted a petition to request the substitution of one of her own two sons for me at the guillotine, reenacting the story of Ton Trong and Ton Mang in the folk tradition of China. In the classical opera there was a theatrical performance concerning the case of a stepmother who petitioned the court to execute her own child Ton Mang instead of her husband's son Ton Trong. Her petition was so moving that the court reconsidered the case and spared Ton Trong's life. My senior mother's request was turned down. According to French law, it was a matter of individual responsibility. Her gesture, her sacrifice for me, and her loving care given to my comrades during the preparation of the insurrection will forever live in my heart. My senior mother . . . she was the only one of her kind in the world. . . .

In retrospect I cannot help finding my secret revolutionary activities in this period laughable and regrettable, because the great task to be undertaken was well beyond my capacity. It was inevitable that the uprising suffer a crushing defeat. First of all, the propaganda, training, and recruiting tasks, which were difficult and complicated, were not carried out with sufficient planning or in the absolute secrecy required. Party organizations in the delta were discovered in large number, partly because of the treason of certain party members. Second, the party leadership was less than fully able and enlightened to lead the revolution to a successful end. Even the critical order to postpone the uprising from Hoc and Chinh arrived too late in my village, as [the VNP vice president] Nhu had already ordered the movement of party members to Yen-Bay. Finally, the population had not been sufficiently "educated" and mobilized. Mao Tse-tung has compared the revolutionary party to fish and the people to water. Without water, the fish cannot but die; without the strong support of the masses, the party cannot survive. However, the uprising can still be considered a wakening call for the Vietnamese people at large.

On July 26, 1930, before Bang learned of the commutation of his second sentence, the French governor general had analyzed in a report to the Ministry of Colonies in Paris the reasons why he did not oppose a commutation of Bang's second sentence:

Nguyen Dac Bang: twenty-one years old, private instructor, born and residing at Son-Duong (district of Lam-Thao). He already received his first death sentence under the March 28, 1930, decree of the Criminal Commission. He was convicted of having (1) joined the Vietnamese Nationalist Party; and (2) been an accomplice to the assassinations committed at Yen-Bay on the night of February 9 by providing arms, scimitars, and bombs for those assassinations.

In my report of April 14, 1930, numbered 30-CS . . . I reiterated that Bang had confessed to having joined VNQDD [VNP], to having had bombs produced at his house, and finally, to having assigned three members of his group to take part in the Yen-Bay attack. I added [in that report] that, although the role of Nguyen Dac Bang was not insignificant, I did not oppose granting him his clemency request.

In accordance with that suggestion, the June 10, 1930, decree [of the French president] commuted Nguyen Dac Bang's March 28 death sentence to that of hard labor for life.

Nguyen Dac Bang received a second death sentence on May 27. He was convicted of (1) having willingly supplied arms (bombs) to armed bands that had attacked and invaded the Hung-Hoa and Lam-Thao posts, (2) having gathered and organized these bands, (3) having participated in the Hung-Hoa event, (4) having fulfilled various duties in the bands that had attacked and invaded the aforementioned posts, and (5) finally, having attempted to assassinate French and indigenous people in the post of Hung-Hoa at the time of the attack.

He has been denied the privilege of attenuating circumstances.

At the beginning of February 1930, Nguyen van Toai, called *Do* [Confucian teacher] Thuy, received an order from the central committee to have bombs produced in connection with the planned insurrection. *Do* Thuy knew that Nguyen Dac Bang, a member of the Son-Duong cell, owned an isolated house at Cao Mai [*sic!*] where one could undertake this clandestine production. Nguyen Dac Bang was consulted, and he readily lent support to the party. Two or three days later, *Do* Thuy and *Ly* [Mayor] Mai brought to his house about one hundred bomb shells, (gun) powder, and all the materials needed for the production of bombs. They notified Bang that it was necessary to work hard: *Xu* Nhu would like to have the bombs ready by February 6 at the latest.

Assisted by his relatives and certain conspirators, Nguyen Dac Bang began the task. As the bombs became available, they were hidden in the rice fields.

On February 6 three parcels containing the bombs and scimitars were sent to Yen-Bay.

On February 9 Bang attended the gathering at *Do* Thuy's house with a full load of bombs and gasoline. He brought along with him a small group of followers whom he had been assigned to recruit.

Bang claimed that his role [in the uprising] was limited to his participation in this meeting and the assignment of certain recruits and that, because of an eye problem, he returned to his house after having excused himself from taking part in the attack. Bang's statements on this point were contradicted by the available information. It has been repeatedly reported that after the departure of the group in charge of the Lam-Thao attack, Bang was still with the group that left for Hung-Hoa a few moments later. Nobody stayed behind. Discipline was extremely strict. No defection could have been tolerated. *Do* Thuy, whose testimony Bang invoked, actually and formally contradicted Bang. He affirmed that Bang complained of an eye problem, but Bang never expressed any intention to part company with the group. Bang told him [*Do* Thuy] on the contrary that it would be shameful of him [Bang] to abandon his comrades at the moment of attack. There is little doubt that Bang participated in the Hung-Hoa attack. But even if his exact role during this attack cannot be determined, he must still assume a heavy responsibility: being an active member of the party, he recruited followers. It was at his house that hundreds of bombs were produced. And it was these bombs that were used by the rebels to attack Yen-Bay, Hung-Hoa, and Lam-Thao.

Nguyen Dac Bang has received two death sentences, but without clear evidence of his [direct] act of violence, it seems that his clemency request can be granted.  (AOM-AP-I, 7F-56)

On November 22, 1930, the teacher Toai of Son-Duong village and four other death row inmates convicted in May by the Criminal Commission at Phu-Tho were led to an open guillotine in the provincial capital of Phu-Tho. They had arrived by train from the Hanoi central prison the previous day. The executions started at 6:00 A.M. on November 22, following one another in quick succession and ending only fifteen minutes later. A few shouted "Long Live the Vietnamese Nationalist Party!" just before being guillotined (Report from Résident Passano of Phu-Tho to the Résident supérieur, AOM-A-RST, 53-436).

Bang was soon sent to the notorious Poulo Condore prison off the coast of South Vietnam. An increasingly large number of VNP and Communist Party members were concentrated in this penal colony in the aftermath of the Yen-Bay and ICP-organized Nghe-Tinh movements, the latter of which involved the participation of half a million Vietnamese in twenty-five provinces (see Luong 1985). In late April 1931 approximately one hundred political prisoners from both parties and over four hundred other convicts were herded onto the steamship *La Martinière* for a thirty-five-day journey to French Guiana in South America. They joined a small number of Vietnamese prisoners who had been sent there in 1922 for having participated in the 1917 anti-French uprising in Thai-Nguyen (North Vietnam). In this sparsely populated French colony, the French National Assembly had, in May 1930, created a special territory called Inini. They hoped to open up the vast hinderland for exploitation and to pull the colony out of a serious recession that had resulted from the collapse of the world market for many Guianese forest product exports (Ballof 1979:3–5). Three special prison camps, Crique-Anguille, Saut-Tigre, and La Forestière, were set up in the interior for Vietnamese convicts to expand the reach of French capitalism. A group of 523 prisoners arrived in French Guiana's capital of Cayenne on June 3, 1931, including Bang and three other native sons of Son-Duong. It was the beginning of a major chapter in their lives, a chapter that hardened them to the realities of the colonial experience.

In the first three years of Inini prison, most prisoners led relatively

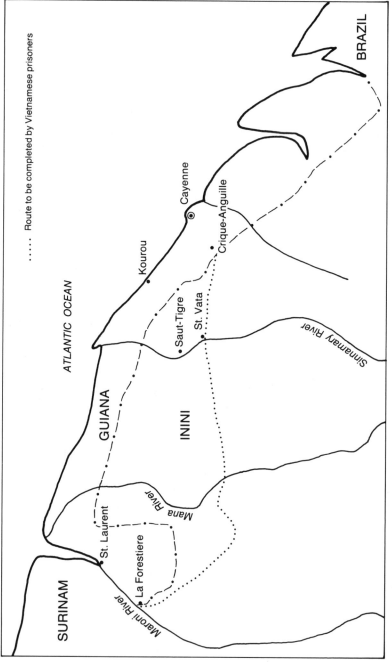

····· Route to be completed by Vietnamese prisoners

BRAZIL

ATLANTIC OCEAN

Cayenne

Kourou

Crique-Anguille

Saut-Tigre

St. Vata

Sinnamary River

GUIANA

ININI

Mana River

St. Laurent

La Forestiere

SURINAM

Maroni River

Map 5. French Guiana

easy lives despite long working hours of nine to ten hours each day. They worked primarily in the prison camps and the surrounding agricultural fields. The prisoners were classified into three categories: (1) clearly reformed prisoners to whom certain favors could be granted, including the remuneration of one franc for each day of labor in cases of employment on agricultural plantations or in administrative work, (2) well-behaved and seemingly repentant prisoners, and (3) those with no sign of improvement. Third-class prisoners who, despite the disciplinary measures of solitary night confinement, still caused difficulties for the camp administration were either separated from other inmates through incarceration in special quarters or assigned to specially arduous tasks (Ballof 1979:10–12). Bang recounted in depth his prison experiences beginning in 1931, when he was sent with approximately 120 fellow prisons to the Forestière prison camp, where he became more familiar with Marxism through dialogues with a fellow inmate from the Indochinese Communist Party:

Within a short period after our arrival in Cayenne, I was transferred together with approximately two hundred [*sic*] fellow prisoners to the St. Laurent prison, a temporary stopping point on the way to our own camp at an abandoned American plantation called La Forestière. Guarded by a platoon of redcapped Senegalese soldiers, we undertook a one-and-a-half-day boat journey to St. Laurent on the St. Laurent River, which forms the boundary between French and Dutch Guiana. Our temporary sojourn in the St. Laurent prison was relatively relaxed since we were allowed to go outside twice a day for showers and sports activities in the prison courtyard. Most of the inmates were French, except for a few Vietnamese who had been sent there in 1922 for having participated in the 1917 Thai-Nguyen uprising. One of them frequently sneaked by to pass on to us French books and magazines. Unfortunately, only a southern common prisoner, Dien [a Communist Party member], and I could read French. Since my fellow inmates were quite eager for news, we three French-reading prisoners decided to publish a weekly newspaper in Vietnamese, *Nhan Hoa* [Humanity in Harmony] for the other prisoners in our group. The attempt, however, was stopped short within three weeks, when the prison warden, Captain Le Large, learned of the development. He gave us a harsh lecture and had all our paper, pens, and ink confiscated.

We arrived at our penitentiary home upstream from St. Laurent within a few weeks of our departure from Cayenne. The river was beautiful with hundreds of islets along the stream. The Forestière plantation, we were told, had been abandoned for lack of labor. As the prison camp had not been completed, we were temporarily housed together with our guards and prison officials in the same abandoned buildings. It was at this point that we began our hard labor. The camp administration broke us up into seven teams, one growing vegetables, two manufacturing tiles, one repairing camp roads, and three in charge of felling trees for timber.

With their knowledge of French, Bang and the Communist Party member Dien were given the interpreter positions in the camp construction teams. Bang subsequently also served as an interpreter for Vietnamese inmates in a St. Laurent hospital until he was discovered to possess leftist books and newspapers, including *L'Humanité* [newspaper of the French Communist Party] and Marx's *Le capital.* He was transferred back to La Forestière in late 1932 to work in the agricultural fields in order to feed the camp population.

Starting in August 1935, Bang and his fellow La Forestière prisoners were gradually transferred to Crique-Anguille to begin a more difficult and turbulent chapter in their lives as road construction laborers. The colonial authorities finally carried out their earlier plan to use Indochinese prison labor for the construction of a new route from Cayenne through the jungles of Inini to the Maroni River on the Surinam-Guiana border. At Saut Vata on the Sinnamary River, more than sixty inmates, already weakened from bad treatment, lack of rest, and arduous work, died from malaria (Ballof 1979:18). The Vietnamese prisoners also began a period of active resistance to French prison authorities when the leftist Popular Front rose to power in France and granted parole to scores of prisoners. They strongly protested France's Doublage Act, which had been adopted to solve the problem of a labor shortage in this French colony: under the act each released prisoner would have to continue to reside in Inini for a time equal to the prison term if it was less than eight years and for life if it exceeded eight years (ibid.:21). But the prisoners were particularly anxious to rejoin the familiar world of kinship and communal ties in their homeland. Bang subsequently became a fugitive protest leader, as he related in his account of the events of this period:

[After the transfer to Crique-Anguille] we began assisting a team of civil engineers, foremen, and French workers previously released from prison in repairing the Cayenne–Crique-Anguille road. The camp administrator, Mr. Sauvant, was fairly liberal minded, along the lines of Phu-Tho's Résident

Colas. He set up for us a small library with old French magazines and Vietnamese books from Indochina. At our request four inmates were also allowed to fish by the riverside to provide us with fresh fish to supplement our diet. We also raised poultry and captured wild animals, which we were allowed to cook to supplement the prison meals. After finishing the road repairs, we began clearing the jungle with our manual labor in preparation for the construction of a one hundred-kilometer road from Crique-Anguille to the Sinnamary River. It took us seven months to finish the job. We were then switched to digging drains along the roads, as tractors and steam rollers were introduced for the main phase of the road construction project. Each day, after we finished the assigned work, we could go hunting and gathering. We truly lived the life of pioneers in those days.

My real trouble with the French authorities began in 1936, when some prisoners were paroled but not allowed to return to Vietnam. Under the Doublage Act of the metropolitan government, former inmates had to stay in Guiana for a period equal to their prison terms. The released inmates were granted land and domestic animals for permanent settlement in French Guiana if they so desired. They were promised that the goverment would pay for their wives and children to join them in the new land. But they were not allowed to return home! All of us were certainly unhappy with this act. We requested an audience with Sauvant, and I served as the spokesman for the group: "We all came from Vietnam, where we were subject to the law of our country. While in Guiana, we are under the Inini territory administration with its own legal system and budget. How can we be sentenced for the second time under the Doublage Act, which was passed in France and applicable only to French prisoners?" Sauvant granted us the point and allowed us to write a petition to the French government. French politics changed quickly that year with the rise to power of the socialists and their coalition partners in the [left-of-center] Popular Front, of which I learned in the French newspapers. The new government also sent a Cayenne attorney to the camp to investigate charges of physical abuse by prison authorities. Interviewed by the attorney, I reported on all the beatings at the Forestière camp, including the abuse of my close friend Dien. A month later, twelve inmates were released. But like their predecessors, they were not allowed to return to Vietnam.

Although Bang's memory failed on the repatriation of these twelve prisoners to Vietnam within one month of their release, i.e., in January 1937, the Doublage Act became a great source of tension in the relations between the Inini prison administration and Vietnamese inmates. Within two days of being informed of their impending release, on December 17, 1936, the twelve Crique-Anguille inmates refused to stay in prison quarters, took off their prison uniforms, and wore only their undershorts. They wrote a note of protest to the prison warden Sauvant: "If to the government of Indochina we are no longer guilty, we do not know on what basis the rule of perpetual residence in Guiana could be imposed on us" (AOM-AP-I, 2-130). Even after their move to Cayenne on December 22, out of skepticism about the French promise of repatriation, these former inmates insisted on receiving their work savings only upon reaching Vietnam and not in Guiana (ibid.). In the meantime their former fellow prisoners at Crique-Anguille wrote another letter of protest to the Ministry of Colonies, then under the socialist Marius Moutet. Toward the end of 1937, in a major episode of unrest in the Inini Indochinese prison camps, they decided on a hunger strike. Because of his knowledge of French, Bang was chosen by fellow prisoners to escape to Cayenne in order to enlist the support of sympathetic leftist politicians. With the help of former Vietnamese inmates and disguised as one of them, Bang successfully contacted leftist local politicians to garner support for the Vietnamese prisoners' demand for the abolition of the Doublage Act. During this period the Ministry of Colonies in Paris also received an individual parole request from the fugitive Bang in a letter from Crique-Anguille dated October 28, 1937 (AOM-AP-I, 9-207). Taking certain liberties with the facts of Bang's prison conduct and appealing to French notions of justice and humanity, Bang's letter illustrates the impact of the dominant discursive practices of metropolitan France on the French-educated native elite:

> Instead of having benefited from an amnesty . . . like all my fellow convicts already released in Indochina in 1936 and like the fourteen prisoners leaving Cayenne on January 2 [1937] . . . I am still in prison . . . frequently and unjustifiably punished.
>
> Toward the end of last August, after having crushed my hopes for amnesty as promised in the program of the leftist parties and discussed many times in the two chambers of the National Assembly, Mr. Jacques Sauvant, the head prison administrator, forced me to work hard and, without any interrogation, ordered me imprisoned in a cell with thirty common prisoners who had refused to carry lumber with three instead of four persons to a team. [This punishment was imposed although] I was not on the spot [and thus not involved in this work protest]. Mr. Daguillon had earlier assigned me to the task of provisioning the second and

third [work] camps. Mr. Sauvant also ordered the cover of the nearby soil-tub removed so that the odor became unbearable. He even decided to send me to the islands.

Having always maintained exemplary conduct and completed the daily task required by the administration and as a political prisoner having struggled for social justice, I feel deeply ashamed and humiliated by this scandalous and groundless punishment. I have complained of this treatment on numerous occasions to no avail to the governor of [French] Guiana.

A major difference [thus] exists [in the treatments of] myself and my [already released] comrades who were convicted for the same ideal, for the same cause, and by the same commission.

I would like to appeal to your spirit of humanity and justice, and to request consideration of a possible pardon, allowing me to return to my native land. I will be enormously grateful.

Finally, I would like to thank you once more, Mr. Minister, my savior, for having saved me from the guillotine with your great activity on the Indochinese Amnesty Committee in Paris in 1930. . . . With the hope that you will save me a second time from the hellish conditions of the Inini prison, where I have suffered a great deal since 1931, both materially and intellectually, I promise to be forever loyal to your government and to live quietly under the socialist regime. The regime has shed the light of peace, liberty, justice, fraternity, and welfare from France all over the world.

Respectfully yours,
Nguyen Dac Bang

On December 12, 1937, the hunger strike broke out in Crique-Anguille (AOM-AP-I, 9-207). It was coordinated by Bang himself from the outside, as Bang related:

As no reply to our letter had arrived within a reasonable period from the Ministry of Colonies, I drafted and sent the schedule of strike activities to the prison camp. When the hour arrived, all inmates stopped working. The camp administrator Sauvant unsuccessfully attempted to persuade my fellow inmates to end their strike. Within three days they were all sent to a Cayenne hospital for treatment. On the second day of the strike, I also returned to Cayenne to follow the developments there. I was told that a large banner had been set up in front of the Communist Party office: *Résolution immédiate de la grève de faim des prisonniers vietnamiens au territoire de l'Inini* [Immediate Resolution to the Hunger Strike of Vietnamese Prisoners in Inini]. Several reports and editorials were also published in local newspapers, the most favorable of which appeared in the *Voice of the People*. Having been informed of an ongoing active police search for me, a fellow fugitive inmate and I disguised ourselves as fishermen or forest hunters during the daytime. [With the help of former Vietnamese inmates working at the governor's palace] we slept at night in the kitchen of the governor's summer mansion or in the servants' quarters at the governor's palace. I was informed that hospital employees had begun force feeding my fellow inmates. Finally, after more than a week, during which all of them had nearly died of starvation, the news reached us that the Doublage Act had been abolished. We then instructed our fellow inmates to stop the hunger strike but to continue the work stoppage on their return to Crique-Anguille.

With the assistance of already released Vietnamese inmates working at the La Mirant plantation, the fugitive Bang found a job at the plantation, first as a sugar cane cutter and later as a land surveyor. However, in 1938, informed of an intensified French search for him, Bang organized an escape to Surinam with two fellow Vietnamese fugitives. Unfortunately for Bang and his comrades, they were arrested by the Dutch police, sent to the Paramaribo jail in the Surinam capital, and returned to Cayenne on a French steamship. The three fugitive inmates received the maximum sentence of two years of solitary confinement. It was during the period of Bang's solitary confinement, in 1939, that the Doublage Act was officially abolished, contrary to Bang's account. Returned to Crique-Anguille at the end of his sentence, Bang escaped again in early 1942. Together with a small number of fugitive prisoners, Bang reached British Guyana later that year and was granted asylum based on the claim of an intention to work for de Gaulle's cause of a free France. With a small gift of gold from two wealthy prisoners-cum-merchants, Bang and his comrades opened one thriving Franco-Oriental restaurant after another in Georgetown, the capital of British Guyana. In 1945 Bang married a local woman of mixed Portuguese and Amerindian descent, who, in the following three decades, actively supported him in the cause of socialist nationalism.

Back in the village of Son-Duong, the French continued repressing incipient resistance to their colonial order. Bang's former favorite student Tiem, later the first president of the Communist Party cell in Son-Duong, was briefly detained because he had written a ballad on Son-Duong history describing in positive terms the VNP uprising and the destruction of the house of a corrupt Lam-Thao district chief. The colonial administration also closely monitored and even banned voluntary village organizations in many parts of the country so as to hinder anticolonial activities within their framework (Ngo-Vinh-Long 1978b: 546–562). These efforts of the colonial government further suggest that local tradition could provide organizational resources for revolutionary activities.

Community members attempted to rebuild their lives after the devastating French repression. Many villagers whose sons and husbands had been sent as prisoners to various corners of the French empire lived in great anguish. Desperate to reconstruct their familial social world, a few dozen households, including Bang's own family, turned to Catholicism. They hoped that the French Catholic priests could exert influence on the colonial administration to gain the release of their family members. The ranks of Catholics in the province of Phu-Tho swelled to 42,000 by the early 1940s, comprising a remarkably high 14 percent of the native population (Cao-Tien-Phung et al. 1985:158).

Out of desperation quite a few family members of political prisoners wrote the French authorities letters that took extreme liberties with the facts. A letter from Bang's senior mother on behalf of her youngest son Tang, officially a juvenile at the time of the Yen-Bay uprising, is still available in the French colonial archival records (AOM-AP-I, 9-206):

Son-Duong, August 1934

The Governor General of French Indochina
His Excellency:

. . . I have a son by the name of Nguyen Doan Tang. At the time of the revolutionary movement, he was a sixth-grade student at the Franco-Vietnamese school in Hung-Hoa. On the twelfth day of the first lunar month [in 1930], with twelve piasters from me, he went to the provincial capital to buy books and school materials. Passing through the Lam-Thao district seat, he saw revolutionary troops in retreat and, despite his youth, ended up being arrested by accident by the mandarins. He was tortured numerous times, although he did not know anything. Suspected of having participated in the revolutionary movement, he was sentenced to twenty years in a correctional camp. I have appealed to the authorities many times without success. I learn that His Excellency has recently assumed the post of governor general.

Would His Excellency reconsider the case for the sake of justice and humanity so that this old woman may be reunited with her son and supported [in her old age]? I will be forever grateful to His Excellency.

Mai thi Luan

In November 1935 the French Catholic priest in Hung-Hoa also wrote a letter on Tang's behalf (AOM-AP-I, 9-206). However, it was not until the rise to power of the leftist Popular Front in France in 1936 that Bang's two brothers together with many other political prisoners were paroled. The parolees were not allowed to leave their native villages and were required to report periodically to the district government. The better-educated junior brother, Tang, taught briefly at a private school in Son-Duong. In an attempt to coopt the better educated among the former political prisoners, the colonial authorities assisted them in searching for steady white-collar employment both within and outside of the colonial administrative apparatus. Tang worked at the French Résident's office and subsequently for the provincial land survey, and his elder brother Gia became a partner in a retail outlet for the French alcohol monopoly in Cam-Khe district.[3]

The cooptation attempt was not totally successful. Despite his French administrative employment, toward the end of World War II, Bang's brother Tang resumed his political activities in the Vietminh front in the provincial capital of Phu-Tho.

The French authorities' efforts at cooptation and the severe penalties for political activism did not succeed in completely extinguishing the flame of Vietnamese anticolonialism. For many activists, including Bang and his brother Tang, prison experiences eventually strengthened their resolve to continue their resistance, notwithstanding probable severe penalties and the apparently small odds for success, based on the lessons of earlier failures. Although the opportunistic conversion of many Son-Duong villagers to Catholicism can be analyzed in terms of a narrow calculus of material costs and benefits, the behavior of those hardened political activists cannot be explained within the framework of logical choice. The strengthened anticolonial resolve contributed to the meteoric rise of the Indochinese Communist Party, which, against serious odds, eventually triumphed in the cause of both national independence and socioeconomic revolution.

≪  ≪  ≪

# PART TWO

·

# The Revolution
in the Village

CHAPTER 4

•

# The Rise
# of Marxist Power

ON SEPTEMBER 2, 1945, to a tumultuous crowd of half a million Vietnamese in Hanoi as well as to the nation and the world at large, Ho Chi Minh declared the formation of the Democratic Republic of Vietnam:

"We hold truths that all men are created equal, that they are endowed by their Creator with certain unalienable Rights, among these are Life, Liberty, and the pursuit of Happiness."

This immortal statement is extracted from the Declaration of Independence of the United States of America in 1776. Understood in the broader sense, this means: "All peoples on the earth are born equal; every person has the right to live to be happy and free."

The Declaration of Human and Civic Rights proclaimed by the French Revolution in 1791 likewise propounds: "Every man is born equal and enjoys free and equal rights."

These are undeniable truths.

Yet, during and throughout the last eighty years, the French imperialists, abusing the principles of "freedom, equality and fraternity," have violated the integrity of our ancestral land and oppressed our countrymen. Their deeds run counter to the ideals of humanity and justice.

In the political field, they have denied us every freedom. They have enforced upon us inhuman laws. They have set up three different political regimes in Northern, Central and Southern Vietnam (Tonkin,

Annam, and Cochinchina) in an attempt to disrupt our national, historical and ethnical unity.

They have built more prisons than schools. They have callously illtreated our fellow-compatriots. They have drowned our revolutions in blood.

They have sought to stifle public opinion and pursued a policy of obscurantism on the largest scale; they have forced upon us alcohol and opium in order to weaken our race.

In the economic field, they have shamelessly exploited our people, driven them into the worst misery and mercilessly plundered our country.

They have ruthlessly appropriated our rice fields, mines, forests and raw materials. They have arrogated to themselves the privilege of issuing banknotes, and monopolised all our external commerce. They have imposed hundreds of unjustifiable taxes, and reduced our countrymen, especially the peasants and petty tradesmen, to extreme poverty.

They have prevented the development of native capital enterprises; they have exploited our workers in the most barbarous manner.

In the autumn of 1940, when the Japanese fascists, in order to fight the Allies, invaded Indochina and set up new bases of war, the French imperialists surrendered on bended knees and handed over our country to the invaders.

Subsequently, under the joint French and Japanese yoke, our people were literally bled white. The consequences were dire in the extreme. From Quang-Tri up to the North, two millions of our countrymen died from starvation during the first months of this year.

On March 9th, 1945, the Japanese disarmed the French troops. Again the French either fled or surrendered unconditionally. Thus, in no way have they proved capable of "protecting" us; on the contrary, within five years they have twice sold our country to the Japanese. . . .

In fact, since the autumn of 1940, our country ceased to be a French colony and became a Japanese possession.

After the Japanese surrender, our people, as a whole, rose up and proclaimed their sovereignty and founded the Democratic Republic of Vietnam.

The truth is that we have wrung back our independence from Japanese hands and not from the French. . . .

For these reasons, we, the members of the Provisional Government of the Democratic Republic of Vietnam, solemnly declare to the world:

"Vietnam has the right to be free and independent and, in fact, has become free and independent. The people of Vietnam decide to mobilise all their spiritual and material forces and to sacrifice their lives and property in order to safeguard their right of Liberty and Independence." (reprinted in Porter 1981:28–30)

Ho Chi Minh's independence speech bore a striking resemblance to the proclamation of the Vietnamese Nationalist Party on the eve of the Yen-Bay uprising fifteen years earlier. Both demonstrated the large degree to which the Western axiomatic emphasis on civil rights (liberty and equality) had shaped the discursive practices of a new generation of Vietnamese revolutionary leaders, although, as earlier noted, within the native sociocultural logic these terms were redefined primarily in terms of the collective rights of the Vietnamese in relation to their colonial masters. More important, both Ho's speech and the VNP proclamation of 1930 appealed to the native population by means of the evocative symbols of unity in a national framework and the fundamental right to socioeconomic welfare within a collective whole. They attempted to respond to both the nationalist aspirations and the concrete needs of the native population. Reflecting both the historical contingencies and the indigenous political culture, Ho also emphasized how the French had lost their mandate as "protector" through their subservience to Japan and their partial responsibility for the death of up to two million Vietnamese.

Ho Chi Minh's declaration of independence in 1945 marked the rise to power of the previously underground Indochinese Communist Party and a major turning point in Vietnamese history. The declaration had been preceded by the seizure of administrative power in August by the Marxist-led Vietminh movement, in virtually all Vietnamese provinces, including the province of Phu-Tho.[1] In the ensuing armed conflict with the French (1946–1954), the Vietminh would strengthen its legitimacy as a party of national independence as anticolonialism grew stronger among the native population. It would gain the allegiance of Vietnamese from all walks of life, including a large segment of the French-educated elite. Furthermore, in the name of national solidarity and building on the reformist sentiment among many members of the Western-educated intelligentsia, the local Vietminh leadership would launch subtle attacks on certain ceremonial manifestations of the class-oriented and male-centered world view, although not without resistance during the course of the Franco-Vietnamese war and afterward.

## THE UNDERGROUND RESISTANCE

The success of the Indochinese Communist Party and the Vietminh movement in 1945 was no small feat, for both Phu-Tho and the neighboring provinces of Vinh-Yen and Phuc-Yen ICP membership totaled only eighty at the time of the seizure of administrative power in August 1945 (Cao-Tien-Phung et al. 1985:112). In the entire district of Lam-Thao, party membership seems to have been restricted to Son-Duong's neighboring village of Kinh Ke. In fact, the ICP had not established its first cell in the province of Phu-Tho until 1939 (Cao-van-Luong 1960:143).[2]

However, since its inception, the ICP had succeeded in building and, after each repression, resiliently rebuilding numerous mass organizations as recruitment channels for the party and structural bases for its activities.[3] In accordance with the ICP emphasis on nationalist and anti-imperialist struggle and its policy of broadened class alliance in the 1939–1945 period—a policy formulated under Ho Chi Minh's influence—in 1939 ICP cadres in Phu-Tho began organizing "anti-imperialist" associations *(hoi phan de)*. By late 1940 the membership in these organizations had reached approximately two hundred and had spread to seventeen localities in Phu-Tho (Vinh-Phu 1971:28). They operated under the guidance of the provincial ICP membership, whose five cells in Phu-Tho at this point comprised nineteen members (ibid.). Following the Japanese invasion of Indochina in September 1940 and Ho Chi Minh's formation of the Vietminh (Viet Nam Doc Lap Dong Minh Hoi, or Vietnam Independence Alliance League) in May 1941, these associations were quickly transformed into "national salvation" *(cuu quoc)* associations in October 1941.[4]

The ICP's Vietminh mass organization strategy touched the Son-Duong area for the first time when a national salvation association was formed in the village of Kinh-Ke in the fall of 1941 (Le-van-Thu 1973:163). This mass organization strategy aimed at identifying the ICP and its associations with the nationalist aspirations of the indigenous population and the concrete needs of the working classes in particular. Depending on the conditions in particular localities, the local associations organized protests against the Japanese coercive purchase of rice at fixed low prices and their requirement of jute cultivation in lieu of secondary food crops,[5] against the draft of young men into the colonial armed forces and the coercive recruitment of laborers for the construction of military facilities (e.g., roads, Phu-Tho and Noi-Bai airfields, and armament factories and warehouses), as well as against French and Japanese imperialism in general. The Vietminh-led protest campaigns helped to increase the visibility of the Vietminh as a rallying point for the disaffected indigenous population in many localities. However, these campaigns also attracted the attention of the colonial regime to the mass organizations and drastically increased the risk of a harsh French suppression. In Phu-Tho, for example, four party members and thirty-seven association members were arrested and tortured in a November 25, 1941, crackdown. Many suspects were required to report periodically to local colonial authorities (Cao-van-Luong 1960:144). As a result, ICP-affiliated organizations survived only in Kinh-Ke and six other localities in the entire province, and the coordination of activities among them became difficult because of the disruption of communication channels (Cao-Tien-Phung et al. 1985:75; Le-van-Thu 1973:163).

However, the ICP possessed a remarkable organizational resiliency—clearly more so than the VNP and other indigenous political groups—and in 1942, the Vietminh mass organizations (the national salvation associations) quickly rebounded throughout the province. Under the leadership of a North Vietnam regional committee member, party cadres even succeeded in establishing new national salvation associations in such industrial enterprises as the tea cooperative plant and the bullet factory (Le-Tuong and Vu-Kim-Bien 1981:164). In the village of Kinh-Ke, national salvation membership increased from five to forty-three in the period from December 1941 to September 1943.

At this juncture the Vietminh began its organizational efforts in Son-Duong through the recruitment activities of a student from a middle-peasant family, Bui Kim Linh. One of Linh's early recruits, a Son-Duong student and the son of a Guiana-exiled VNP activist, briefly related Linh's conversion to the revolutionary cause:

Linh studied at one point at the Thang-Long school in Hanoi [where the well-known Vietnamese military strategist Vo Nguyen Giap had taught in the 1930s]. Among his teachers was the elderly Thuc, who possessed a strong revolutionary spirit. Through his teaching, Mr. Thuc succeeded in heightening the political consciousness of many of his students, Linh among them. Receiving special guidance, he returned to Son-Duong at a time when [Vietminh] cadres were also making efforts to raise the political awareness of people in this area [i.e., in Kinh-Ke village].

In regular consultation with the Vietminh leaders in Kinh-Ke, Linh began to explore the possibility of organizing a national salvation association in his native village based on the Vietminh organizational motto "investigate, propagandize, train, organize, and [lead to] struggle" (Son-Duong 1987; Le-van-Thu 1973:164). In the investigation phase the Vietminh activist would target poor peasant youth and, as in the village of Kinh-Ke, family members of executed and imprisoned Vietnamese Nationalist Party members (Le-van-Thu 1973:164). Informal and individual discussions would then be held with prospective political activists on local, national, and international issues, particularly the high cost of living and the protest movements against the draft, corvée, and high taxes. In Son-Duong Linh also transmitted ballads critical of gambling and large expensive village ceremonies, reminiscent of a VNP leader's critical comments regarding the large funerals in Nguyen Dac Bang's household in the late 1920s. The more progressive elements would subsequently be recruited, trained, and organized into three-member Vietminh cells, each of which comprised an established member and two new recruits (Son-Duong 1987; Le-van-Thu 1973:165). They would then be taught the methods of covert operation and how to deal with the enemy when under arrest, and assigned, among other things, the task of leaflet distribution. With this organization and method of recruitment Vietminh activities spread from Kinh-Ke not only to Son-Duong, Ban-Nguyen, and other villages in Lam-Thao district, but also to other communities in Thanh-Thuy and Tam-Nong on the other side of the Red River.

Once organizational momentum had been regained, struggles against foreign capitalists began flaring up in certain localities. In Doan-Hung district in May 1942 under Vietminh guidance, peasants successfully demanded a rent reduction and the return of appropriated land from a French plantation owner. In the same year workers at the Viet-Tri paper factory also successfully demanded overtime pay, a wage increase, paid holidays, and protection against wartime inflation through the purchase of such basic commodities as rice and cloth at fixed prices (Cao-Tien-Phung et al. 1985:76).

In a by now familiar pattern, French suppression quickly followed these campaigns, resulting in the arrest of almost all the provincial party leaders (Le-Tuong and Vu-Kim-Bien 1981:165). On October 2, 1943, the repression reached the villages of Kinh-Ke and Son-Duong: an ICP member and seven national salvation association members were arrested in the two villages. The top Vietminh organizer in Son-Duong, Linh, was arrested that day together with two recruits on the information provided by a previously imprisoned VNP activist (the executed Confucian teacher Toai's younger brother) and another recruit (Son-Duong 1987:16).[6]

Bang's cousin Te, a landless laborer, talked about his life and his assistance to Linh in Son-Duong for a brief time during this period:

In the early 1940s, after six years in the village of Vinh-Lai, my job as an annual live-in worker was terminated. I returned to Son-Duong to live with my mother. I went to work as a seasonally employed laborer (from the third to the eighth lunar month every year) for the wives of [the late] Canton Chief Chi. No longer receiving any payment in kind as in the earlier position, I was fed and paid fifteen piasters a month.

*How much did paddy cost in those days?*

Paddy cost about thirty piasters a quintal [one hundred kilograms].

During this period as a seasonally employed laborer, I became well acquainted with Brother Linh in the village. On one occasion, without dwelling on the reason, Brother Linh asked me to accompany him to Kinh-Ke and then asked me to serve as a sentry for a meeting once we got there. One day a number of Kinh-Ke villagers were arrested. On learning of this development, I hurried to see Linh to make inquiries, only to be entrusted with a stack of printed materials, including a map, books, and magazines with the hammer-and-sickle emblem. I knew that Mr. Kieu Hien, a student at the Thang-Long school in Hanoi, had recently brought back to the village a huge stack of propaganda leaflets. Moving the entrusted materials from one corner of the house to another for hiding, I eventually decided to burn them out of concern about being arrested. I was scared because I had earlier witnessed the torture of Mr. Kieu Hien by the authorities.

Another Son-Duong native, Le van Tiem, who had been Bang's favorite student and had assisted him with leaflet printing in 1930, and who later became the president of the Son-Duong Communist Party branch, spoke of his teaching background and his peripheral activities in the incipient Vietminh organization of Son-Duong:

[After obtaining the certificat d'études primaires at the age of eighteen and working as a private tutor in neighboring Phung-Nguyen village for three years] I managed to obtain an official teaching position. I taught for eight years in the village of Quynh-Lam, approximately six or seven kilometers from Son-Duong. In the early 1940s, in a switch with me, a native of that village who taught in the village of Ngu-Xa neighboring on Son-Duong requested a transfer back to his native village.

In 1942, soon after my assumption of the Ngu-Xa teaching post, Bui Kim Linh, a former student of mine, recruited me into the local Vietminh organization. I was the first recruit. Vietminh activities in Son-Duong at the time were limited mainly to building up the local organization to a dozen members so that activities could begin. Other Vietminh members in Son-Duong secretly distributed anti-French leaflets from time to time. However, the activity was limited in scale, as villagers had whispered concerns about attracting French attention.

Less than a year after I became a Vietminh member, Linh was arrested. I escaped imprisonment only because Linh refused to reveal the local Vietminh membership. However, with a revolutionary spirit not yet too strong and being concerned about my family's livelihood at the time, I became inactive.

Thanks to Linh's and other arrested activists' discipline under torture, the Vietminh organizations in both Son-Duong and Kinh-Ke were protected. Linh was given a three-year sentence and subsequently died in the central prison of Hanoi in August 1944. The momentum of the organization in Son-Duong slowed down considerably when the mayors of Son-Duong and the tiny village of Thuy-Son (later a part of Son-Duong) were removed from office for not reporting on Vietminh activities and one of the two informants was appointed deputy mayor, and as a number of activists and sympathizers either fled to other villages or, like the teacher Tiem, became immobilized out of concern about future arrests. With the repression of the early 1930s obviously still vivid in the mind of many villagers, the crackdown in 1943 temporarily halted overt anticolonial activities.

In contrast, in neighboring Kinh-Ke, where ICP members were protected by village authorities, the development of the Vietminh organization went forward. The village became the coordinating point for anticolonial resistance in the entire province. The Vietminh membership in Kinh-Ke (est. pop. 850) continued to increase from 43 in September 1943 to 87 in early 1945 (Le-van-Thu 1973:165). Under Vietminh influence the village became increasingly defiant toward the colonial authorities, refusing to pay taxes in 1944.[7] Visiting cadres from Kinh-Ke reestablished contacts with Vietminh organizations in Doan-Hung, Phu-Ninh, and Tam-Nong districts. They succeeded in recruiting into national salvation associations young students, soldiers, and even civil servants in provincial offices such as the court, the French Résident's office, the treasury, the post office, the geographical survey, and the ammunition warehouse (Cao-Tien-Phung et al. 1985:76–77; Cao-van-Luong 1960:145, 153). In Kinh-Ke on January 7, 1945, three hundred Vietminh members from four districts (Lam-Thao, Thanh-Son, Thanh-Thuy, and Cam-Khe), including the village of Son-Duong, were exhorted to mobilize local populations at the appropriate moment chosen on the basis of particular local conditions in order to widen the Vietminh's appeal. As a sign of the intensified preparation for the anticipated conflict, a self-defense militia team was organized in Kinh-Ke in the aftermath of the January 7, 1945, meeting in order to provide support for future mass struggles.

The Vietminh gained further momentum when the Japanese over-threw the French colonial administration in Vietnam on March 9, 1945, and then became unpopular with their continued tax collection and coercive rice purchases despite the poor fall crop of 1944. Famine spread throughout north Vietnam, including the village of Son-Duong. This catastrophic event was estimated to claim from half a million to two million lives in northern Vietnam. Despite the smaller magnitude of the famine in the province of Phu-Tho compared to other locations, one of the three mass graves of famine victims in the provincial capital contained more than five hundred bodies (Le-Tuong and Vu-Kim-Bien 1981:172). In Son-Duong the Japanese removal of approximately one hundred tonnes of paddy led to a famine among numerous poor peasant families. Although the famine was alleviated to a certain extent by large paddy loans from the wealthiest villager, the wife of the former canton chief Chi, almost ten families left their native village in search of food, and three or four villagers reportedly died (Son-Duong 1987:17). The landless cultivator Te reported on his strug-gle for survival at this critical time:

In 1945, because of the scarcity of rice, my family had to mix banana-tree bulbs with steamed cereal in order to fill our stomachs. To increase our food supply, I had to carry ashes to the mountainous region of Thanh-Son on the other side of the Red River to exchange for manioc—two baskets of ashes for a three-liter basket of manioc. I even had to collect discarded lichee seeds, which we cooked, peeled, and pounded in order to add flavor to the manioc used as a rice substitute in soup. Even so, I considered my family fortunate because many people starved to death in the area.

The Vietminh accordingly intensified the campaign of struggle to denounce the Japanese and their collaborators, and launched a movement to seize public rice stocks in response to the concrete needs of poor peasants. They also formed guerilla units in preparation for local insurrections and for the seizure of district and provincial administrations as soon as conditions turned favorable (Le-Tuong and Vu-Kim-Bien 1981:166).

Throughout the spring and summer of 1945, either orally or in leaflets, Vietminh cadres denounced the Japanese and their Vietnamese collaborators at large gatherings such as the Hung King shrine festival in Lam-Thao district; certain periodic local markets in Thanh-Thuy, Tam-Nong, and Lam-Thao; and even a pro-Japanese youth gathering in the provincial capital in August (ibid.: 167; Cao-Tien-Phung et al. 1985:89; Cao-van-Luong 1960:150).[8] Starting in May 1945, Vietminh cadres in Phu-Tho also mobilized the poor to seize rice stocks in various locations and to resist tax collection by the pro-Japanese government: "Keep the rice! Destroy the enemy's granaries! No need to pay taxes on our land. Do not tolerate the theft of our rice! Fellow countrymen, join the Vietminh!" (Le-Tuong and Vu-Kim-Bien 1981:166). In Lam-Thao district, from their Kinh-Ke village stronghold Vietminh cadres led peasants to seize rice stocks in the villages of Ban-Nguyen, Thach-Son, and Tien-Kien as well as in the town of Hung-Hoa on the other side of the Red River (Le-van-Thu 1973:169). Large meetings were also convened in Thanh-Son and Thanh-Thuy districts in May to exhort the local populace to prepare for an uprising (Cao-Tien-Phung et al. 1985:90).

The growing intensity and success of the Vietminh-organized activities increased the significance of the Vietminh as a rallying point for the local population. After the Japanese coup in March, a small number of Vietminh members in Son-Duong together with scores of other activists from the rest of the province were sent to the Hien-Luong guerilla base in Ha-Hoa district for training.[9]

The Japanese made numerous efforts to repress the movement. In the village of Kinh-Ke, where the Vietminh leadership was planning a large regional meeting for early May, the Japanese, with the collaboration of informers, arrested twenty-four activists (Le-van-Thu 1973: 170). In the provincial capital, the Japanese arrested and tortured twenty-four young activists in June in order to crack down on the distribution of tax protest leaflets and the covert financial and arms purchasing activities of the Vietminh. However, Vietminh strength was solid enough that these repressions, although briefly disrupting Vietminh activities, did not succeed for long in displacing the Vietminh organizations in either place.

In July and August, in order to expand their guerilla forces in the province, the Vietminh made several seizures of arms from lightly guarded administrative posts (e.g., Phu-Ninh on July 30, Ha-Hoa on August 2, Doan-Hung on August 8, Thanh-Son on August 11, Thanh-Thuy on August 15, and Lam-Thao on August 17). The self-defense unit of Kinh-Ke village participated in the last two events in coordination with its counterparts from three villages of Thanh-Thuy and four other villages of Lam-Thao.[10] The Vietminh even succeeded in enlisting the support of the provincial security forces in preparation for the seizure of administrative power (Cao-van-Luong 1960:155–156).[11] Throughout the province of Phu-Tho the district administrative apparatus began to collapse. One district chief joined the Vietminh (in Ha-Hoa), two surrendered (in Lam-Thao and Phu-Ninh), another was assassinated (in Thanh-Thuy), and others abandoned their posts for refuge in the countryside.

In the aftermath of the Japanese unconditional surrender on August 15, mostly through mass demonstrations supported by armed guerillas and village self-defense forces, the Vietminh officially took over district administrations in Phu-Ninh (August 15); Cam-Khe, Doan-Hung, and Thanh-Ba (August 17); Tam-Nong and Yen-Lap (August 18); Hac-Tri and Lam-Thao (August 20); and Thanh-Thuy (August 22). Many Son-Duong villagers participated in the demonstration that culminated in the transfer of the Lam-Thao administration to the Vietminh, although quite a few participants were less than fully aware of the nature of their action, as related by the landless laborer Te:

In August 1945, when the area was flooded because of a broken dike, I saw a large gathering of people with flags in the fields preparing to leave for the district seat. Not understanding politics and simply looking for fun, I asked to join them and heard a few speeches in the district seat. It was [during this demonstration] that the Vietminh took over the administration of Lam-Thao.

In order to carry out their plans for a general uprising, riding the wave of success in various Phu-Tho districts and taking advantage of the highly symbolic seizure of administrative power in Hanoi on August 19, on August 21 the Vietminh delivered, among other demands, an ultimatum to the Japanese authority in Phu-Tho demanding the disarmament of Japanese troops and the transfer of the provincial administration.[12] On August 22, armed guerillas and peasants marched from all over the province to the provincial capital of Phu-Tho in order to exert indirect pressure on the Japanese and pro-Japanese Vietnamese officials. Despite complications and tense negotiations, on August 25 the pro-Japanese provincial administration made the official transfer of power to the Vietminh.[13] On the same day, under pressure, Emperor Bao Dai in the puppet Hue court declared his abdication of the throne; and in the village of Son-Duong, under the guidance of the Lam-Thao district Vietminh leadership, a new village administration, called the People's Provisional Revolutionary Committee, was established. The colonial era formally came to an end when Ho Chi Minh declared the formation of the Democratic Republic of Vietnam in Hanoi on September 2, 1945.

## THE WAR OF NATIONAL LIBERATION

From a historical perspective, the seizure of administrative power represented only the first in a series of victories for the Vietminh. For nine years challenges would come not only from outside forces in the international arena, but also from a minority of the indigenous population who would collaborate with foreigners, both Chinese and French, in their opposition to the Marxist-led Vietminh. In response, the Vietminh would rely heavily upon their legitimacy as the first government of national independence and would skillfully combine the reformist and activist traditions represented by Phan Boi Chau and Phan Chu Trinh, respectively, of the earlier generation of anticolonial leaders. Historical events in both the village of Son-Duong and the country at large would be shaped by the violent encounter between the forces of capitalist imperialism and the growing momentum of a nationalist Marxist movement.

In North Vietnam the first major challenge came with the arrival of 150,000 anticommunist Chinese troops in September 1945 under an Allied agreement to disarm the 30,000-strong Japanese army.[14] Following the Chinese troops came a challenge from Vietnamese carpetbaggers: Vietnamese Nationalist Party remnants and other anticommunist politicians returning from exile in China. By this time the VNP had been reduced to a relatively small contingent. They no longer had a base among the peasant and worker masses in the country, and their socialist cause had been shed in the search for power under the shadow of Chinese troops. A more serious challenge was the French attempt to reincorporate Indochina into their colonial empire and the ensuing Franco-Vietminh war from 1946 to 1954.

In the province of Phu-Tho anticommunist Chinese troops occupied the two major towns of Phu-Tho and Viet-Tri. An official Communist Party source claims that they also connived with, if not actively supported, the VNP in its attacks on the Vietminh forces in these two towns in November and December 1945 (Cao-Tien-Phung et al. 1985:119).[15] The VNP occupation of Viet-Tri and its presence in Phu-Tho lasted until June 1946 in a local modus vivendi. This understanding stemmed from Ho Chi Minh's efforts from October 1945 onward, in preparation for a possibly protracted conflict with the French, to find a peaceful end to the Chinese occupation and to include the indigenous opposition in a new national coalition government.[16] In the village of Son-Duong the Vietminh-VNP conflict had little bearing on the support of the local population for the Vietminh, despite the flight of the two Franco-Japanese–era informers on Vietminh activities and the Vietminh's later "elimination" of these two individuals (Son-Duong 1987:16). The banner of nationalist socialism in Son-Duong had long been captured by the Vietminh owing to a decade-long absence of VNP activities in the community, the activism of local Vietminh cadres in response to the nationalist aspirations and concrete needs of the local population, and the legitimacy of Ho Chi Minh's government as the first national independence government in almost a century.

In the spring of 1946 Chinese forces gradually withdrew from Vietnam in accordance with a February 28, 1946, Franco-Chinese agreement by which the French would return to northern Vietnam as the replacement for Chinese troops.[17] In an atmosphere of worsening relations between the Vietminh, on the one hand, and the VNP and allied parties, on the other, the withdrawing Chinese troops were quickly followed by many anticommunist VNP and allied party leaders. In June 1946 the Vietminh mobilized three thousand troops in attacks on VNP armed forces in the towns of Phu-Tho and Viet-Tri. It succeeded in driving the troublesome VNP opposition permanently out of the province (Cao-Tien-Phung et al. 1985:135; Hoang-van-Dao 1970:400, 403–406).

The conflict with the VNP notwithstanding, the Vietminh theme of national unity and Ho's ideologically powerful declaration of independence captured the hearts and minds of virtually all Vietnamese. The Vietminh had reinforced the theme of national unity in November 1945, when it formally dissolved the ICP in a tactical move. No less significant were its well-polished mass organizational skills, its ability to coopt traditionally influential Vietnamese and to involve local populations in the cause of "national salvation" and socioeconomic reforms. In late 1945 the Son-Duong village administration organized young activists into *cuu quoc* (national salvation) associations (youth, peasant, and women's) under the umbrella of the village Vietminh organization. In early 1946, as the need arose for a broadened coalition and the wider participation of all progressive elements in preparation for possibly protracted struggle with the French, additional *cuu quoc* associations (Catholic and Buddhist) were formed in the village as a part of the larger Lien Viet (Viet Alliance) front. Although association membership figures are not available, these associations together with the association of combatants' mothers formed soon after the outbreak of the Franco-Vietminh war seem to have involved virtually all adult villagers.

Influential villagers were coopted to serve as leaders either within the *cuu quoc* associations or in the village, district, and provincial administration. The political activist Tang, Bang's brother and a roommate of the first chairman of the Vietminh provincial administration, reportedly became the director of the provincial economic office and later on the head of military supplies for the provincial defense police *(canh ve)* battalion in 1946. Despite his lack of formal Communist Party or Vietminh affiliation, Bang's former student Le van Tiem, a teacher, was drafted to become the vice chairman of the People's Provisional Revolutionary Committee (deputy district chief) in Lam-Thao and later to fill the position of president in the local Communist Party cell:

It was by accident that my activity in the movement resumed in August 1945. At the time, I was seeking refuge in the Lam-Thao district seat since the area was flooded. The Red River dike had been broken. On the evening of my arrival, I joined the crowd as the Vietminh took over the district seat. They drafted me to serve as vice chairman [deputy district chief] of the People's Provisional Revolutionary Committee in Lam-Thao district, under Mr. Tran Quoc Sang of Thach-Son village, because they found me a competent person of integrity. I was nominated despite my lack of desire for the position.

One of my main tasks as vice chairman was to take charge of dike repair from Phu-Tho to Viet-Tri. I informed prospective contractors and subsequently supervised the work of the chosen one to ensure the high quality of the work. The other major task involved judicial duties because there was no court at the time. Wherever I went, people listened to my reasoning. They respected me as a teacher, and local problems got solved quickly. I was well liked at the local level.

*Did you and the committee encounter any major insoluble problems in those days?*

I do not recall any. All the litigations got resolved. I did well as vice chairman thanks to my prestige in the district as a teacher.

*Was there any opposition to the Vietminh?*

Fortunately, it became inactive, although we also had to assure them that there would be no recriminations.

The first president of the People's Provisional Revolutionary Committee in Son-Duong was also a Sino-Vietnamese teacher and a former mayor. He was in turn succeeded by three French-trained teachers from privileged backgrounds. Among the successful and Vietminh-supported candidates for the village people's council in 1946 was the third wealthiest villager, the wife of the late mayor An. Similarly, *cuu quoc* associations in the village were led by well-educated and progressive villagers from the more privileged social strata. In other words, in mobilizing the local population the Vietminh relied heavily on the respect for education in the indigenous sociocultural framework. However, in order to broaden their bases through *cuu quoc* associations, they also sought to include women and peasants in public activities. In the

1946 elections to the National Assembly, the provincial people's committee, and the village people's committee, women could, for the first time, participate in official political activities. The broad-based membership of both the Vietminh front and local governmental bodies dramatically increased the participation of Son-Duong villagers in the search for solutions to major short- and long-term problems both within the village and beyond.

In search of solutions to short-term problems, the new Vietminh government made powerful appeals to Son-Duong villagers for unity and national salvation. In the face of persistent hunger caused by the August flooding in the district, the village administration and *cuu quoc* associations mobilized well-off families to donate rice to other villagers, organized the population to repair the damaged dike system, and encouraged peasants to assist one another in planting fast-growing secondary staple crops in order to replace the lost rice harvest. Starvation was consequently averted as the local food supply in the fall of 1945 reportedly increased by 150 tonnes over the preceding year (Son-Duong 1987). The national government also canceled poll, market, and ferry taxes (Cao-Tien-Phung et al. 1985:124). Villagers responded enthusiastically to the appeals of the new national government for donations to the "Independence Fund," "National Defense Fund," and "Gold Week" in order to finance basic administrative operations and the expansion of the armed forces for the cause of national independence. Well-off villagers donated money to arm the new thirty-man self-defense force in Son-Duong at the same time that a provincial defense police force *(canh ve)* was created. Although Son-Duong's population amounted to less than 0.4 percent of the 500,000 inhabitants in Phu-Tho and Vinh-Yen, Gold Week donations from Son-Duong in the fall of 1945 totaled 0.5 kilogram of gold and 1 kilogram of silver, amounting to a significant 2 percent of the gold donations from the two provinces (cf. Cao-Tien-Phung et al. 1985:125; Son-Duong 1987:21).

In the name of national salvation, the *cuu quoc* youth association and the village administration in Son-Duong also launched campaigns to increase young villagers' physical activities, to raise the literacy level of community members, and to eradicate such problems as gambling, theft, and superstitious practices among certain quarters of the local population. With the slogan "Be Strong for the Fatherland," *cuu quoc* activists organized sports teams and daily soccer practices in order to channel the physical energy of Son-Duong youth during the slack seasons. Responding to Ho Chi Minh's nationwide appeal to "destroy illiteracy as an enemy," the Son-Duong village administration and the local *cuu quoc* youth association launched a literacy campaign, resorting not only to ideological exhortation ("It is patriotic to become literate") and social pressure (invitations by beating drums to specific households), but also to indirect negative sanctions (conducting literacy tests at the village gate to embarrass less eager villagers). Within a year the movement expanded from a single class in the communal meeting hall to fifty classes with a total of 1250 students, including women and the elderly. This enrollment amounted to 2.4 percent of the total provincial literacy enrollment (53,324) although Son-Duong villagers comprised only 0.6 percent of the Phu-Tho population of 290,000. By the end of 1946, 70 percent of illiterate villagers had been certified to pass the literacy tests (Son-Duong 1987:22). In addition, with popular support, the village administration adopted strong measures to eradicate gambling, theft, and "superstitious" practices. Gamblers were forced to attend funeral processions for their playing cards and to publicly shout "down with gambling." Second-time theft offenders were required to hang stolen objects (e.g., cucumbers or fruit) from their necks in procession through the village. Shamans had to report at the communal meeting hall, where they were firmly asked to destroy their altars and to abandon their practices.

With the theme of unity within both communal and national frameworks, young *cuu quoc* activists also took a leading role in instituting major long-term reforms, occasionally triggering acrimonious debates within the community. In order to forge a greater sense of unity and to overcome territorial parochialism, the local Vietminh front, under the leadership of modern-educated young activists, pushed the hitherto separate villages of Son-Duong, Dung-Hien, and Thuy-Son to organize a joint worship of their identical village-guardian deities. The administrative divisions also broke down, as they were subsequently merged into one village. For the cause of stronger communal unity within an egalitarian framework, local young activists attempted to undermine the class-oriented and male-exclusive institution of communal house feasts through public criticism and subversive satirical ballads. With input from district-level Communist Party leadership, this reform campaign started with young activists' critique of the unegalitarian tradition of food distribution according to which higher-ranked male villagers received the more honored portions of sacrificial animals (e.g., the cockscomb was distributed to the highest-ranked notable), lower-ranked male villagers had to crowd onto a lower communal house platform around fewer food trays, and villagers without titles simply could not participate. Later demands were made for the abolition of the feasting system altogether and for the division of communal land among the poor families in the village (cf. Hunt 1982:153). In response to a question on opposition to the reform processes, a major leader in the village at the time reported:

Under the general guidance of party authorities and with the agreement of other villagers, we also distributed communal land to landless cultivators. Through discussion in the district seat among village representatives, we decided to mobilize people to simplify such ceremonies as funerals and weddings and to scale down wasteful village feasts. We did not encounter any opposition even from the former notables, because they did not dare to raise any objections to such widely supported ideas in public meetings.

In the name of national salvation, the Vietminh reform campaign eventually emerged triumphant over century-old institutions, although not without a cost to village harmony. The first president of the People's Revolutionary Committee, a former Sino-Vietnamese teacher and a mayor during the colonial period, resigned in protest. In fact, a total of four villagers, all teachers, succeeded one another in this office within a sixteen-month period (Son-Duong 1987:25–26).[18] Still, the hierarchical model was gradually weakened in favor of collective welfare. The local Vietminh front's *relative* success in its *equality-oriented reform* campaign may have been facilitated by the three universal suffrage elections of 1946, in which voting rights were no longer restricted to men of wealth and education and in one of which a woman (the third wealthiest villager in Son-Duong) was elected as a Vietminh candidate. The themes of unity and national salvation and the Vietminh's organizational successes reinforced each other. They not only laid the groundwork for the formation of a local Communist Party branch in Son-Duong, but also enhanced the legitimacy of the Vietminh in preparation for the protracted Franco-Vietminh war, during which the support of local populations would prove critical for the success of the Vietminh's guerilla warfare strategy.

French troops returned to North Vietnam in March 1946 under the provisions of a Sino-French agreement. Relations between the French, on the one hand, and the vast majority of the Vietnamese population and the Vietminh, on the other, were unusually tense, despite numerous negotiation sessions between the two sides throughout 1946.[19] The First Indochina War broke out on December 19, 1946, when Ho Chi Minh issued a call to the people, urging them to join the national resistance against the French in the aftermath of French provocations in Hai-Phong, Lang-Son, and Hanoi in November and December:

> For the sake of peace, we have made concessions [to the French]. But the more conciliatory we are, the more aggressive the French colonialists become. They are determined to reconquer our country. No! We would rather sacrifice everything. We are determined not to lose our country and not to be enslaved. Dear compatriots, we must rise up. Male and female, old and young, regardless of religion, political party, ethnicity, all Vietnamese must rise up to fight French colonialists and to save the fatherland. Those with guns will fight with guns. Those with swords will fight with swords. Those without swords will fight with picks, shovels, and sticks. Everybody must do his or her best to oppose colonialism and to save the country! (Cao-Tien-Phung et al. 1985:144)

Like the Aid-the-King proclamation King Ham Nghi had issued six decades earlier in his flight from the capital, Ho's call for resistance against foreign invaders struck a deep emotional chord among the indigenous population. As Vietminh forces launched counterattacks on French troops in Hanoi and other towns in North Vietnam, Ho's government and the Vietminh military command withdrew gradually toward the base of resistance in the mountainous area of Thai-Nguyen, Bac-Can, and Tuyen-Quang in order to lead the resistance to the French attempts to reestablish a colonial system. The Vietminh also dispersed equipment and supplies to resistance bases. Quite a few printing plants, major warehouses, and a military hospital were moved to the province of Phu-Tho (Cao-Tien-Phung et al. 1985:177).

During the first phase of the resistance (1947–1950), in order to slow down technologically superior French troops while building up their own forces, the Vietminh relied on the "scorched earth" resistance tactic, a strengthened rural defense system, and a guerilla warfare strategy. The Vietminh destroyed roads, bridges, and rail lines; created obstacles to the movement of the French navy and paratroopers; and, in order to eliminate sheltering facilities for French garrisons, burned barracks and large buildings in provincial towns, including Phu-Tho, Hung-Hoa, and Viet-Tri in the province of Phu-Tho. Within a year, according to present Vietnamese sources, the Vietminh had heavily damaged 530 kilometers of roads and 2585 buildings in Phu-Tho and the neighboring provinces of Vinh-Yen and Phuc-Yen (Cao-Tien-Phung et al. 1985:182). As defensive measures in the large area under their control in Phu-Tho, the Vietminh strengthened village defenses with elaborate systems of hedges and trenches, organized the hiding of food, launched a "three nos" policy among the rural population (hear nothing, see nothing, and know nothing in response to strangers), as well as temporarily dispersed the population (ibid.:191–194). In the village of Son-Duong able-bodied male villagers were organized into a thirty-man self-defense squad in 1947, and two militia squads were formed with female and elderly volunteers. Gates were erected even at the entrances to small alleys, and trenches five feet high were constructed throughout the village (Son-Duong 1987:38). The Vietminh also started to build up the guerilla and regular armed forces more quickly. By 1949 average village guerilla strength had increased to the company level, as able villagers from the age of eighteen to forty-five were drafted into the local guerilla force. Many guerillas also received better training and volunteered for local regular units *(bo doi dia phuong)*. As a result, not counting companies at the district level, the provincial regular forces increased to one battalion (approximately three hundred soldiers) (Cao-Tien-Phung et al. 1985:161–164). Eighty Son-Duong villagers joined the regular Vietminh forces during the period from 1947 to 1950.

The first phase of the Franco-Vietminh war (1947–1950) was highly reminiscent of the first war of resistance against the French in the late nineteenth century: the Vietminh relied primarily on guerilla warfare to disrupt the logistical movements of the French in their offensive campaigns in Phu-Tho and elsewhere. In contrast, the French attempted to take maximal advantage of their own tactical mobility and superior fire power. In Phu-Tho, the two sides clashed for the first time in May 1947, when six hundred French paratroopers landed in Phu-Tho and Viet-Tri and damaged the Vietminh forces in both towns but withdrew within five days under the Vietminh guerillas' constant harassment.

The real test of the Vietminh's guerilla warfare strategy came later in the fall of 1947, when the French launched a major campaign with

12,000 troops in an attack on the Vietminh's resistance headquarters in the mountains. The colonial forces had hoped to destroy the Vietminh quickly by capturing the Vietminh government and military command and heavily damaging the Vietminh's regular army in the process. On the western front of this campaign, the French occupied strategically located Viet-Tri and, in October 1947, moved their troops to Tuyen-Quang along the Clear River (Song Lo) (Pham-Gia-Duc 1986:160–190). In conjunction with this major offensive, the French swept through the districts of Thanh-Son, Thanh-Thuy, and Yen-Lap in southeastern Phu-Tho (Cao-Tien-Phung et al. 1985:185–189). The Phu-Tho campaign was aimed at disrupting a major line of communication between Central Vietnam and the Vietminh headquarters in the northern mountains (through the midland provinces of Hoa-Binh and Phu-Tho). After successfully taking a number of target towns with limited Vietminh resistance in the provinces of Bac-Can and Thai-Nguyen, French troops faced insurmountable logistical problems in this mountainous area of northern Vietnam, where Vietminh guerillas constantly harassed them in a pattern reminiscent of the nineteenth-century resistance. Because of the Vietminh's adept use of guerilla warfare and the grass-root support for the resistance, within two months the French had to withdraw their troops without achieving their objectives. Their illusion of a quick and easy reconquest of northern Vietnam was shattered. In Phu-Tho, thanks to the proximity of the major supply lines in the delta and the availability of river transportation channels, the French succeeded in holding on to certain major locations in the southeastern part of the province, despite the Vietminh guerillas' infliction of fairly heavy casualties on the French troops along the Clear River.[20]

Over the next three years, the French launched numerous military campaigns in the province of Phu-Tho with four basic objectives: (1) to hold on to the occupied territory as a source of manpower and food supply, (2) to damage the Vietminh's economic and military buildups, (3) to strengthen the defense of the ethnic Muong province of Hoa-Binh and the Red River delta, and (4) to disrupt the Vietminh's communications with north central Vietnam. These efforts were successful only in the limited sense that Vietminh control in certain areas became contested. In November 1948 the French launched a paratroop attack on the strategic town of Viet-Tri, which they were able to hold for the next six years. After a 1500-soldier campaign in the districts west of the Red River (Thanh-Son, Thanh-Thuy, Tam-Nong, and Cam-Khe) in February 1949, the French launched a 2600-troop operation two months later into the more economically important eastern districts (Hac-Tri, Lam-Thao, Phu-Ninh, and Doan-Hung) in order to damage an important Vietminh economic base, seize the Vietminh's regional command, and destroy part of the Vietminh's regular forces. French forces swept through the area of Son-Duong in both of these operations, and on both occasions the village guerilla unit laid ambushes for the French troops. The first involved coordination with the provincial forces and reportedly resulted in two French and one Vietminh casualty in the rice fields of Kinh-Ke village (Son-Duong 1987:39). In the second operation in April 1949, the French did not engage Son-Duong's guerilla force and quickly retreated after seizing ten cattle and burning one house (Son-Duong 1987:40). The elderly and children of Son-Duong village subsequently moved to safer areas in Thanh-Ba and Phu-Ninh districts.

Although they were unable to expand their control into much of the province, by early 1950 the French had set up pro-French administrations in thirty-one villages in the southeastern districts (Thanh-Son, Thanh-Thuy, Tam-Nong, and Hac-Tri) and were able to exert significant influence on forty-four others, either arresting or forcing into the underground ICP members as well as Vietminh guerillas and cadres in these localities (Cao-Tien-Phung et al. 1985:206, 208). In these villages the French also instituted a draft and recruited heavily among native Catholics for local intelligence and administrative services. However, the French presence in southeastern Phu-Tho and occasional military forays into the area had no direct impact on village life in Son-Duong and the local support for the Vietminh, as a village leader at the time reported:

In defense the village was well protected with a strengthened bamboo hedge and fortified gates that once closed were simply impenetrable. The French conducted two or three mop-up operations through this area during that time, once even doing a house-to-house search in the village [in August 1950]. During this search, I had to hide under the water lentils in a village pond.

*Were you informed by villagers at the ferry landing point in Ban-Nguyen of incoming French operations?*

We got sufficient warning from the skittish French soldiers themselves, who fired noisily into the air when approaching the village. Armed with only a few guns, local guerillas might also follow the French firing with a few more shots to give additional escape warnings to one another. Our communication network did not exist then. However, the French did not really disrupt village activities since they seldom spent more than a few hours here. Area markets were held less frequently in those years, but Son-Duong did not specialize in marketing activities. As an agricultural village, we simply resumed our work in the fields after their departure.

Despite these French operations, villagers maintained their full confidence in the Party and the Vietminh. Supported by their families, party cadres worked willingly without any salary in those days. When we needed men for the armed forces, villagers volunteered without any complaint. The number of volunteers always exceeded the quota from higher authorities. When regular armed Vietminh units passed through Son-Duong, villagers donated food. Whenever the district or local administration needed financial contributions, as we levied no taxes at the time, we simply asked for assistance from well-off families, especially from the third wealthiest villager, the most generous and enthusiastic Mrs. Ai An [mother of Ai and the wife of the late mayor An]. These families would contribute anything from rice to the sizable sum of a few hundred piasters. Support was widespread, from both the rich and the poor. We held large public meetings where the party members in attendance easily reached one hundred, just like at a public festival, without any need to be concerned about security.

With the strong support of local populations and by means of guerilla warfare as well as the occasional deployment of the newly formed regular forces, the Vietminh succeeded in inflicting casualties upon the French, at times heavy casualties, thus containing the effects of the French "pacification" campaign and politically destabilizing the area under temporary French control. In order to further complicate the logistics for the French in the southeastern districts, a partial trade embargo was imposed with a prohibition on rice, corn, and cattle exports to the area under French control.[21] The Vietminh continued to ambush French forces during the French mop-up operations and to launch small-scale attacks on French posts. Prefiguring the guerilla warfare in the South Vietnam of the late 1950s and 1960s, the provincial Vietminh leadership also organized armed underground propaganda and assassination teams in occupied territory, assassinating 67 pro-French local officials and arresting 255 others in fifty hamlets in the period from December 1949 to March 1950 (Cao-Tien-Phung et al. 1985:210). These small-scale offensives were occasionally combined with the use of the Vietminh's new regular forces, as during the April 1949 campaign, when the Vietminh mobilized one regiment and six battalions to eliminate almost one-third of the French attack troops (ibid.:197). As a precursor to the guerilla warfare strategy in the south in the 1960s, this pattern of armed activities partially succeeded in limiting French influence to the southeastern districts and at times reverted the control of a number of communities to the Vietminh.

Throughout this period as well as through the second phase of the Franco-Vietminh war (1951–1954), the village of Son-Duong lent solid politico-military support to the Vietminh and remained firmly under Vietminh control. The firm support for the Vietminh in Son-Duong and the general success of the guerilla strategy in the province of Phu-Tho were intricately linked to the Vietminh's in-depth organizational efforts and more generally to their successful mobilization of the population through nationalist appeals and by means of the political economy of reforms. Bang's cousin Te, the landless laborer, discussed his life in the first two years of Vietminh power and the reason for his decision to join the local regular Vietminh forces:

After the revolutionary forces had seized power, I joined the village self-defense unit and became a squad leader in 1946. I also eventually managed to get married around this time, in early 1947, at the age of twenty-seven. The marriage was certainly quite late because of our poverty. Our fortune improved slightly because my wife brought to our family 1.2 *sao* of rice fields and my mother also received an inheritance of 1.8 *sao* from my maternal grandmother. However, I still had to work for an additional year after my marriage as a live-in laborer, because I had to pay off the wedding debts and also because we had a total of only 3 *sao* in those days. The wedding costs had been substantial, including a bride price of forty or fifty piasters plus a wedding banquet. Despite the contributions from relatives at the banquet, I still had to borrow to pay for half of the expenses. I repaid the debts with my income from another year's work as a laborer.

In late 1947 I volunteered for the regular army because my wife could take care of my mother at home then. Although I was the only son of my parents, I volunteered for the armed forces anyway out of the desire to end the oppression by foreigners. The citizen of a conquered country suffers many miseries.

*How did your mother and wife react to your decision?*

Inspired by patriotism, they were quite supportive, albeit not without some concern for my safety.

One year I was assigned to cut the telephone line on the other side of the river in the Hung-Hoa area. I was also instructed to wait on an alluvial soil area after completing the task for transportation across the river. But after finishing the assignment, I waited for almost the entire night without seeing anybody. Getting scared at the approach of morning and running out of other solutions, I decided to cut down three banana trees and tie the trunks together with the telephone wire, and I also made sure to bring along a roll of telephone wire as evidence of my successful completion of the assigned task. Knowing neither how to swim nor how to navigate, I ended up being swept away by the current and only reached the other side at Ban-Nguyen. Boiling with anger, I decided to skip my company command and reported at the battalion headquarters. Putting down the telephone wire, I told the battalion commander: "I am quitting the army now to return to my home village!" They inquired, and I told them: "Yesterday, they [the company command] assigned me to cut the telephone wire on the other side of the river. However, they failed to pick me up as promised and abandoned me to the mercy of the enemy patrol. My mother had only one son. If I die, it will be the end of the line! I am not going to stay in the army!" The battalion commander asked me to stay on there and sent a representative to my company to ask whether all the company's soldiers were present. The company commander [reportedly] replied: "Yes, except for those on vacation and on assignment." A specific inquiry was made about me, and he reported that I had left for assignment only earlier in the day! The battalion officer retorted: "You lie! Having completed your assignment last night, he is now with the battalion! How could you take him to the other side of the river for the assignment and abandon him there?" The battalion commander consoled me and allowed me to stay with them for three days before returning me to the company.

After that event, I returned and fought alongside my fellow soldiers. In those days, I was quite brave, if not at times foolhardy. Once, during a reconnaissance mission of the enemy's mop-up operation in Cao Mai [Lam-Thao district seat], I saw a black enemy soldier fall asleep with his machine gun next to him. I made the offer to my squad leader to snatch the machine gun. He prevented me from doing that out of concern for my life. After two battles with the French forces, in recognition of my bravery, I was admitted as an official member of the Party. That was in 1948. Despite the occasional confrontation with French troops, I managed to take literacy classes during my four years as a soldier, finishing the equivalent of three grades and learning how to do calculations.

Around 1947, Bang's politically conscious brother Tang was transferred to the supplies department of the Vietminh's military medical services. Bang's nephew by his elder half-sister, who had grown up in a wealthy family, discussed the context in which he, too, had joined the Vietminh armed forces:

I joined the People's Army in 1949, when the Vietminh came to our class to urge us to make our contributions [to the cause of anticolonial resistance]. Teacher and students, we all went. We all felt strongly about the cause of national independence. I was sent to China for training as an officer candidate. As soldiers, we had no shoes, wore latania leaf hats, received no salaries, and walked all the way to China.

Upon inquiry regarding her participation in the local guerilla force, the old lady Thanh explained:

No, I did not participate in the guerilla forces, because I only knew how to work the soil and provide for my family. However, my younger brother, at that point still single, volunteered for the armed forces. Determined to join, he did not dare to tell me. Although he saw me when I went around searching for him, he did not even respond to my call. He returned three years later and got married at my suggestion.

In the first phase of the Franco-Vietminh war, the village of Son-Duong sent eighty of its own sons to the Vietminh regular forces. Villagers responded enthusiastically to the Vietminh's call to arms, even though their own tangible benefits were negligible, if any (cf. Popkin 1979). By 1948 the village had also organized a well-trained village guerilla platoon. Donations were solicited, partly through the association of combatants' mothers *(hoi me chien si)*, in order to provide food and purchase weapons for both local guerillas and regular force soldiers. The wife of the late mayor An donated a few *mau* of rice fields for village guerillas to cultivate to obtain their food supplies. Voluntary contributions amounted to fifteen tonnes of rice and over one million piasters in resistance bonds in the 1946–1950 phase of the resistance alone (Son-Duong 1987:38).

In the village of Son-Duong, in order to strengthen mass support in the context of guerilla warfare and the French reciprocal trade embargo, the Vietminh began the initial steps toward greater economic self-sufficiency and improving the long-term economic well-being of the peasant masses. Toward the former goal, the village administration encouraged the growth of cotton and the development of a cottage textile industry to meet the needs of the population and the growing armed forces in the Vietminh area. Cotton was consequently grown on approximately a dozen *mau* of Son-Duong land; 60 percent of village households spun thread, and 15 percent of the households engaged in weaving with over one hundred looms.

More significant were the long-term efforts to improve the welfare of the peasants and to strengthen their support in the long war of resistance. Enacting the government's July 1949 land decree, the Son-Duong village administration officially lowered the land rent by 25 percent to 37.5 percent of the crop and abolished secondary rents (gifts to landlords at New Year's and other occasions).[22] It also sold communal land to poor peasant households with less than half a *mau* of rice field and in 1949, under the guidance of the new local party branch, formed one of the seven experimental agricultural cooperatives in the province (Cao-Tien-Phung et al. 1985:247). In May 1950 the Vietminh government took further steps in the collectivist direction by decreeing an upper limit of 18 percent interest on cash loans and 20 percent on loans in kind as well as the abolition of peasants' pre-1945 loans and loans whose interest payments had doubled the principal (Hoang-Uoc 1968:67). Although the cooperative experiment failed within two years, because of internal conflict regarding the use of cooperative resources and the distribution of crop yield (Son-Duong 1987:33–34), the limited socioeconomic reforms of the 1947–1950 period generally improved the well-being of Son-Duong villagers in the lower strata and strengthened their support for the Vietminh in the prolonged conflict with the French.[23]

The Vietminh-initiated reforms resulted in strengthened support for the Vietminh among the large majority of the local population. This support provided the basis for the formation of the local Communist Party branch during the first phase of the Franco-Vietminh war. In the province of Phu-Tho the ICP expanded rapidly at the local level after the outbreak of the war, probably in an attempt to provide a stronger and potentially independent local leadership in the context of guerilla warfare and a possible disruption of communication with higher authorities. Sixteen Son-Duong villagers were recruited in the second half of 1947 into a joint seventy-member party branch dominated by members of neighboring Ngu-Xa village. In 1948 a separate Son-

Duong branch was formed when Son-Duong was reconstituted as an independent administrative unit and renamed Viet-Cuong (Strong Viet). The recruitment was aimed at all prospective contributors to the cause of national salvation regardless of their class backgrounds, as related by the teacher Le van Tiem, president of the Son-Duong party cell from 1948 to 1950:

Despite my success in the district administration, I did not continue as a vice chairman beyond the [two-year] term because of a conflict with party members in Kinh-Ke village. Because I had not become a party member, they wanted me to follow their advice on numerous issues. I was considered junior to them in terms of revolutionary knowledge and experience. I refused to continue on for a second term in the administration despite their draft. It was because of this conflict that I was not admitted into the party organization at the district level.

I returned to Son-Duong, where we were supported by our daughter from her weaving job, and I joined the village administrative council, though I declined the invitation to become chairman. I was among the first admitted into the Son-Duong party organization in August 1948—an organization that had earlier been a part of the Ngu-Xa party cell. I had not been invited to join the Party earlier because, given my prestige as the teacher in Ngu-Xa and with my network of pupils and their parents, I would have become party secretary. Ngu-Xa party members did not want to lose the position to a member from another village. Throughout the years, the people of that village were more concerned about village positions than about education. That was why only one Ngu-Xa villager obtained the *certificat d'études primaires.*

In December 1948 I became the Son-Duong party secretary. Party membership expanded rapidly in the village under my leadership. Under the guidance of higher party authorities and on the basis of the gender equality principle, we recruited a number of active female villagers, like Mrs. Canh [the first wife of Tang, Bang's half-brother], who later became the secretary of the Party's women's cell. However, the top party leaders were all male, because, if nothing else, being encumbered by children and family obligations, female members could not deal flexibly with wartime conditions and could not quickly escape from the French if necessary.

In retrospect, the expansion was not conducted with sufficient attention to the Party's criteria of membership, because we did not have a firm understanding of those [class background] criteria. We did not understand well the party authorities' suggestion of targeting poor and landless peasants for party membership. Out of poverty and the lack of both education and good public speaking skills, many members of these social strata did not at all aspire to become party members. In contrast, former notables all wished to join the Party, but we selected only the few who could make the best contributions to our cause. Like we invited the wife of [the late] Mayor An, who had contributed generously to the revolutionary cause, to join the Party. She declined, citing her old age and her prayer sessions at the pagoda.

The three members of the modern-educated intelligentsia still in the village, those with the *certificat d'études primaires* like myself, all became party members because, with our prestige, our advice to other villagers was frequently followed. Similarly, many teachers were also recruited into the Party because of their education, their speaking skills, and the prestige that they commanded as members of the teaching profession. I can recall only a few cases of teachers who were not invited to join the Party: one because of his competitive and argumentative style of interaction and two others because of their distance from other villagers.

In those days we simply recruited the most active, energetic, and hardworking villagers, including certain former notables. The only restriction was that present and former members of other parties could not be admitted without the approval of higher authorities. Whatever background people might have, once admitted into the Party, they were devoted and conscientious members. Whatever class-based ideological differences there might be, they seldom mattered because even those former notables among party members contributed significantly to party activities.

Communication with higher authorities in general was limited. Meetings were convened in the district seat on the average once every quarter for the party guidelines to be transmitted and for us to report on local conditions. The guidelines were usually quite general. As a result, we simply did our best at the local level. With some luck, the local implementation would conform to the party policy. Without luck, we might err. District party leaders were understanding, because our errors arose not out of bad will but out of enthusiasm.

It has to be said that nobody in the Party had a good understanding of class analysis in those days, myself included. I did my best at leading introductory-level discussions among party members on Marxism, dialectics, and historical materialism from what I learned in district-level party meetings. The understanding, however, was not in depth.

Under Tiem's leadership and with quarterly membership targets from higher authorities, by October 1950 party membership in Son-Duong had quickly expanded to 143, including 23 women. This expansion paralleled the increase in national party membership: from 5000 in 1945 to approximately 700,000 in 1950 (White 1983:193).

Within the framework of national salvation and in a radical departure from tradition, a fairly large number of members for the elite party organization were recruited among the more dedicated activists from landless and poor peasant backgrounds in the mass organizations and in the guerilla campaigns. However, thirteen former mayors, deputy mayors, and landlords with progressive attitudes and significant local influence were also admitted in this recruitment drive (Son-Duong 1987:30). The percentage of party members from landlord, rich, and upper middle peasant families well exceeded 46 percent. With an ongoing party recruitment drive, membership in Phu-Tho and neighboring Vinh-Phuc-Yen increased from 80 at the time of the formation of the Democratic Republic of Vietnam, to 1003 by the end of 1946, and to 33,846 by the end of 1949 (approximately 16,000 in Phu-Tho and 18,000 in Vinh-Phuc) (Cao-Tien-Phung et al. 1985:112, 138, 147, 210, 237). In general, the Communist Party and the Vietminh leadership in Son-Duong were more committed to national liberation than to the logic of class conflict within the Vietnamese social formation. Their ranks were dominated by young male activists, generally from privileged backgrounds; they carried out limited village reforms in order to strengthen the war of anticolonial resistance rather than out of a full understanding of dialectical materialism. With only limited communication from the national and provincial party leadership, the local party apparatus provided direct local policy guidance for the Son-Duong village administration and mass organizations in the context of an intensified war of national independence.

Because of a combination of national and international developments, the course of the Marxist-led national independence struggle and socioeconomic transformation took a sharp turn after the third national party congress in January 1950. In the international arena, the nature of the Franco-Vietminh conflict became submerged in the international cold war. Mao's triumph in China in October 1949 had reinforced the United States' concern regarding the spread of communism. As the Vietminh received increasing military aid from China, the United States intervened more forcefully with direct financial and logistical support for France to defeat the "communist" Vietminh movement.[24] By 1954 U.S. aid had increased to cover 78 percent of the cost of the war to the French side. Within Vietnam, under U.S. pressure the French granted the Bao Dai government (1948–1955) limited autonomy in order to compete with the Vietminh on nationalist appeals. In the areas under their control, in the context of the Vietminh's socioeconomic reforms in 1948–1950, the French were also able to secure the collaboration of many landlords.

The Vietminh's socioeconomic policy became increasingly class-oriented, as a result of both the internal dynamics of the war and the French ability to gain the collaboration of the indigenous landlord class in the occupied areas. With its expanded armed forces and the need for regular revenues in order to sustain the war effort, in 1951 the Vietminh reintroduced land taxes with a progressive tax schedule. Taxes varied from a rate of 6 to 10 percent for poor peasants to a rate of 30 to 50 percent for large landholders, with a tax surcharge of 25 percent on land rent (Hoang-Uoc 1968:70ff.). Large landholders resorted to various measures: cultivating the land directly with hired labor, reducing or even eliminating the official land rent in exchange for covert rent payments or free labor, selling less fertile land at depressed prices, and dispersing holdings through bequests to children or other relatives (ibid.:70–81). Many landholders in Son-Duong divided up their properties as a result of the Vietminh land tax structure in the 1951–1954 period. Within the Party, under the December 1951 directive of the central committee of the officially reemerging Communist Party (now called the Vietnamese Workers' Party), the local party branch launched a critical self-examination campaign in 1952–1953. It expelled fifteen members for not having a sufficiently clear understanding of class and for not fulfilling their party obligations with sufficient devotion (cf. White 1983:193). Twenty-four other party members were expelled for a variety of reasons in minor purges from December 1950 onward, resulting in a decline in party membership from 131 in the fall of 1950 to 91 in 1953.[25] In September 1952 the local Vietminh front conformed to party-imposed quotas in its slate of candidates for the village council: landless, poor, and lower-middle peasants made up two-thirds of the Vietminh-endorsed candidates; party members and women, respectively one-third and one-sixth of the endorsed and elected candidates to the council. Although these class-oriented moves undoubtedly caused some anxiety among the upper strata of the village, they further consolidated support for the Party among the peasant masses and contributed to the recruitment of soldiers for the Vietminh's offensive military strategy in the second stage of the war (1950–1954).

On the battlefield, reinforced by Chinese supplies, the Vietminh began launching more conventional attacks on French posts along the Vietnam-China border in 1950, routing the French troops in Cao-Bang and Lang-Son in September 1950. According to present Vietnamese sources, eight thousand troops in the French colonial forces, mostly African and European, were killed, wounded, or captured in this campaign together with three thousand tonnes of ammunition and military supplies (Phuc-Khanh and Dinh-Luc 1986:143). As a result of this serious defeat and the Vietminh's strong counterattack in Phu-Tho, the French withdrew from minor posts in the province in order to consolidate their positions in Ha-Nong and Viet-Tri (Cao-Tien-Phung et al. 1985:219). With its many warehouses, hospitals, ammunition plants, and a reconstructed road network, Phu-Tho had by this point become a major back-up area for the Vietminh. The French countered the Vietminh offensives with occasional large search-and-destroy operations as well as more regular air attacks and ground bombardment of Vietminh positions in the province (especially in late 1951 and in 1953). Toward the end of the war, in 1953, commando teams were sent in to destroy Vietminh economic and military installations.

In late August 1950, for example, the French launched a ten-day two-thousand-troop Chrisalide campaign into Lam-Thao, Thanh-Ba, and Ha-Hoa districts. Although encountering strong resistance and suffering 160 casualties, the French reportedly inflicted heavy damages in these areas of the province with their reported policy of killing all, burning all, and destroying all (Cao-Tien-Phung et al. 1985:217–218). In Son-Duong a French force swept through part of the village, arrested twelve villagers, and shot one. The French forces withdrew, however, after encountering a strong protest against their rape attempts, before getting to the Son-Duong guerillas' ambush positions (Son-Duong 1987:40). In October 1952 the French launched their three-division Lorraine campaign along major routes in Hac-Tri, Lam-Thao, and Doan-Hung districts, destroying economic targets through rice seizures and arresting and killing many people.[26] In this last major battle in the province, the Vietminh countered the French's Lorraine campaign with a combination of guerila and conventional warfare, reportedly inflicting two thousand casualties on the French (Cao-Tien-Phung et al. 1985:271–274). They also dispersed warehouses, industrial plants, military hospitals, and civilian populations, and constantly moved troops to avoid making them easy French bombing targets (ibid.:278–280). As direct military engagements in the province became less frequent, the Vietminh in Phu-Tho temporarily lent troops to the neighboring provincial commands in Son-Tay, Vinh-Phuc, and Yen-Bay in 1951 and to Son-Tay in 1954 (ibid.:230–231, 325–326). They also increased the mobilization of local populations for military campaigns elsewhere.

Son-Duong suffered most heavily during the French indiscriminate bombing and terror campaign of 1951 (when it was bombed once in April, twice in May, and once in December), during which seventy-eight houses were destroyed, the communal meeting house was partly damaged, and over thirty civilian villagers died (Son-Duong 1987:44). The soldier Te, formerly a landless laborer, described the situation in the aftermath of the most heavy bombing on May 23, 1951:

In 1951 the village was bombed a few times. Particularly horrible was the May 23 napalm bombing. It was spring harvest time in the village. Since my company was stationed in [nearby] Son Vi village at the time, I requested a quick visit to the village, only to see many deaths. The village had built an extensive system of trenches, which were unfortunately full of water [from the rain]. As a result, many villagers had not taken advantage of the trenches and bomb shelters during the bombing. I bought a wounded cow for my company and had to ask for a ten-day leave to take care of my family, since my house had been burnt down. During my leave, [there were so many corpses that] I had to bury relatives even at night. Being unable to locate their whole bodies, we buried only their intestines, which we found on trees in their gardens. We even found in our yard the head of a neighbor whose body could not be found. Many villagers also died from profuse bleeding from not-so-serious wounds because of the lack of medication and bandages. The scene and the smell of death were so horrible that after burying two or three villagers on the same day, I could no longer swallow food. . . . When I left the village at the end of my leave, I worried quite a bit about the members of my family, because we had not been able to rebuild our house and they had to stay in the pagoda temporarily. Later that year I was granted a release from military service. I returned home. However, because of my well-known bravery as a soldier, I was drafted by the village in 1952 to command the village guerillas for two years.

Fortunately for Son-Duong villagers, the 1951 bombing episodes were the last time the village was directly damaged by the Franco-Vietnamese war. It escaped damage during the Lorraine operation of October 1952, the biggest French operation of the eight-year military conflict.

Son-Duong managed to fulfill its fiscal and manpower obligations toward the state. It sent the provincial government 150 tons of paddy in 1951, the first year of Vietminh land taxes, to support the growing Vietminh armed forces. (The taxes amounted to an estimated 30 percent of village paddy production at the time.) One hundred of its sons joined the Vietminh armed forces and left for the front in the 1951–1953 period, increasing the number of men to 180 for the entire war. A large number of villagers served as civilian porters for Vietminh military campaigns throughout this period: 50 or 60 were porters for the fall–winter 1950–1951, June 1951, October 1952, and Upper Laos 1953 campaigns; and 200 for the Hoa-Binh campaign in November 1951 (Son-Duong 1987:45). In the winter and spring of 1954, Son-Duong provided 270 civilian porters, both male and female, for up to six months in order to transport military supplies through difficult terrain for the final, historic Dien-Bien-Phu campaign against the French. For this final campaign the populations of Phu-Tho and Vinh-Phuc were mobilized en masse and reportedly provided 73,000 civilian porters (28 percent of the porters for this campaign), 4,789 cattle, 500 tonnes of pork, and more than 5,000 tonnes of rice, peas, peanuts, and sugar, among other things (Cao-Tien-Phung et al. 1985:324). The Vietminh mobilized 49,500 combat soldiers and 55,000 support troops for this campaign to attack a 16,500-strong French garrison near the Vietnam-Laos border. Despite the massive 23,000 casualties (including 8,000 dead) on their side, the Vietminh inflicted 5,500 casualties (1,500 dead) on the French garrison and forced the surrender of the French post command on May 7, 1954 (Harrison 1982:124).

In Phu-Tho, under constant Vietminh sniping and bombardment and as a result of the Dien-Bien-Phu defeat, the French decided to withdraw from their Viet-Tri and Ha-Nong posts the following month. This withdrawal marked the end of the French colonial presence and the Franco-Vietminh war in Phu-Tho. During the costly military conflict the Vietminh in Phu-Tho claimed to have inflicted 4,800 casualties on the French and pro-French Vietnamese forces; destroyed 54 trucks, 8 tanks, 34 boats, and 2 planes; and captured a large number of guns, over 2,000 land mines, and 26 tonnes of ammunition (*Nhan*

*Dan,* Feb. 25, 1955). The population of Phu-Tho reportedly contributed 64,000 tonnes of paddy, the cash equivalent of 42,600 additional tonnes, over 700 tonnes of meat, 18.5 million labor days (to destroy communications in the early period and rebuild them later on), as well as more than 10,000 soldiers for the People's Army (ibid.). Of these contributions, the village of Son-Duong made good its share with hundreds of tonnes of paddy as taxes, 15 tonnes of paddy for military supply, 1,500 labor days for the destruction and subsequent reconstruction of roads, and 180 soldiers for the war of national independence itself (Son-Duong 1987:44–45).

On July 21, 1954, the Geneva Agreements and Final Declaration temporarily divided Vietnam into two zones at the seventeenth parallel: the north as the Democratic Republic of Vietnam under Ho Chi Minh's government and the south as the Republic of Vietnam under the former puppet emperor Bao Dai of the Hue court. The accords banned the introduction of foreign troops and called for a referendum on the unification of the country within two years. The village of Son-Duong enjoyed a decade of peace as it underwent probably the most fundamental socioeconomic transformation in its history.

≫    ≫    ≫

Throughout the Franco-Vietminh conflict the cause of national independence, which forged a unity among Son-Duong villagers in their support for the Vietminh, remained a powerful driving force in the political career of their compatriot Nguyen Dac Bang, exiled halfway around the globe in British Guyana. In pursuing this cause, over the years Bang participated in numerous activities in support of Ho Chi Minh's government, formed a close relationship with Cheddi Jagan, the leader of the powerful socialist People's Progressive Party in Guyana, and made an official visit to Cuba, a landmark of his political life.

Bang related his reactions on hearing news of an independent Vietnamese government under Ho and also spoke of his political activities in support of the Vietminh during the course of the Franco-Vietminh war:

In July 1946 I received a letter from a former fellow prisoner in Cayenne [an ICP member], informing me that a Vietnamese government delegation had just arrived in France to conduct diplomatic negotiations with the French at Fontainebleau. Having written to the delegation regarding the possibility of repatriation for Vietnamese residents in South America, he had not yet received an answer. He urged me to write.

I was most pleased to learn of this development in our homeland. At my friend's suggestion, I sent a letter to Paris:

> To the Government Delegation of the Democratic Republic of Vietnam:
>
> We, the Vietnamese in exile in South America, would like to extend our warmest fraternal greetings to the delegation of the government of Vietnam. We wish the delegation a brilliant success at the Fontainebleau conference in order to achieve the independence and unification of our fatherland and to restore happiness to our race. We are extremely happy and proud to be citizens of independent Vietnam and to see the dishonor of being enslaved come to an end. We pledge to unite ourselves firmly and to do our best to support the government of the Democratic Republic of Vietnam in the heroic struggle to liberate our homeland. We also wish to express our desire to return to our homeland as soon as possible and to participate directly in the struggle of our people.
>
> For the independence, freedom, and unification of Vietnam
> Fraternally yours,
> On behalf of all Vietnamese in S. America,
> Nguyen Dac Bang
> President of the Union of Vietnamese in South America

Within three weeks, right on the first anniversary of independence on September 2, I received a telegram from Paris, urging us to strengthen our solidarity while waiting for repatriation. I was most delighted to receive this first official telegram from the Vietnamese delegation but kept wondering about the signature, Ho Chi Minh. "Who is Ho Chi Minh?" I asked myself. I hastily brought the telegam to every Vietnamese in Georgetown, trying to figure out who Ho Chi Minh was. In the months that followed, through letters from the representative of the Vietnamese government in Paris and the newspaper *Lao Dong* (The Worker) of the Vietnamese in France, I learned that Ho Chi Minh was actually Nguyen Ai Quoc. I was thrilled with the news because in 1932, from the misleading information in *Le péril rouge en Indochine,* my comrades and I had grieved at Nguyen Ai Quoc's death and had mistakenly held a one-day fast in his memory.

From that point onward the thriving restaurateur Bang maintained regular contact with Vietminh supporters in France and England. He raised funds among his fellow Vietnamese and sent the contributions through the *Cuu Quoc* newspaper in London and the Vietminh-supporting Union of Vietnamese in Paris. Bang also organized an annual independence day celebration for Vietnamese and their friends in Georgetown, displaying the DRV flag. Most significant was the 1961 celebration that Guyanese Prime Minister Cheddi Jagan and many cabinet members attended, partly out of ideological support for Ho Chi Minh's national independence struggle and partly because of Bang's good relations with Jagan. This rapport grew out of an anticolonial solidarity. Jagan was of Indian descent, and in 1947 Bang had sent a greeting to the Indian community on the occasion of Indian independence. Although Bang was not able to join the People's Progressive Party because of his alien resident status, Bang's wife had been a member from the time of the party's formation.

In 1962 the Vietnamese Foreign Ministry invited Bang to Cuba to strengthen relations with Vietnamese nationalists in Guyana. Bang reported on this landmark event of his political career:

[On the day of my arrival in Havana in August 1962] I received the Vietnamese ambassador in an informal meeting lasting for hours in my hotel room. I found out that he had also been a political prisoner in Poulo Condore and, surprisingly, a fellow inmate of my brother Gia. I briefed him on the support of the Vietnamese in the Guyanas for the government of the Democratic Republic of Vietnam and for the National Liberation Front [NLF] of South Vietnam: "Although thousands of miles away, the Vietnamese in South America have their hearts in the homeland. They have keenly followed the situation in our country. Since 1945 they have wholeheartedly supported our government in Hanoi and the NLF. They all admire President Ho Chi Minh, who has sacrificed everything for the liberation of Vietnam. . . . Always steadfast in their love for the fatherland, they have put the interests of the Vietnamese people above their individual interests. They remain united as ever and determined to support the Party and the government in the struggle for the liberation of our country."

In the days that followed I accompanied the ambassador during the visit of [Guyanese] Minister Hubbard to the Vietnamese embassy and on the ambassador's courtesy call on the minister. I also accepted the minister's invitation to a meeting with Guyanese students in Cuba. On the fifth day I arrived at the Havana hotel to attend the Vietnamese national independence day reception in the grand reception room on the twenty-second floor. It was splendidly decorated with flags, banners, and pictures of the leaders of Vietnam. While

waiting for guests, the ambassador and I stood on the balcony and looked out
at the lights of Havana. "While in Con-Son [Poulo Condore] prison in
1931," he told me, "it was impossible to dream of being here tonight on this
balcony looking out at a city in the Americas." "Yes," I replied, "we are here
tonight thanks to the heroic struggle and the deep patriotism of our people."
It was a memorable evening attended by high-ranking Cuban officials, Minister Hubbard of Guyana, and numerous diplomats. I was introduced to many
Cuban officials and to the ambassadors of China, the Soviet Union, and
France.

Bang's trip to Cuba was not only a landmark in his political career, but
also represented the triumph of Ho's government in winning the hearts
and minds of Vietnamese nationalists during the Franco-Vietminh war
and the period of American intervention in Vietnam.

When the American war reached its peak in the 1965–1968 period,
as Son-Duong villagers strengthened their resolve against the second
major foreign force in twenty years, so did an exiled native son in British Guyana. Bang worked closely with Dr. Cheddi Jagan, the former
prime minister, and played an active role in the Guyana-Vietnam Solidarity Committee to sponsor events in support of the DRV and against
the American war efforts. In 1967, at the height of the war, he organized local Vietnamese, recruited his own children, and participated
with Jagan and other progressive Guyanese in demonstrations in front
of the U.S. diplomatic mission in Georgetown. He also helped organize a weeklong exhibition on Vietnam when a delegation of the Provisional Revolutionary Government of South Vietnam attended a non-
aligned foreign ministers' conference in Georgetown in 1972. Some of
these activities were reported in *Nhan Dan,* the official organ of the
Vietnamese Communist Party, as well as in local Guyanese newspapers. These activities constituted only a small part of the growing outcry in the United States and the world at large against the American
war in Vietnam—an outcry that contributed to the American withdrawal in 1973 and the end of the war in 1975. Bang related his last
major political celebration of an independent and soon-to-be-unified
Vietnam, a goal he had valiantly fought for four and a half decades earlier:

When peace did finally arrive in Vietnam on April 30, 1975, I was overcome
with joy and relief. Together with a few other Vietnamese still alive in
Georgetown, we raised our national flags and displayed banners, "Salute to
the Final Victory of the Heroic People of Vietnam." We organized a recep-

tion at my hotel restaurant, Fraternity, for all my Guyanese friends in order to express our thanks to them for their years of continued support for the struggle of our people.

With a few friends of mine, including Professor Clive Thomas from London, England, Professor Walter Rodney of the University of West Indies, Dr. Ramsay of the University of Georgetown, and Editor Clinton Claymore of the *Mirror* newspaper, I went on a speaking tour. We held several gatherings in the Penitence market square and many other places [in Georgetown] to speak to the people of Guyana about the liberation of Vietnam. The Guyana-Vietnam Solidarity Committee and other progressive organizations also held similar speaking sessions to salute this historic victory, a victory not only for the Vietnamese people after a century of heroic struggle, but also for all the progressive forces in the world.

≪    ≪    ≪

The Marxist-led Vietminh movement enjoyed overwhelmingly strong support from Son-Duong villagers as well as the broader Vietnamese population during the course of its conflict with the French from 1945 onward. Villagers readily lent support to Ho Chi Minh's government despite the high cost of their action, the few foreseeable tangible benefits in the early years of the Franco-Vietminh conflict, and the small odds of success. Vietminh supporters faced potentially severe losses because of superior French military technology, and the material benefits to poor villagers were restricted to the elimination of taxes and a small share of the village's limited amount of communal land. Their choice, then, is not reducible to a narrow and universal matrix of material costs and benefits. Even the utilitarian theorist Popkin remarks that "the Vietminh mobilization is a clear case of the importance of contributions, some of which were not stimulated by any expectation of future selective payoff. It emphasizes how important internalized feelings of duty or ethic can be" (Popkin, 1979:223).

At the critical juncture of modern Vietnamese history from 1940 to 1954, national independence constituted, for the overwhelming majority of both Son-Duong villagers and the larger Vietnamese population, an objective of utmost importance. In the first decade of this period the objective was pursued at an incredibly high cost and with practically negligible concrete benefits as well as against serious odds. Within the framework of national independence, the revolutionary leadership sought to enact democratic ideals such as universal suffrage as well as to move slowly toward the socialist and collectivist vision of political economy with rent controls, progressive land tax schedules, and the experimental formation of an agricultural cooperative in Son-Duong. It can be argued that along with the Vietminh's nationalist appeals and their legitimacy as the first national independence government, their close attention to the concrete subsistence needs of the population and the political economy of reform made a major difference in the strength of their support. It constituted a fundamental difference between the abortive VNP uprising in 1930 and the successful Vietminh movement in 1940–1954. The dynamics of the Vietnamese revolution cannot be understood exclusively in terms of nationalism, although national independence did constitute the primary objective for the majority of Vietnamese in the 1946–1954 period. Nor can they be seen as a concomitant search for democracy among the Western-educated elite (cf. Emerson 1960: chap. 13). Neither can they be analyzed primarily as a reaction by the peasantry to the violation of a subsistence ethic by the colonial regime (cf. Scott 1976). Such a massive violation of the subsistence ethic existed in 1944–1945 in northern Vietnam and did not necessarily lead to agrarian unrest. Despite massive starvation, unrest rarely broke out in localities without the organizational efforts of the Vietminh (see also Ngo-Vinh-Long 1978b).

Certain Western Marxist analyses to the contrary notwithstanding, the objective of national independence was no less important to the native intelligentsia than to the worker and peasant masses (cf. Murray 1980:36–37; Ngo-Vinh-Long 1978b). In fact, as seen both in the village of Son-Duong and beyond, the leadership that played a critical role in mobilizing and coordinating the revolutionary potential of the population came largely from the Western-educated intelligentsia (see Woodside 1976:303; Emerson 1960). As emphasized in chapter 2, in order to understand the roots of the modern Vietnamese revolution, it is necessary to examine both the inequality and contradictions within the capitalist imperialist system and the local tradition itself. The importance of the latter will be highlighted in the conclusion of this book through a systematic discussion of the spatio-temporal variations in local tradition and revolutionary strength within Vietnam in the past century. The importance of the local tradition is also reflected in the persistence of its structural tension into the present period, which constitutes the focus of the following chapter.

# CHAPTER 5

•

# The Revolution
# in the Village, 1954–1988

On June 30, 1987, the village of Son-Duong organized a formal ceremony to receive the third-class labor medal from the national government. The village was commended for a wide variety of achievements,
ranging from agricultural production and a rapid decline in birth rate
to measures of economy in life-cycle rituals. Invited to the ceremony
were not only incumbent high-ranking cadres from surrounding villages, the district, and the province, but also retired high-ranking cadres from Son-Duong and the oldest villager from each of the four hamlets to represent the rest of the population. In a departure from local
tradition in the colonial era, the four elderly villagers were chosen
solely on the basis of age, regardless of gender and class backgrounds.
The squealing of hogs was heard from early in the morning, when they
were brought from all over the village to the residentially based agricultural production teams for butchering and distribution to village
households. Each villager, child or adult, would receive three hundred
grams of pork as part of the celebration.

The celebration marked the culmination of a long process of revolutionary transformation. Significant progress had been achieved despite
the painful memories of a small number of villagers, occasional policy
reversals, and the hardships of the American war.

Agricultural productivity had increased dramatically from 430 kilograms of paddy per *mau* per crop (1.2 tonnes per hectare) in 1954 to an
average of 1.4 tonnes per *mau* (3.9 tonnes per hectare) for most of the

1985–1988 period.[1] Experiments with a new variety of rice in the village promised to increase the yield to 2 tonnes per *mau* (5.55 tonnes per hectare per crop). Equally significant in terms of agricultural production was the considerably more intense use of land, thanks to the completion of the Lam-Thao–Hac-Tri water control project and the construction of feeder canals starting in 1957. Before the canals were constructed, village fields had yielded only one staple crop annually. By 1988 most of the land yielded three crops. The crop rotation index, which indicates the average number of staple crops on agricultural land, had accordingly increased to 2.6. Since 1985 the village had added the important cash crop of peanuts to the annual cycle of planting and harvest. Grown mainly for foreign markets, the peanut crop provided villagers with sizable cash incomes. The peanut acreage correspondingly grew from 50 *mau* in 1985 to 151 *mau* in 1988.

Depending on altitude, four main crop rotation patterns exist on the 744 *mau* of village fields managed by the agricultural cooperative (see figure 2). In fields at the highest altitude, two rice crops are grown between the first and the eighth lunar months, followed by a corn crop for the remainder of the year (crop rotation pattern 1). In other high fields (199 *mau*), rice is cultivated from the beginning of the fifth month to the end of the eighth month of the lunar calendar *(lua mua),* corn and vegetables from the beginning of the ninth month to the end of the year, and peanuts from the beginning of the first month to the beginning of the fifth month (crop rotation pattern 2). To the extent that crop cycles may overlap, as in the case of the corn and rice crops in the fall of each year, the seeds of the second crop are sowed for germination on a layer of soil in the yard until the completion of the harvest of the other crop. In low-lying fields, rice is cultivated twice a year: from the beginning of the eleventh month to the middle of the fourth month for the winter–spring crop *(lua chiem)* and from the beginning of the fourth month to the middle of the ninth month for the summer–fall crop *(lua mua)* plus whatever villagers can grow within a month and a half on the land (crop rotation pattern 3). The first and third crop patterns are used on 311 *mau* of village fields. In the lowest fields (190 *mau*), rice is grown only once a year in the spring and summer (from the first to the sixth lunar month). For the rest of the year the flooded fields supply villagers with fish as another food source (44 *mau* are reserved for the cultivation of rice seedlings). Corresponding to the intensification of land use, the average amount of chemical and organic fertilizers invested in each *mau* has increased to 3.5 tonnes a year (9.7 tonnes per hectare), including 200–250 kilograms of chemical fertilizers purchased from state enterprises and 3.25 tonnes of organic fertilizers from water lentils, and human and animal waste.

The intensification of land use came hardly a moment too soon. The acreage under cultivation had declined by 19 percent between 1954 and 1988 (from 1009 to 820 *mau*) because of the conversion of agricultural fields into residential land, water control canals, cooperative stock-houses, collective livestock farms, and paddy-drying courtyards. (Of the 820 *mau* of cultivated land in 1988, 744 were collectively owned, and 76 constituted the so-called five-percent land allotted to individual households as garden plots.) Throughout the same period, Son-Duong's population had increased from 2144 to over 4000 people, 3828 of whom resided in the village. The rest were mostly male villagers who had temporarily left for armed and other government services. In the face of growing demographic problems, in 1961–1962, 1973, and 1976, the village had sent members to clear new land in the mountain valleys of Thanh-Son district on the other side of the Red River as well as to the Yen-Bay region of neighboring Hoang-Lien-Son province. All these attempts had failed within a year because of material hardships and family separations.

In the search for a more balanced food-population ratio, the village of Son-Duong was more successful in increasing crop yield and slowing village population growth. The village birth rate dropped from 3 percent in 1980 to 2.3 percent in 1986 and the first half of 1987. The

LUNAR CALENDAR MONTH

| | 1 | 2 | 3 | 4 | 5 | 6 | 7 | 8 | 9 | 10 | 11 | 12 |
|---|---|---|---|---|---|---|---|---|---|---|---|---|

Crop rotation pattern 1   | ← rice*(chiêm)* → || ← rice*(mùa)* → || ← corn → |

Crop rotation pattern 2   | ← peanuts → || ← rice*(mùa)* → || ← corn → |
(Alternative pattern 2)                                                         [vegetables]

Crop rotation pattern 3   *(chiêm)* → || ← rice*(mùa)* → |          | ←rice

Crop rotation pattern 4   | ← rice → || ← fish → |

FIGURE 2. Main crop rotation patterns in Son-Duong

annual population growth stood at a relatively modest 1.5 percent for this eighteen-month period. The secretary of the Son-Duong Communist Party branch discussed the mobilization of village women in the campaign for birth control:

Before 1983 Son-Duong couples had an average of five or six children each. A couple usually had their first child within a year of marriage. The large number of children resulted partly from villagers' desire to have sons to continue their patrilines. Newlywed couples rarely waited before conceiving, because most of the grooms were soldiers on short vacations for their weddings. In 1983, under orders from above, we encouraged population planning: ideally, a couple would wait five years before their first child, and births would be spaced at five-year intervals. On the one hand, we worked with the village clinic staff in setting the numerical target for intrauterine device placements and with the pediatrician at the district hospital regarding more technical matters. On the other, we asked the labor teams to examine the family situations of team members and to visit the families in need of better population planning in order to persuade the appropriate child-bearing-age wives to go to the clinic for IUDs. For our part, we have decided to grant a one-month leave and a waiver of corvée labor to any woman who has an abortion and has an IUD inserted. She is also given twenty-five kilograms of paddy, the amount a delivering mother would receive from the cooperative. Any woman who gave birth to a fourth child would neither receive the food assistance nor be granted the waiver of corvée labor after delivery. The only exception is when the devices are defective, like on one occasion when the Saigon IUDs in use here had a 70 percent defective rate.

Villagers now understand the need to restrict the number of children to two or three for their own benefit and for society at large. When the plan is not followed, it is most often because a couple has had no son by the third or fourth birth. It is also difficult to enforce the rule of a five-year waiting period. Young couples want to have children within one to two years of marriage, especially because their parents exert pressure on them. It is the rural folk mentality. And once they have the first child, a couple wants other children all in a row. Despite these problems, the birth rate has declined from 3 percent in 1980 to 1.7 percent in 1986.[2]

Public facilities in Son-Duong had considerably expanded even before 1983, when the crop yield began to rise sharply. Village roads, although still unpaved, had been widened and were properly drained during the rainy season. In 1987 cars and trucks could pass through the main village road on a shortcut route to the industrial town of Viet-

Tri, although it still took a lot of concentration on the part of skilled drivers to avoid the large potholes in certain parts of the road. Older villagers frequently remarked to visitors on how the roads had improved from the pre-1945 period, when during a heavy rain they had had to hold on to the branches from the bamboo hedges along the roads and to wade in muddy water up to their knees to get from one point to another. In 1987 the village clinic, which was first set up during the war of resistance against the French, was staffed by two physician's assistants, a pharmacist's assistant, a nurse, and an administrator. It also included an Oriental medicine room. The staff readily made house calls on request. The village school had begun offering junior high school classes as early as 1958–1959, being the third in the district to do so. By 1987, with 42 teachers, it offered up to grade twelve and had enrolled 1001 male and female students.[3] The three nursery schools in the village also enrolled 120 pupils. The equal access to education for boys and girls stood in sharp contrast to the almost all-male enrollment of 35 students in the three-grade village school on the eve of the August 1945 uprising.

Beyond public facilities, most Son-Duong villagers emphasized the significant physical improvements in their living quarters as part of the revolution in the village. As easily observed from the village roads in 1987–1988, almost all the houses in the 675 housing compounds were constructed of brick and tile. The Son-Duong party branch gave a figure of 98 percent for the proportion of brick houses in 1987. As the village credit cooperative offered mainly short-term loans and loans for collective projects, these new houses were constructed with bricks produced in villagers' backyards and paid for by villagers' considerable savings and informal loans through credit associations, as discussed by Bang's cousin Te:

In 1977 we completed the construction of a new brick house. We began planning for it as early as 1975, when I organized a ten-member rotating credit association to provide a financial cushion for members' unexpected funeral and wedding expenses. My fellow members suggested that I take the credit first. It cost me only cigarettes and tea, not a dog for a meal for them as I had thought. I received half a tonne of paddy and used it the following year to buy timber. My wife and I carried sand from the river bank on baskets hanging from a shoulder pole because we did not possess an oxcart then. We also molded and kiln-dried most of the bricks ourselves. When somebody unexpectedly offered to purchase our removable house for the asking price of 1100 piasters, we decided to go ahead with the construction of the new house.

*How many members does your household have?*

We have nine members altogether: my wife and myself; our eldest son, his wife, and their three children; and our second son and his wife. Our daughters moved out upon marriage. Our eldest son and his family stay in the same house with us, and our other son and his wife stay in the thatch house just over there on the same piece of land.

Most village houses in 1987–1988 were equipped with their own wells, and many had brick outhouses and outdoor bathing rooms. In 1985, according to the village administration, the percentages of houses with wells, brick outhouses, and outdoor bathing rooms had reached 94 percent, 71 percent, and 49 percent, respectively. For transportation, village households possessed on average two bicycles each (in comparison to one for the entire village before 1945). Most also owned oxcarts for the transportation of grain and construction materials, instead of relying on the traditional method of carrying them in two baskets hanging on a pole. The physical improvements within villagers' household compounds were significant in comparison to the conditions on the eve of the August 1945 uprising, when there existed only five brick houses, six private wells, and no outhouses and bathing rooms in the entire village. In a message to what he perceived to be a hostile Western world, a former president of the Son-Duong agricultural cooperative emphasized to me that since 1954 the new brick houses in the village had required an estimated investment of 26 million bricks, 402,500 tiles, 1820 tonnes of timber, 6600 tonnes of coal, 3432 tonnes of firewood, and 338 tonnes of lime.

Beyond the physical improvements and the considerably better access to public services, the village party leaders emphasized to visitors the radical reforms to life-cycle ceremonies that they had instituted in 1986. The village prohibited the serving of cigarettes at wedding and funeral receptions, restricted the servings at funerals to tea and areca palm nuts, limited the number of wedding banquet trays to ten (sixty guests), and placed a ban on villagers' butchering of their own hogs for weddings.[4] In order to reduce the costs of these life-cycle events and to simplify the complex sequence of rituals, the village administration specified that (1) wedding rituals were to be held in the village office; (2)

Photo 1. Main village road

Photo 2. Sheltered part of the village market

Photo 3. Open village market

Photo 4. Old-style village house

Photo 5. Modern village house

Photo 6. Interior decorated in traditional style

PHOTO 7. Interior decorated in revolutionary style

PHOTO 8. Woman working at one of the few remaining mosquito-net looms in the village

PHOTO 9. Herbal pharmacist measuring ingredients

Photo 10. Washing dishes by the household well

Photo 11. Abandoned collective livestock farm marks the shift from collective agriculture to decentralized household production

engagement ceremonies should require no more than five packs of cigarettes, half a kilogram of tea, and a few dozen areca palm nuts, instead
of virtually unlimited demands by the bride's family for items to be distributed among its relatives and acquaintances; and (3) in the case of
death, the corpse would be buried within half a day. In return, the village cooperative provided free of charge a coffin, ten packages of
incense, and burial services for any deceased member. The village per-
forming arts group provided free entertainment at the brief wedding
ceremony at the village office. The rationale for the reforms, according
to the local party secretary, was to avoid the extraordinarily high costs
of traditional ceremonies, which included status-oriented banquets and
the distribution of elaborate engagement gifts.

A well-off family probably managed a traditional ceremony all right. However, many others went heavily into debt on wedding and funeral occasions.
If we take a small family with two children, in the old days, six major costly
banquets would have to be given: the wedding banquets for the two children,
the funeral banquets for the parents, and two reburial banquets three years
after each funeral. The costs were quite burdensome, especially if we take into
account most parents' efforts to build houses for their junior sons. [Both in
the past and the present, parents' house is bequeathed to the first son.]

In the summer of 1987 the administration's ceremony regulations
were generally observed in Son-Duong. Occasional attempts to circum-
vent the rules involved conformity to them in letter but not in spirit:
restricting the number of wedding banquet guests at any moment to
sixty by having only ten food trays but giving two or three consecutive
banquets; or not directly butchering one's own hogs but selling a hog
to the village marketing cooperative for butchering on condition that
most of the meat be sold back. Religious services were also simplified
to two monthly prayer sessions held by approximately two hundred
devoted elderly women at a dilapidated local Buddhist pagoda. The
only village nun had passed away many years before, and most village
Catholics had abandoned their religion as early as the late 1930s, well
before the rise of Marxist power in Son-Duong. Worship of the village
guardian deities had long been abandoned, ever since the French bombing of the communal house in 1951 and the subsequent destruction of
the remainder of the building, authorized by the village leadership. The
neighborhood groups (giap) had also ceased to exist in their capacity as

ritual-centered units. Although the twenty production teams of the agricultural cooperative were formed on the basis of residential proximity like the *giap,* they functioned as production units and not as ritual-centered ones. Of all the village organizations dating from the colonial period, only the credit associations, the patrilineages, and the elderly Buddhist group survived into the late 1980s. Most important among the new village institutions were the agricultural, sales and purchasing, and credit cooperatives, reflecting the rise of the collectivistic ideology.

The aforementioned changes in the village are all the more remarkable as many young male villagers had been absent for at least three years in connection with the intensified U.S. war in Vietnam (1964–1975) and then the Sino-Vietnamese and Cambodian armed conflicts of the past decade (1978–1989). Three hundred sixty young men joined the armed forces in the 1965–1975 period, and another 350 joined between 1976 and 1984. After the period of intense destructive warfare between 1965 and 1972, when over one million tons of bombs were dropped by the U.S. airforce on North Vietnam alone, and the triumph of the Marxist-led movement in the south in 1975, bringing the independence and national unity that had been out of reach for two decades, Vietnam invaded Cambodia in December 1978 to put an end to the reported armed intrusions by the China-allied Khmer Rouge forces. Then, in February 1979, partly in retaliation for the Vietnamese armed initiative in Cambodia, China invaded Vietnam with over one hundred thousand troops. Although Vietnam quickly routed the Khmer Rouge from most of Cambodia, and China withdrew after one month of intense fighting along the Sino-Vietnamese border, the continuation of armed conflicts with the Khmer Rouge and China required the imposition of a draft and constant Vietnamese vigilance, which remained in effect in 1988.[5] Accordingly, young male villagers were required to spend three years in the armed forces. Although many veterans returned to the village to fill the top positions in the Party, the village administration, and the cooperatives, many others had not come back because new opportunities for veterans were available elsewhere and because of casualties of the war. As a result, the active local labor force—predominantly an agricultural labor force—was lopsided with women, as seen in table 4. The imbalance in the sex ratio in 1987 was also quite significant for the village population as a whole, albeit not as great as for the agricultural work force (see table 5).

## Table 4. Demography of the active agricultural labor force in Son-Duong, 1987

| AGE RANGE | MALES | FEMALES | TOTAL |
|---|---|---|---|
| 16–17 | 25 | 47 | 72 |
| 18–27 | 126 | 234 | 360 |
| 28–40 | 150 | 318 | 468 |
| 41–45 | 50 | 130 | 180 |
| 45–retirement* | 130 | 302 | 432 |
| Total | 481 | 1031 | 1512 |
|  | (32%) | (68%) | (100%) |

*The retirement age was 55 for women and 60 for men.

## Table 5. Sex ratios in four hamlets of Son-Duong village, 1987

| HAMLET | MALES | FEMALES | TOTAL |
|---|---|---|---|
| Chung-Chinh | 582 | 627 | 1209 |
| Dai-Dinh | 350 | 480 | 830 |
| Dai-Tu | 396 | 474 | 870 |
| Dung-Hien | 403 | 498 | 901 |
| Total | 1731 | 2079 | 3810 |
|  | (45.5%) | (54.5%) | (100%) |

Underlying the aforementioned concrete changes in Son-Duong is a fundamental transformation in the village political economy. The transformation involved a destruction of the dominant classes of the colonial social formation and the emergence of the Communist Party, the "representative of the proletariat," as the dominant force in communal affairs. The means of agricultural production were mostly collectivized, except for draft animals and the household garden plots. The class-structured rigid distinction between mental and manual labor was no longer maintained, because many university-educated cadres, mostly retirees, were also engaged in animal husbandry, among other things, in order to improve their households' living conditions. Some female villagers played active roles in the public arena. At the height of the egalitarian and collectivistic ideology in 1954–1958, a female villager had occupied the powerful party secretary position. In 1985 the local party membership stood at 186, including 37 women (20 percent). It was overall an aging membership. The average age of party members had risen to 53 in 1985, since only 15 new members had been admitted in the 1975–1985 period. There were 80 retirees among party members in 1985 and 87 out of a total of 196 in 1987. The party membership elected a 17-member leadership committee *(dang uy)*, of which two members (11.8 percent) in the summer of 1988 were women, cadres in charge of women's affairs and birth control. However, real power at the local level lay with the all-male five-member executive committee of the party branch *(thuong vu dang uy)*. The committee included a secretary, an assistant secretary (the president of the village administration), and three other members (the vice-president of the administration in charge of village security, the president of the agricultural cooperative, and an assistant to the local party secretary). The local Communist Party branch provided policy guidelines for the village administration and the agricultural, credit, and sales and purchasing cooperatives. Comprising only village residents, the party executive committee had a considerably greater input into the daily affairs of the village than a board of directors does into the administration of a North American corporation. It was no coincidence that the most important public space in the village was the meeting hall of the local Communist Party organization.

In Son-Duong, the rise of collectivism and the greater participation of women in the public domain notwithstanding, the male-centered hierarchy of the colonial and precolonial eras persisted both within the communal framework and in the kinship system. The narrative on birth control quoted in this chapter, in discussing the villagers' preference for sons, points toward the persistence of this male-centered model in kinship and gender relations in the village. The model of hierarchical relations also structured both the internal organization of the local Communist Party and the dominant relation of the Party to the rest of the community. As a reflection of the dominance of the Communist Party and the persistence of the hierarchical model, the linguistic form *dong chi* (comrade), originally restricted to party circles, has become a term of address selectively used to convey respect and formality among the larger population both within the village of Son-Duong and beyond.

≫  ≫  ≫

The process of transformation that has taken place in the village of
Son-Duong since 1954 has not been free of tension. It has involved a
dialectical relation between the principle of radical collectivism espoused by the Marxist state for most of this period and, despite the
elimination of the colonial class structure, a hierarchical sociocultural
model centering on the kinship unit. The official collectivist ideology
of the state has emerged dominant in the northern social formation. It
underlies the radical transformation of the village political economy
that has occurred through the land reform program and the subsequent
collectivization of the means of production. However, the pace of
change has not been uniform, and the path of transformation has not
been unidirectional.

In June 1954, as the French were to withdraw from their last two
military posts in the province of Phu-Tho in the aftermath of the Dien-
Bien-Phu defeat, a land reform team arrived in Son-Duong to accelerate
the momentum of the Vietminh's egalitarian socioeconomic policy. It
included no village member so as to minimize the impact of the extensive village network on the reform process. The team arrived with a
specific directive from higher authorities: "reliance on landless and
poor peasants, solidarity with middle peasants, alliance with rich peasants, and gradual and discriminate destruction of feudal exploitation,
all to enhance production and strengthen the armed resistance"
(Hoang-Uoc 1968:141).[6] In a radical departure from tradition, instead
of staying in well-off households like other important visitors, the team
based itself through *ba cung* (eat, live, and work together) with landless
and poor peasants. It sought to raise the consciousness of the poor villagers and to conduct a classification of village households into the five
aforementioned categories (see also White 1983). Among the poor villagers approached was Bang's cousin Te:

In 1954 the rent reduction team arrived in Son-Duong. They initially
inquired of me who the landlords were in the village. I replied: "I do not
know how to determine whether somebody is a landlord or not." The team
then asked for my assistance in gathering information in the village of Vinh-
Lai [on the rent conditions there for its future work] at a time when the
enemy was stationed exactly on the other side of the river. I did not succeed in
requesting the transfer of the assignment to somebody else, because nobody
dared to accept this dangerous assignment.

The classification of households involved two main criteria: the size of landholding and the degree of exploitation through usury, hired labor, or land rental:

1. Households were classified as landlords if they owned sizable amounts of land and exploited others through usury and nonhousehold labor in the cultivation process (i.e., through sharecropping and hiring labor). Labor was considered to come primarily from external sources if more than two-thirds of the manual labor on family land came from "outsiders." The category of outsiders included not only workers beyond the household concerned, but also secondary wives, adopted children, and sons-in-law who had been treated as landless laborers (Hoang-Uoc 1968:146ff.). Depending on their support for the Vietminh during the Franco-Vietminh war and their treatment of laborers, sharecroppers, and debtors, landlord households were further differentiated into brutal landlords, neutral landlords, and resistance-supporting landlords.[7]

2. Rich peasant households relied primarily on household labor in the cultivation of their fairly sizable landholdings but still regularly exploited other people through usury, hired labor, and land rental.

3. Middle peasant households had sufficient control over the means of production for their livelihood and relied primarily on their own labor. They engaged only occasionally in hiring labor or renting land to or from others.

4. Poor peasant households did not have sufficient means of production. They were exploited through usury, land rental, and employment by members of other classes.

5. Landless peasant households had no land. They were heavily exploited by other classes, primarily through usury and employment.

The arrival of the land reform team harbingered turbulent times ahead for the large landholding families of Son-Duong. The team sought to destroy the exploiting classes through the redistribution of their holdings to poorer peasants and to purge the local party branch of members with "exploiting" class backgrounds. In the context of the Franco-Vietminh war, these steps aimed at further consolidating the support for the Marxist-led Vietminh government among the peasant masses and at weakening the landlord stratum—in the Party's analysis, the indigenous class most sympathetic to colonial control (Hoang-Uoc 1968:86–95). The policy sought to destroy the class differentiation process in order to strengthen national unity and collectivism in the long term, although its method of overt class struggle was not rooted in the local tradition.

The first measure of the land reform campaign in Son-Duong required landlords to reimburse their sharecroppers for the difference between the actual rents and the government-specified rent (at 37.5 percent or a 25 percent reduction from the pre-1945 period). Their loans to other villagers were canceled if these dated back to the pre-1945 period, if interest payments had doubled the principal by April 1953, or if they had been made to villagers who had sacrificed their lives during the Franco-Vietminh war. Since the government's rent reduction policy was not applied in Son-Duong until 1949, landlords had to reimburse their tenants and sharecroppers for rent differentials primarily in the 1945–1949 period. A total of two tonnes of rice and over one million piasters were redistributed to 1600 villagers in the first phase of the campaign.

In the subsequent land reform period, in the public denunciation sessions organized by the local peasant association, four households were classified as brutal landlords, twenty-two as landlords, and ten as rich peasants. This classification was based on landholdings and labor conditions in 1949 in order to discount landowners' "illegitimate" dispersal of their properties and change in land exploitation method in response to the government's rent reduction and progressive-land-tax policies. Dispersals were considered legitimate if they involved bequests to children or main heirs, sales to meet family needs during disaster, or transfers to commercial and industrial ventures (Hoang-Uoc 1968:169). Little evidence was available on any major and systematic efforts in the village of Son-Duong by the landlord and rich peasant households to undermine the land reform classification through kinship or patron-client ties with poorer villagers (cf. White 1981: ch. 7).

The thirty-six households in the landlord and rich peasant categories comprised 7.82 percent of the village households. The percentage of landlord households in Son-Duong (5.65 percent) exceeded the 4 to 5 percent guideline suggested by higher authorities to land reform teams (Hoang-Uoc 1968:157). At the other end of the spectrum, 70 percent of Son-Duong households were classified as poor or landless. These figures indicate a greater polarization in Son-Duong in wealth differentiation and land reform classification than in the province of Phu-Tho as a whole (table 6).

The brutal landlords in Son-Duong were imprisoned after trials in the people's court. All their property was confiscated. The son of one

## Table 6. Household classification during land reform (percent)

| | LANDLORD | RICH PEASANT | MIDDLE PEASANT | POOR PEASANT | LANDLESS LABORER | NONAGRI-CULTURAL |
|---|---|---|---|---|---|---|
| Phu-Tho | 4.06 | 2.66 | 30.40 | 37.05 | 17.11 | 7.36 |
| | 6.72 | | 30.40 | 54.16 | | |
| Son-Duong | 5.65 | 2.17 | 21.97 | | | |
| | 7.82 | | 21.97 | 70.00 | | |

Source: M. Lambourg, L'économie actuelle du Vietnam Démocratique, reprinted in White 1981:423.

colonial-era mayor who was classified as a brutal landlord fled to the south at this point, his longstanding Communist Party membership notwithstanding. The son of another "brutal landlord" related his traumatic experiences during land reform:

My father did not own enough land to rent to anybody. We had only three *mau*. However, he was classified as a brutal landlord because of his land management for one of the wealthiest villagers and his occasional beatings of other villagers during his term as a village administrator. I was a Vietminh cadre at the time of this land reform campaign. I was ordered to return to the village, although fortunately my wife and I had been considered a separate household and classified as a poor peasant family. The land reform cadres told me to advise my father to reimburse the excess rent that he had collected. I went to see my jailed father in the communal house. I did not have the courage to address him with the pronouns *may* (thou) and *tao* (I/me) [which implied the total denial of kinship relation], as the land reform cadres thought I should have done. Looking away from my father, I said quietly: "Sell whatever possible for the rent reimbursement." [The deletion of the subject implied great disrespect.] I was crying hard inside at the time. On the trial day, under pressure from the land reform cadres, my close relatives and even my wife denounced my father and addressed him with the pronouns *may* and *tao*. He was subsequently imprisoned. In this entire episode, the physical loss meant relatively little in comparison to the emotional trauma and the damage to the social fabric. After my wife passed away, in my absence, my children moved her tomb away from my father's because of the bitterness in their relationship after her public denunciation and her indirect rejection of their kinship tie by the terms of address used during the trial. Even nowadays, I still do not feel comfortable in the presence of the relatives who denounced my father and addressed him with the terms *may* and *tao* on that trial day more than three decades ago. It is still embarrassing for us to interact.

The wife of the late mayor An, the third wealthiest villager who had strongly supported the Vietminh since 1945 and had declined an invitation to join the Party in 1948, was classified as a regular landlord instead of a resistance-supporting one. Her property was appropriated together with that of other landlords.[8] As quite a few villagers whispered to the field researchers in 1987, she committed suicide at this point. (The land reform guidelines specified that regular and resistance landlords' land and other means of production would be purchased by the state with payments over a ten-year period and 1.5 percent annual interest on the purchase price [Hoang-Uoc 1968:163–164]. Resistance landlords would be allowed to donate land to the state so as to escape the tension of denunciation sessions [ibid.:166–167].) Bang's half-sister's husband, a mayor in the colonial era and a Communist Party member during the Franco-Vietminh war, was classified as a regular landlord. Although his two sons had been serving as soldiers in the Vietminh armed forces, all his property, except for a buffalo stable, was appropriated. One of the sons reported on his family conditions during and in the aftermath of the land reform:

My father had been an active party member during the war. My house had been a frequent meeting place for the party leadership, and my father had been elected treasurer because of our wealth. . . . I volunteered for the People's Army in 1949 and was sent to China for training. We all felt strongly about the cause of national independence. As soldiers, we had no shoes, wore latania-leaf hats, received no salaries, and walked all the way to China. . . . When I observed the land reform in China, I wrote to my father to warn him to get rid of some land. . . . I was not home during the land reform, but it was reported that our property was all appropriated except for a buffalo stable. The stable was returned to our family only after some villagers had commented that my younger brother and I had been serving in the armed forces. My family was given a tiny piece of land in a village cemetery, where they grew corn. My younger sisters collected manure on the village roads and sold it to provide a supplementary income for the family. Yet, after the sale they were stripped of the money by the authorities and reportedly told: "Manure belongs to peasants." Few people dared to see my family in those days. My brother, at the time stationed not too far from Son-Duong, had to sneak back to see my family at night. A few villagers who took a pity on my family hid small bags of rice and a few corn cobs under their shirts. They reportedly called in from the outside, "Is the bastard landlord home? He'd better be home!" and discreetly threw the food inside if no other villagers were around. . . . We were later reclassified as rich peasants and eventually down to middle peasants. Even so, in 1958, when I was granted a vacation, I did not dare to return to Son-Duong. I spent my vacation elsewhere.

Bang's brother Gia, who still owned 2.4 *mau* and cultivated an additional *mau* as a "gift" from his wealthier half-sister, was classified as a rich peasant. Most of Gia's land, like that of other rich peasants, was purchased by the state for redistribution to other cultivators. As a reflection of the intense struggle during the land reform, Gia's senior daughter-in-law and his sister-in-law, the leading female Communist Party member in the village, reportedly denounced and strongly insulted Gia in public denunciation meetings by their use of the personal pronouns *may* and *tao* with him. Bang's other brother Tang and his wife, respectively an army officer and the leading female party member in the village, were not adversely affected by the land reform because, ironically, they had lost their share of the family rice fields through Tang's gambling in the early 1940s.

In accordance with land reform guidelines, the confiscated, appropriated, and coercively purchased lands from landlord and rich peasant households in Son-Duong were distributed to landless, poor, and middle peasants. Cadres, soldiers, and workers serving the revolution, whether deceased, invalid, or on active duty, were counted as peasants if their families resided in the countryside and qualified for land as landless, middle, or poor peasant households (Hoang-Uoc 1968:172). The poor peasant Te (one of Bang's cousins), who had been recruited as a land reform cadre and assigned to work elsewhere in the province, received over one *mau* for three adult family members:

We received 1 *mau* for three adults, on the basis of about 0.3 *mau* for each adult in our category. We received neither grain, because as a cadre I did not dare to ask for it directly, nor cattle, because we had bought one earlier.

The family of the former Communist Party secretary Tiem was classified as "petit bourgeois," although through his wife's labor on the land and their ownership of only over one *mau* for a large household, they received slightly over one *mau* of rice fields. The old lady Thanh, whose property had increased to 2.2 *mau* by this time, was classified a middle peasant family. She received no land:

At the time of the land reform, we received no land because we had been classified as a lower-middle peasant family with our 2.2 *mau*. I told the land reform cadres that we should be classified as poor peasants. Our holding had increased to 2.2 *mau* only shortly before the land reform because another family had sold us 0.11 *mau* out of concern about the land reform program. We received only a large copper tray with a hole, which I returned to the original owner upon the reclassification of her class background.

An estimated 300 *mau* of rice fields from landlord households were redistributed to landless, poor, and lower-middle peasants on the basis of the number of adult workers and the current holdings of the households. According to village statistics, the average rice-field holdings of landless and poor peasants increased significantly after the land reform (table 7).

Working from its base in the peasant association, the outside land reform team also organized a drastic purge of the local party branch in order to bring an end to its domination by the landholding class. Within the framework of the land reform program, the team had been authorized to educate party members on class perspective, to purge the local party membership of the elements from the landlord and rich peasant categories still engaged in exploitative practices, and to recruit actively among landless and poor peasants. Party members from landlord and rich peasant families who had firmly carried out party policies could be spared in the purge. However, according to party directives, they would have to be transferred outside the community in order to mimimize their impact on the relations between the party and the masses at the village level. In the village of Son-Duong, forty-two party members were expelled in an indiscriminate purge. In other words, 46 percent of party members were purged because of their landlord and rich peasant backgrounds, although by the least stringent cri-

**Table 7. Rice-field holdings of landless, poor, and middle peasants before and after the land reform of 1954 in Son-Duong**

|  | PERCENT OF ADULT VILLAGERS | HOLDINGS BEFORE LAND REFORM (MAU) | HOLDINGS AFTER LAND REFORM (MAU) |
|---|---|---|---|
| Landless peasants |  | 0.033 | 0.4 |
| Poor peasants | 70 | 0.2 | 0.48 |
| Middle peasants | 22 | 0.4 | 0.57 |

teria, at the time of land reform the landlord and rich peasant households made up no more than 13 percent of the local population. The
high percentage of party members from these backgrounds after the
earlier class-oriented party purge in 1952 clearly indicates the dominance of landlords and rich peasants in the village sociopolitical structure and in the support for the war of national liberation from 1946 to
1954 (cf. Wolf 1969:292). Thirteen new party members were admitted
from the ranks of villagers of landless and poor peasant backgrounds in
1954. And in another departure from the male-oriented and class-structured model of hierarchy in the colonial era, a female party member
became the party leader (party secretary) from 1954 to 1958. As a result
of the land reform, the radical egalitarian and collectivist ideology
emerged dominant not only within the communal framework of Son-
Duong, but it also restructured household relations, especially among
the elite, because many daughters-in-law played a major role in
denouncing their husbands' parents for exploitative practices.

The party purge and the land reform program totally shattered the
unity of the earlier years of the Franco-Vietminh war. Like their counterparts in other communities, many Son-Duong villagers from landlord and rich peasant households had joined the Vietminh in the cause
of national independence and had been consequently admitted to the
Communist Party. A North Vietnamese authority on land reform has
analyzed party conditions throughout North Vietnam in 1953 as fol-
lows:

> In terms of ideology, a large number of party members possessed a
> nationalistic spirit, actively participated in the anti-imperialist move-
> ment, but did not have a sufficient class awareness and did not under-
> stand the division between landlords and peasants. The influence of
> landlords' and rich peasants' world views was still fairly strong among
> many party members. In terms of organization, party cells still had
> members from exploiting classes [3 to 4 percent], some of whom occu-
> pied positions of authority in the party branch and village administra-
> tion in a number of localities. (Hoang-Uoc 1968:180)

In the aftermath of the land reform campaign, the tension in Son-
Duong was extraordinarily high between embittered landlords, rich
peasants, and expelled party members, on the one hand, and their
denouncers and the remaining party members, on the other. When

Bang's brother Tang, reportedly a Dien-Bien-Phu veteran, returned to Son-Duong on a short vacation in 1955 and suddenly died, his god-brother (the chairman of the village Vietminh front during the war) and his brother Gia were accused of poisoning Tang and three other Son-Duong villagers. Gia was reclassified a "reactionary rich peasant" and his adopted brother, a reactionary landlord. Both were imprisoned. Although allowed to keep the thatch house and the garden land, Gia lost all his rice fields. The high tension in the local community rever-berated beyond the communal framework, because many high-ranking party members and cadres at the district and national levels came from relatively well-off families in the countryside.

In 1956 the Communist Party and the goverment of the Democratic Republic of Vietnam launched a rectification program throughout North Vietnam to correct the excesses in the earlier local implementa-tion of the land reform policy. In the summer of 1956, as the leading advocate of the class alliance policy in the Vietnamese Communist Party, Ho Chi Minh lent his personal prestige to the rectification of land reform excesses. On August 18, Ho took the initiative by writing to the rural populace:

> The status of those who have been wrongly classified as landlords or as rich peasants should be reviewed.
>
> Party membership, rights and honors should be restored to party members, cadres, and others who have been wrongly convicted. . . .
>
> Unity is our invincible force. In order to consolidate the North into a solid base for the struggle to re-unify our country, our entire people should be closely and widely united on the basis of the worker-peasant alliance in the Vietnam Fatherland Front. It is all the more necessary for veteran and new cadres of the Party and Government to assume identity of ideas, to be united and single-minded, and to compete to serve the people.   (translated in White 1981:430)

In an unprecedented forty-day session in September and October of the same year, the rectification program was ratified by the party cen-tral committee (White 1981:432). In Son-Duong, because of his absence from the village during the land reform, the party member Te, in his capacity as the assistant secretary of the peasant association, was appointed to rectify the earlier excesses. Of the twenty-six families originally classified as landlord households, seven remained in the land-lord category, and five and fourteen were reclassified as rich and middle peasants, respectively. The wife of the late mayor An, who had committed suicide, was posthumously reclassified as a resistance landlord. The ten originally classified rich peasant households, including Bang's brother Gia's, were reclassified as middle peasant families. The households reclassified as rich and middle peasants had some of their previously appropriated property returned. Gia and the nominally adopted son of his father were released from prison. However, redirecting pent-up hostility toward his earlier denouncers, Gia reportedly almost resorted to physical violence with them. Each member of a reclassified household was granted rice fields approximating the holding of a middle peasant. He or she regained the rights to vote and to stand for election to the village people's council. However, party guidelines on alliance with rich peasants notwithstanding, rich peasants were not allowed into peasant associations, administrative committees, village guerilla forces, or security forces. Members of landlord households continued to suffer the consequences of the land reform classification for years, since landlords' children, no matter how bright, were not admitted to institutions of higher education, although they were employable in nonsensitive positions in the state apparatus. Starting in 1957, as a result of the party central committee's rejection of class background as the primary criterion of party membership (White 1981:435), the local party branch gradually readmitted twenty-nine of the forty-two expelled party members, bringing the number of party members to ninety-six. Over time, ten of the thirteen new members admitted during the land reforms were dropped from the party branch for "unethical conduct" and insufficient political knowledge.

Despite the rectification of land reform errors, the land reform radically transformed the colonial class structure as a strategic step toward a collectivistic political economy. It also consolidated the position of the Communist Party among the rural masses and led to concrete improvements in the lives of the vast majority of peasants. These gains were further strengthened in 1957, when a major irrigation system with feeder canals was built in the Lam-Thao–Hac-Tri delta, increasing the food production in the village by 14 percent from 1953 to 1957. The land reform and the water-control project transformed the peasant masses not only in material terms: from an attitude of resignation, many of them came to have a positive outlook on the larger world. This new outlook was reinforced by the state in its labor mobilization slogan during the 1957 canal construction: "Squeeze water from the earth, and replace heaven in making rain." The overt deferential behavior of peasants toward landlords, of which the pattern of addressing men of wealth by their formal titles constituted an intrinsic part, was eliminated as well.

By 1957, the socioeconomic structure of Son-Duong in particular and of northern Vietnam in general had been fundamentally transformed with the elimination of the colonial landholding class and with the supremacy of the Communist Party as the representative of the proletariat. The male-oriented, kinship-centered, class-structured model of hierarchy in the local tradition was seriously undermined in favor of a radical egalitarian and collectivistic ideology in the land reform process.

The village party history concluded on the land reform program:

> The rent and land revolution achieved significant results in (1) overthrowing the feudal landlord class, the objective of the people's nationalist democratic revolution; and (2) eliminating forever the feudal land ownership by landlords and distributing land to poor and landless peasants. . . . In the process of land reform, we made serious errors (1) in not having sufficiently educated the masses, leading to people's and many cadres' loose understanding of the party's policy; (2) in not differentiating the enemies in accordance with party policy, creating anxieties and disunity in the countryside; and (3) in not relying firmly on the guidelines of party reorganization, causing upheaval in the local apparatus with an emphasis on the expulsion of party members and not on their education as well as with the reliance on the peasant association and "correct background" cadres at the expense of the village administration and the local party leadership.          (Son-Duong 1987:48–49)

The radical collectivist principle truly gained ascendancy the following year when the Vietnamese Workers' Party and the government of the Democratic Republic of Vietnam launched the cooperative program in 1958. On the one hand, the program was aimed at solving the problem of a resurrected socioeconomic differentiation within the peasantry. On the other, the Party and the state sought to increase agricultural production and to procure resources for an accelerated industrialization process within a centrally planned and collectivist political economy. In Son-Duong the cooperative program was launched with the formation of labor exchange teams, whose membership ranged from three to eighteen households. However, because of an emphasis on voluntary participation, membership in the labor exchange program had its ebb and flow, with many members withdrawing at one point (Son-Duong 1987:51). In 1959, under party guidance, party members were instructed to take the lead in persuading their families to join a cooperative as well as in convincing their relatives and other villagers. Two hamlet-level cooperatives were established in 1959, followed by two others the following year. All the means of agricultural production (rice fields, draft animals, and farm instruments) were pooled, except for the 5 percent of cultivable land that could remain in the possession of cooperative members for household use as residential, gardening, and animal husbandry land. Cooperative members initially received their share of the crop according to both their labor input and their contribution of land and draft animals to the cooperative.

The process of cooperative formation was not completely smooth. Although not overtly resisting collectivization, quite a few Son-Duong villagers were not enthusiastic. Most eventually joined the cooperatives, but up to 15 percent of members withdrew at one point (Son-Duong 1987:52). The old lady Thanh, who had moved from a landless laborer to a middle peasant position by the time of the land reform, commented on the process:

We were better off after the land reform. Within a few years, a cooperative program was launched because they said: "Otherwise, many poor and land-less peasants may sell their land and end up destitute again." We were among the first to join. We did not waver at all, unlike some other families that withdrew and rejoined. My husband headed the inspection team for the cooperative, which left us no choice. We had some difficulties at the beginning. On the one hand, villagers who did not want to join cursed us behind our backs: "Those party members are crazy!" We also had some difficulty with village criers who took grain from cooperative land without permission and were ready to beat up those making an issue about it.

The former landless laborer Te, the first president of the Chung-Chinh cooperative, elaborated on the process of cooperative formation:

When the rectification program was completed, I was recruited to head a labor exchange team. It was 1957–1958 then. I exhorted peasants to join on the basis of mutual assistance. Each team had fifteen to eighteen households. Those with cattle helped those without. It was also at this time that I was selected as a member of the party leadership committee in the village.

When the village started establishing an agricultural cooperative, the party committee asked me to become the president of a cooperative. I replied: "I do not know how to do it. I know neither how a cooperative functions nor what it means being a cooperative president." But they told me: "You should accept the responsibility. The district administration will provide the necessary guidance."

*How were the living conditions of your family at the time?*

Honestly, we were doing well economically at the time when I was drafted to head a cooperative. We owned a head of cattle and more than one *mau* of land. Although our house was not big by any standard, after receiving the land from the land reform campaign, we managed to save enough money for bricks and to pave our courtyard for drying paddy. However, the Party initiated the cooperative program to increase agricultural production. The Party also actively promoted [formerly] poor and landless peasants to more important positions at the time. As party members, we had to clear the path with enthusiasm in order to provide good examples for other villagers, no matter how we actually felt in our hearts. Practically no choice was available on the matter. I ended up being the president of Chung-Chinh cooperative, the biggest one in the village both in terms of membership and the amount of cattle and land, for three years.

The cooperative had no office at the beginning. My house became the cooperative office where even the general meetings for all cooperative members were held. My wife and my mother had to serve tea for cooperative members for about three years until I stepped down from the president's position. Despite my lack of knowledge, fortunately it was not too complicated to run a cooperative in those days, because villagers were quite honest. We assigned people to carry paddy to drying courtyards, to take it in overnight, and eventually to check it into the cooperative warehouse, all without weighing the paddy before or after. If members had been greedy, we could have lost quite a bit with such a loose system of control. But believe me, members were not at all devious. . . . We did well as a whole. I remember a request one year from a district cadre for the paddy consumption of households within the cooperative and whether production met members' needs. I estimated monthly consumption at thirty-three kilograms of paddy for each adult. [We did well by this standard. . . .]

Our family received over one tonne per crop, although my job as the president of the cooperative was considered the equivalent of only fifteen labor days and thus earned me only ninety kilograms of paddy per crop. A labor day was worth six kilograms of paddy when the crop was divided in those days. The rest of our paddy share came from our land and cattle stocks in the cooperative. We received 25 percent of the crop yield from our land, and a four-labor-day credit for every 0.1 *mau* plowed by my buffalo. Our share of the paddy crop was quite good in those days, because we simply divided the crop among ourselves according to a labor-day credit system after reserving the seeds for the next crop and fulfilling the paddy obligations to the state. We made no provision for future investments. As a sideline, with a 0.3 *mau* garden, my family also grew vegetables and raised pigs. My mother was able to enjoy the fruits of the revolution for a few years before passing away in 1962. In general, my job turned out to require more activism and devotion than sophisticated formal training.

In all those years the only major complication arose when a number of villagers decided to resign their membership in the cooperative. They were calculating middle peasants who wanted to leave the cooperative after a not-so-great harvest, even though each of those families had a paddy reserve of easily half a tonne to one tonne. The higher authorites initially dragged their feet on the return of the land and cattle to those peasants. Village militia even intervened when those peasants tried to get back their cattle and cultivate their land. We also attempted to estimate their grain reserves and made debt claims on the reserves after leaving those peasants just enough for their survival. They were allowed to leave the cooperative, but they eventually reapplied for membership. Their new membership applications were accepted after they agreed to our condition that if they ever left again, they would lose all their land and animal contributions to the cooperative. It was certainly a triumph for the principle of collective labor over that of individual labor. By 1962 every villager had joined a cooperative.

A member of the Chung-Chinh cooperative described his background and explained why he withdrew from the cooperative and reapplied for membership:

My grandparents had six children, three sons and three daughters. Until 1951 my father and two uncles all lived in the same wooden house with their mother and their own families, except for a period when an uncle of mine lived in Yen-Bay. They split up and built three separate houses only when our house was destroyed by French bombing in 1951. Before 1954 our livelihood came from cultivation and weaving. Our family was poor. When my family and those of my uncles still shared the same house, we sharecropped 0.3 *mau* of rice field. We split the crop half and half with the landlord because we provided the seeds and the draft animal ourselves. We did not have enough to eat. My mother and my uncles' wives had to collect cow dung and human excrement for sale as fertilizer. My father also worked as a shaman, although he earned only his food and contributed little to the family budget. I went to school for one year only.

At the time of land reform, we were classified as a poor peasant family and received a few *sao* of rice field. Our lives improved considerably because we no longer worked for other people. We joined the Chung-Chinh cooperative because the entire village joined one cooperative or another at the time. But we resigned our membership, as many other families did, because we found cooperative work too restrictive. We had to show up at a certain hour. Although we got back the land, we lost our cow with this resignation because of some change in cooperative management personnel. We managed to buy a buffalo with small loans from relatives. We rejoined after one agricultural season and contributed the buffalo to the cooperative. We eventually adjusted to the work hours in the cooperative. Despite the numerous debates at one point among cooperative members about how many points a task should be given, we were pleased as cooperative members, especially in the earlier days, when a labor-day credit yielded four to five kilograms of paddy.

In general, the cooperative program proceeded fairly smoothly in Son-Duong, as in most northern villages. Over the next fifteen years, the principle of collectivism gained further ascendancy with the establishment of the credit and purchasing cooperatives and the further collectivization of the means of production. In 1966 the village merged four hamlet-level cooperatives into two larger ones. They were further merged into a villagewide cooperative two years later for better planning and resource utilization. It was a relatively smooth process, as highlighted in the party member and former landless laborer Te's continued narrative:

When the cooperatives were merged, I headed the inspection team and joined the management committee of the new cooperative. In the context of war, the higher-level cooperative in Son-Duong had fewer problems than cooperatives elsewhere. I told members of another village: "Your village [cooperative] has three fathers, while we have only one. Despite the earlier division of Son-Duong into three villages [before 1945], we had the same customs and worshiped the same guardian deities. The earlier administrative division in Son-Duong merely resulted from the conflicting interests of village notables in the past [in the nineteenth century]. In your case, you had three different contests at the annual village festivals: rice cooking, wrestling, and group singing. You had three different traditions; hence the problems with a higher-level cooperative."

The idiom of kinship in Te's discussion of the smooth merger process in Son-Duong suggests that far from being submerged in the egalitarian and collectivist ideology at the time, the hierarchy-centered kinship ideology still persisted as a relatively important parameter of the village structure.

As part of the concentration of production resources, smaller livestock farms were concentrated into a large one. By 1971 the collective farm had increased its stocks to 300 breeding ducks and 3000 for meat and eggs, as well as 20 breeding sows and 300 regular pigs. Hog husbandry annually produced 300 piglets, 1.5 tonnes of pork, and a large quantity of manure for the rice fields. The labor system was changed from working-day credits to credits for specific tasks. Cooperative members' shares of the harvest depended only on their labor contributions and no longer on their contributions of land and draft animals as at the time of hamlet-level cooperative formation. By 1965 the yield per crop had increased from 500 to 700 kilograms per *mau* (i.e., from 1.4 to 1.95 tonnes per hectare), where it remained stable throughout the duration of the U.S. war. Thanks to the increase in double-cropped acreage, paddy production increased from 780 tonnes in 1965 to 940 tonnes in 1972. As a result, despite the population increase, paddy production per person remained approximately 310 kilograms throughout this seven-year period. The village was able to contribute 3140 tonnes of paddy to the war effort of the Democratic Republic of Vietnam from 1965 to 1975 through its tax obligations and through low-price sale to the state.

However, partly as a result of the need to minimize the risk to human lives in large gatherings during the intensive U.S. bombing of the north (1965–1968), the production process was decentralized through a contract system. After the merger of smaller cooperatives, although planning became increasingly centralized and resources were concentrated, the agricultural work itself was contracted out to production brigades (corresponding to the earlier hamlet-level cooperatives). It was further contracted to interhousehold task-specialized teams that, upon the completion of the work, allowed their members to take care of their own household gardens. This decentralization of the production process took place during a three-year period when, after the village of Son-Duong was damaged on the very first day of the

U.S. bombing in the province in June 1965, 620 U.S. fighter squadrons reportedly dropped tens of thousands of tons of bombs on Phu-Tho and neighboring Vinh-Phuc (Vinh-Phu 1971:108). The village rebuilt bomb shelters; organized fire, excavation, alarm, and emergency medical teams; trained the village militia in shooting at low-flying attack planes and the entire population in capturing parachuting pilots; and dispersed village classes throughout the four hamlets. Wearing thick thatch hats, young students took lessons sitting halfway inside classroom trenches in order to minimize the risk to their lives. During this period, in order to gather information, sabotage the economy, and weaken the North Vietnamese people's will, the United States reportedly sent South Vietnam–based commando teams to the province as well as dropped propaganda leaflets and counterfeit North Vietnamese bills (Vinh-Phu 1971:108–109). These measures by the United States were to no avail, as the solidarity among villagers increased in support of the war effort, both in terms of resources and manpower. The state and the Party appealed to Son-Duong youth with its dictum "Three Readinesses, Three Capacities": for men, readiness to fight, to join the armed forces, and to be assigned to whatever task the country deemed necessary; and, for women, capacities to take care of the family and encourage male family members to fight in the war, to take charge of production and other tasks on behalf of departing male fighters, and to serve the war and prepare to fight. Three hundred sixty men were sent to the front between 1965 and 1975. As a result, women played an even greater role than before in the production process. Households with insufficient labor and too many consumers were sold paddy at preferential prices by the cooperative.

In early 1968, toward the end of the intensive U.S. bombing campaign, the village of Son-Duong became part of the new province of Vinh-Phu, created through the merger of Phu-Tho and neighboring Vinh-Phuc. Toward the end of the three-year U.S. bombing campaign in 1968, certain localities in Vinh-Phu experimented for the first time with a system of household contracts, especially in livestock husbandry. In the Dong-Xuan cooperative (Lap-Thach district) households on contract with the cooperative for pig husbandry were allotted a certain amount of cooperative land to grow food for the pigs. They would receive labor-day credits for meeting the production quotas (e.g., twenty-three labor-day credits for a fifty-five-kilogram pig and half a tonne of manure), 80 percent of the surplus above the quota, or a penalty of 40 percent of the deficit in case of falling below the production target (*Vinh-Phu,* April 12, 1968, 2–3).[9] The collective hog stock consequently increased from three in 1961 to almost two hundred in early 1968, not counting the sizable private stocks of cooperative members. The provincial leadership extolled Dong-Xuan's exemplary achievements. Other villages were exhorted on a weekly basis to follow Dong-Xuan's innovation by the provincial party newspaper *Vinh-Phu,* which carried a large headline caption: "Learn From, Catch Up, and Bypass Dong-Xuan; Struggle to Achieve Three Major Objectives: Each laborer cultivating one hectare, producing five tonnes of paddy, and raising two hogs." The household contract system quickly spread to the rest of the province, including the village of Son-Duong, where it was adopted for swan husbandry. By October 1968, 618 cooperatives in Vinh-Phu (more than half of its agricultural cooperatives) had entered the production competition with Dong-Xuan. In certain cooperatives, especially in Kim-Anh, Lap-Thach, Vinh-Tuong, and Yen-Lang districts, households even contracted with the cooperative for transplanting, tending, and fertilizing both rice and secondary crops (*Vinh-Phu,* March 21, 1968, 1; *Vinh-Phu* July 30, 1968, 1). However, party ideologues at the provincial and national levels quickly smothered the movement:

A good contract system responds to the basic needs of socialist management: to create conditions conducive to a continuous increase in labor productivity and, most importantly, to strengthen the collective economy, as well as to perfect the new [socialist] relations of production . . . and simultaneously to conquer the small-producer mentality. . . .

As the party leadership committee of Binh-Xuyen district has recognized, the [household] contract system easily becomes a total contract system in which cooperative members receive paddy fields for their own cultivation of vegetables and secondary crops on contract with the cooperative. . . . This is a decentralized management method that weakens the collective economy and incidentally enlarges the household economy sector. It is contrary to the principle of socialist management. It is a symptom of rightist thinking. (*Vinh-Phu,* November 1, 1968, 2)

The ideologues suggested instead the limitation of contracts to small production teams—a method that, in their opinion, fostered both the collectivistic ideology and the exchange of technical knowledge (*Vinh-*

*Phu,* November 1, 1968, 2; November 22, 1968, 1; December 13, 1968, 2). The leadership of the party branch and the cooperative in Son-Duong was directly reprimanded for allowing household contracts in swan husbandry.

As a further consequence of the collectivistic ideology, the purchase price for paddy that the state commercial apparatus offered to coopera- tives fell increasingly behind the inflation-prone cost of living. By 1970 the paddy price offered by the state amounted to only 25 percent of the going rate at local rural markets (Pham-Cuong and Nguyen-van-Ba 1976:104). The radical collectivist ideology remained dominant in the public domain as late as 1978. When the household contract system was reintroduced in 1978 for the cultivation of secondary staple crops in certain localities, the party secretary of Vinh-Phu province report- edly declared in a provincial party meeting: "It is better to let the fields lie fallow than to allow household contracts."

The local covert resistance to the radical collectivistic vision of politi- cal economy emerged strongly after the end of the U.S. war in 1975, when cooperative members increasingly turned their attention to the household garden plots. If a major war with a Western superpower strengthened Son-Duong villagers' solidarity and collectivistic orienta- tion, agricultural production in the village suffered a serious setback in the 1978–1981 period as the yield per hectare dropped from an average 2 tonnes in the preceding fifteen years to approximately 1.5 tonnes per crop. The declining productivity stemmed from a decline in the returns from cooperative work caused by two sets of factors. First were the decrease in cultivated surface due to various public work projects, and the absorption of population growth at the unabated annual birth rate of 3 percent into the local agricultural work force. The yield from the land was consequently divided among a larger number of cooperative members. Second were the continuing decline in the state's purchase price for paddy (as low as 12 percent of the market value) and the greater scarcity of subsidized consumer goods after Chinese aid was cut off as a result of the Sino-Vietnamese conflict (Ngo-Vinh-Long 1988; see also White 1988; Fforde 1989:194–197). In a vicious cycle, the diminishing returns from cooperative work led villagers to pay greater attention to their household garden plots. Despite the adoption of high-yield crop varieties, the return on a cooperative labor-day credit declined steadily to below two kilograms by the late 1970s from approximately six kilograms at the onset of the cooperative program in 1958–1960. The former cooperative president Te noted the problems:

In Son-Duong, despite the lack of conflicts rooted in tradition [among the merged hamlets and lower-level cooperatives], the yield per labor day in the higher-level cooperative dropped steadily to an average of 1.7 to 1.8 kilograms of paddy. This problem stemmed from population growth and the decrease in cultivated acreage. The village population kept increasing. At the same time, cultivated acreage had dropped owing to the construction of irrigation canals, the collective livestock farm, collective paddy-drying courtyards, and collective warehouses. [Furthermore] cooperative members received points for the work on contract [to the task-specialized teams]. They consequently showed up late and tried to finish the work as soon as possible so that they could take care of their gardens and other economic activities at home.

In the summer of 1979, for the first time in half a century, Nguyen Dac Bang returned to his homeland from Canada, where he had resettled in 1976 with his family. He made a second extended visit in early 1983 to experience again the New Year celebrations of his youth. Bang's extensive account of his encounter with the land and people of his youth after half a century of exile adds many details to the picture of life in the village in those difficult years of the radical collectivistic economy:

My feeling was indescribable when the Aeroflot plane landed at Hanoi's Noi-Bai Airport on my first trip. My chain of thought was full of anticipation of the re-encounter with the land and the people of my youth. However, because our departure from Moscow had been delayed by a few days, I did not meet my relatives until the following morning, when I ran into my senior brother Gia on the hotel staircase on the way down to breakfast. It was an emotional encounter after half a century of absence, as tears streamed down our faces and as we happily wept at being able to see each other again.

[The following day, returning to Son-Duong] I was led to our ancestral land, where I saw nothing but a poor thatch house. Like the pagoda, the meeting hall, and, as I found out later, also our ancestral hall, much of the five-room brick house of my youth had been destroyed by French bombing during the Franco-Vietminh war. The only reminders of the house of my youth were the brick gate, the brick yard, and the house steps. From the house came joyful screams of "Grandfather Bang is home at last." In the next half hour even more people came to the small house already full of relatives.

. . . Visitors came forward one after another, introducing themselves as the children of such and such persons. The passage of the decades notwithstanding, I was still able to pass muster as I told them where I thought their parents and grandparents had lived in the days of my youth. They were quite pleased at seeing me home, able to recollect the events of the past, my advanced age and the half century of absence notwithstanding. . . .

It was an eventful first night in Son-Duong because of the loose village security and the dilapidated condition of my ancestral house. It rained hard during the night. In the heavy rain, water poured down through the leaky thatch roof into the house. We had to change our sleeping location from one corner to another! The house was also broken into during the rainstorm. A few hoodlums from the village anticipated a successful night, thinking that as an overseas Vietnamese from North America, I had brought back a large amount of cash. Sleeping on the same bed with me in the altar-cum–guest room, the main room of the house, my brother's grandsons were awakened by the noise and caught the burglars in the house.

Retaining his pleasure-seeking lifestyle, my brother Gia had done little to maintain our ancestral home. As the head of my branch of the Nguyen Doan patrilineage, [my senior brother] Gia and his wife had lived [in our ancestral home] together with his second son and the latter's family. Having been in conflict with his father, Gia's eldest son Thuy had long before moved to the village of Phu-Ho, a former hilly plantation about fifteen kilometers away, where he had a lot of children by his second and third wives. . . . The condition of my ancestral house was particularly deplorable because the majority of village houses had been constructed of bricks by the time of my visit. The living conditions in the countryside had improved a great deal over the past. The village fields were double-cropped, because the government had built a long irrigation canal from the Lam-Thao district seat to Viet-Tri.

After my first day in my home village, I went with relatives to the Ngu-Xa market, which was held every morning. The periodic market of the old days in my village was no longer held. In our area only the Ngu-Xa and Cao-Mai markets had stood the test of time. The trip was not bad because [even after the heavy rain] the village roads were still not too muddy. They had been enlarged and leveled. Although it was not yet possible to drive a car all the way into the village, the roads were no longer flooded in the rainy season.

God, [even] the peasants [at the market] had started talking about my return! Marketing activities were less lively than in the old days, [partly] because there already existed a purchasing and sales cooperative in every village. The merchandise was composed simply of vegetables, frogs, fish, eels, poultry, and other small items that villagers raised, caught, or produced in the small household economic sector. It was mainly old people who sought to earn supplementary incomes [for their families] with paltry amounts of whatever it was in their baskets. The peddlers at Ngu-Xa market still divided themselves into different areas: one for fish, eels, and frogs, another for poultry and meat, and another for vegetables.

Although the shelves of the cooperative store were virtually empty except for fish sauce, soybean sauce, other minor items, and occasionally meat, the Ngu-Xa market was simply not as lively as in the old days. The socialist government considered private commerce exploitative in nature. The land had been collectivized, being divided only into ten large fields at the time of my first return. Such a collectivist economy only fostered passivity on the part of the people. Take draft animals. The cooperative had only a few for plowing. One member used one one day, another member the following day, and another the next. The buffalo were overworked and fed little. They could not but die one after another. At one point, the second son-in-law of my deceased senior brother Tang even had to pull the plow in the field himself because of the shortage of buffalo. The only private land was the household garden plot where fish, fowl, and pigs were raised and where fruit and vegetables were grown. The government allowed only small-scale private enterprises, such as [cottage] brick industries and housing contract work. For example, Gia's first son Thuy had worked as a housing contractor for some time. If you wanted to have a house built, you would call him over for measurement, design, material delivery, and construction labor. He simply hired workers for his contracted projects.

*Hiring workers?*

Yes, the government had allowed it well before my first return home. The second daughter of my other brother Tang could produce bricks on order for other villagers. Noncollective economic activities were still allowed, but nowhere close to the scale of the past. I repeatedly said [in Vietnam] that with the continuation of the same collectivistic economy, the buffalo would all die in Vietnam!

The declining productivity of the collective fields in Son-Duong village encapsulated the problems on the national scale, since in the 1978–1980 period Vietnam suffered a severe food shortage. It resulted partly from bad weather and partly from the state's low purchase price for paddy. As a result, no sooner had the Vinh-Phu party leadership declared it better to let the fields lie fallow than to allow household contracts than the national party leadership and the state authorized the household contract system in agriculture in 1981 in a complete policy reversal. Under this system the household, under its two-to-five-year contract with the agricultural cooperative, was responsible for rice transplanting, crop tending, and harvest. In other words, the household was responsible for 70 percent of the labor input in agricultural production, for which it received labor point credit (Nguyen-Huy 1980:11). In principle, the agricultural cooperative still provided for plowing, irrigation and drainage work, the spreading of fertilizer, seeds, and the spraying of insecticide, although in Son-Duong, the household also took care of plowing. Collectively owned land was allocated primarily on the basis of the household's adult work force. To ensure an equitable allocation, under this system each household received small pieces of land of varying quality in different parts of the village (ibid.).[10] The state also increased its purchase price for paddy to a level only slightly below the local market price.

The application of the household contract system in November 1982 brought about a dramatic increase in agricultural productivity and food production in Son-Duong, because cooperative members could retain the increased yield above the cooperative quota. Average yields reached 1.3 and 1.5 tonnes per *mau* (3.6 and 4.2 tonnes per hectare), respectively, for the summer–fall and winter–spring crops, with the quotas set at 0.88 and 0.94 tonne per *mau*. Corn production averaged 1 tonne per *mau* with a quota of 0.6. Peanuts yielded 0.6 to 0.7 tonne per *mau*, with quotas varying from 0.3 to 0.4 tonne, depending on the field. When the crop was damaged by natural calamity, the cooperative revised the quotas downward accordingly. For example, as the winter–spring crop in 1987 was adversely affected by a drought, and as productivity declined by an average of one-third, the quota was lowered by 42.5 percent. Instead of 0.94 tonne, the household on contract delivered only 0.55 tonne on an average production of 1 tonne per *mau*. Similarly, in the fall of the same year, when the average yield dropped further to 0.86 tonne, the quota was lowered by 47.5 percent to 0.46 tonne. Members also received back part of the crop delivered on contract to the cooperative on the basis of their labor point credits for work performed on the contracted land. However, out of what cooperative members kept over and above the cooperative quotas and what they earned from the cooperative through the labor point credit system, they had to purchase additional fertilizer to maximize the crop yield. This complex system is illustrated in a cooperative member's description of his income sources in the spring of 1987:

In my family my wife is counted as the only active adult member of the cooperative. I have reached the retirement age. Our eldest daughter has already married outside the family. Our eldest son, a veteran, works away from home, and one of his younger brothers is now in the armed forces. Three of our children still go to school at present. With only one active cooperative member, our household receives 0.6 *mau* of land contracted with the cooperative. To supplement our income from the cooperative, we also contract for the care of a cooperative buffalo. Our rice harvest last month yielded only 0.6 tonne of paddy from 0.6 *mau* of rice field because of the drought. The cooperative agreed to lower the quota by 43 percent, which means that we delivered 330 kilograms to the cooperative as a part of the contract. On the other hand, we earned 90 labor-day credits for the work done on the contracted 0.6 *mau*, on the standard basis of 15 credits for 0.1 *mau*. Our work involved transplanting, cultivating, crop tending, harvesting, and drying the paddy. Because of the smaller amount left to the cooperative after paying for retired members' pensions, taxes, chemical fertilizers, seeds, and irrigation water fees, the quantity of paddy for each labor-day credit dropped to 0.5 kilogram from an average of 1.2 kilograms in previous crops. The cooperative consequently owed us only 45 kilograms of paddy for the work on the 0.6 *mau* and 100 kilograms for our tending of a cooperative buffalo. Substracting this amount from the revised quota on 0.6 *mau* of contracted land, we still owed the cooperative 185 kilograms. We therefore kept 415 kilograms.

On top of our share of paddy, we also received a cash equivalent of over 30 piasters per labor-day credit from the cooperative's export of peanuts [i.e., 7800 piasters for six months for 290 credits]. On the other hand, we had to spend about 120 kilograms of paddy [about 4800 piasters] to buy additional chemical fertilizers for our 0.6 *mau*. Otherwise, the yield would not have reached 100 kilograms per 0.1 *mau*, because the cooperative provided only 3 kilograms of chemical fertilizer per 0.1 *mau*. The paddy we received last spring was just enough for a family of five. Fortunately, we earn quite a bit from our hog husbandry. The piglets born of our two breeding sows are usually exchanged with the cooperative for an average of 1.4 tonnes of paddy a year, although this spring I have been selling quite a few piglets to people from other villages for cash. We also have twenty ducks. We sell eggs to villagers for 20 piasters an egg. In addition, we have a brick kiln that can bring in up to 30,000 piasters a year. The elder of our two teenage daughters can earn quite a bit in her spare time in the summer. She would take a bus to a market about twenty kilometers away, buy wood for retail sale in the local market, and earn 500 to 700 piasters a day [i.e., the equivalent of 12.5 to 17.5 kilograms of paddy at the official local price or slightly less at the open market price]. For thirty years of service in the armed forces, I also receive a small pension worth about 5 kilograms of rice a month.

After the spring harvest of 1987 the cooperative delivered 148 tonnes of paddy to the state for the annual tax bill, for an average of 200 kilograms per *mau*. The cooperative also owed state agencies approximately 250 tonnes of paddy for chemical fertilizers and the water control maintenance fee for the year ending in May 1987. According to the secretary of the local party branch, the incomes of villagers derived from cooperative work alone averaged an equivalent of 475 kilograms of paddy per person in 1986, when the crops were reportedly average. (This figure includes the share of cash, peanuts, and corn from cooperative work.) It more than doubled the 1980 average income, which stood at 220 kilograms of paddy per person. On the assumption of no change in village obligations toward the state and state agencies between 1986 and 1987, the estimated paddy production in Son-Duong reached 1414 tonnes of paddy in 1986, of which tax levies amounted to 10.3 percent.

The party member and former cooperative president Te gave a more general overview of the development of the household contract system in the village:

[Despite the overpopulation problem] the crop yield has increased dramatically, from 600 kilograms of rice per *mau* at the time of the introduction of household contracts in 1982 to an average of 1.5 tonnes per *mau* nowadays. At present, [with the household contract system] some cultivators have even increased the yield to over 2 tonnes per *mau*, while the cooperative quotas are set at 0.94 and 0.88 tonne respectively for the spring and fall crops. For example, in the spring crop of last year [1986], the yield per *mau* from our contracted land reached 2 tonnes. We had to hand over to the cooperative only 0.94 tonne to meet the quota specified in the contract with the cooperative for the spring crop. However, I actually kept almost 1.5 tonnes because I also received seeds as well as paddy for the work performed on the contracted land.

*How much land does your family contract with the cooperative?*

With three main laborers, we contract 1.7 *mau* for the winter–spring crop, 1.3 for the summer–fall crop, and about half a *mau* for the winter corn crop.

We harvest 90 to 100 kilograms of corn for each *sao* and, paying no taxes to the state, keep 60 to 70 kilograms for ourselves.

I would say that nowadays of every one hundred households, ten are truly well-off, twenty possess some surplus, fifty have sufficient means to feed their members, and only twenty face the problem of making ends meet. These twenty households may have less domestic labor [because of the draft], spend beyond their means, or not want to acquire new technical knowledge. It may be necessary to group them together for collective help, because household contracts or not, they have trouble improving their lives because of their obstinacy.

With the household contract system, provincial food production in Vinh-Phu increased by 20 percent to 364,000 tonnes within the three-year period to the end of 1983 (*Nhan Dan,* June 14, 1984, 2). This rebound from the nadir of the late 1970s was paralleled by similar developments across the country as the production of food crops increased to 18.2 million tonnes in 1985 from 14.4 million tonnes in 1980.

The spectacular success of the household contract system in agriculture notwithstanding, there were also minor difficulties in its implementation, both in the village of Son-Duong and elsewhere. A small number of villagers in Son-Duong complained of the decline in the yield per labor point credit, a decline from an average of 1.2 to 2 kilograms in the mid-1980s to 0.5 kilogram of paddy in 1987. Both within and beyond the village of Son-Duong, village leadership did not infrequently draw upon the resources of the cooperative for public projects and village cadres' salaries. The yield per labor point credit diminished as the paddy stock to be divided among cooperative members dwindled. From the perspective of the cooperative management, many villagers showed a lack of responsibility in their use of collectively owned draft animals. Although the cooperative invested money to purchase sixty-four buffaloes between the spring of 1986 and the spring of 1987 in order to increase the collective plowing force, it lost approximately thirty buffaloes in 1987 because they were overworked and underfed. Because of lack of technical knowledge, shortage of labor, or insufficient resources to purchase fertilizer, approximately 10 percent of the contracting households could barely produce above the production quotas and could not make ends meet. By early 1988, 26 percent of the 822 contracting households (214 households) owed the cooperative 110 tonnes of paddy because they had food shortages. Beyond Son-Duong, in the province of Ha-Nam-Ninh in the lower delta of northern Vietnam, many cultivators took the decisive step of returning the contracted land to their cooperatives after experiencing diminishing yields per labor point credit and an increase in their production quotas. The return of the land led to a serious food shortage in this province in the spring of 1988.

To provide additional incentives for cultivators to increase crop yields and raise national food production above the 1985 figure of 18 million tonnes, the national leadership reformed the household contract system in early 1988. Party Directive 10 prohibited village administrations from tapping cooperative resources for their cadres' salaries. It also prohibited the cooperative from increasing production quotas without a technological change and a corresponding higher crop yield. Most important, it guaranteed cooperative members a long-term lease on the contracted land and at least 40 percent of the production quota for their fulfillment of the transplanting, crop tending, and harvesting tasks. (Had this policy been applied in the fall of 1987, given the revised production quota of 46 kilograms per *sao,* Son-Duong cultivators would have received 18.4 kilograms per *sao* instead of the actual 6.75 kilograms for their 15 labor points.)

In order to raise food production, the village leadership in Son-Duong refined the household contract system in the spring of 1988. Agricultural households were divided into three categories: poor contractors (70 households), average contractors (412 households), and good contractors (350 households). Poor contractors were defined as households whose crop yields usually fell below the norm of 1.4 tonnes per *mau* and who could not pay back their paddy debts to the cooperative. Average contractors usually produced within the norm, and good contracting households clearly exceeded it. Village fields were also divided into three categories:

1. The first category *(ruong khau)* included 260 *mau* of rice fields that were divided among all households on the basis of the number of consumers in the village (3828). Each person, child or adult, was thereby entitled to two-thirds of a *sao.* The cooperative divided agricultural taxes as well as the irrigation water, crop protection, and insecticide expenses for these 260 *mau* among the village households on the basis

of their holdings in this category. The cooperative leadership expected that with the annual crop rotation index of 2.5, the two-thirds of a *sao* (0.06 acre) would produce 210 kilograms of food (including both rice and secondary food crops). Allowing 20 kilograms for taxes and other expenses, each person would retain 190 kilograms a year, or 15 kilograms a month.

2. The second category *(ruong lao dong)* included 369 *mau* that were divided among the average and good contracting households on the basis of the active household work force (women from sixteen to fifty-five years old and men from sixteen to sixty). The cooperative provided irrigation water, crop protection, insecticide spraying, and 13 kilograms of fertilizer per *sao*. The cooperative in turn received half the production quota figure of 90 kilograms (i.e., 45 kilograms for a normal crop), of which 80 percent (36 kilograms) went toward taxes, water fees, insecticide, fertilizer, and crop protection. In the estimate of the cooperative leadership, the cooperative would retain 20 percent of the production quota (9 kilograms per *sao* for a total of 33 tonnes of paddy per crop) for its obligations toward retired cultivators, as an operating fund, and for management expenses.

3. The third category *(ruong tang san)* included 110 *mau* of the most fertile rice fields for which only the 350 good contracting households were allowed to bid. The cooperative provided an additional 12 kilograms of fertilizer for each *sao* of contracted land in this category. In return, the production quota was set at 170 kilograms per *sao* for each crop, of which the cultivator was entitled to one-half.

The cooperative promised not to raise production quotas for at least five years. Barring a change in household size and contracting status, contracting households were also guaranteed the same pieces of land for twenty years as an incentive for them to make long-term investments in the fields. In 1989, primarily as a result of reform refinements in the previous year, national food production increased to 20 million tonnes. Vietnam resumed the export of rice after a hiatus of about forty years and regained its status as the third major rice exporter in the world. Its rice exports exceeded 1 million tonnes in 1989 and 1990.

As part of the decentralization process, the agricultural cooperative in Son-Duong sold, in spring 1988, its entire herd of 108 buffaloes to members at the going market price of 0.5 tonne of paddy each. Any group of five cultivators without a draft animal was given priority in this program. Buyers were required to pay half of the amount after the spring crop and the other half after the fall 1988 and spring 1989 rice harvests. Including additional buffaloes purchased by individual households from other communities, the draft animal force of Son-Duong had increased to 382 by the end of the summer of 1988. As part of the general trend, the collective livestock farm had been abandoned since 1982. The farm buildings had all been dismantled except for the frames. The largest cooperative paddy-drying courtyard was rented to a private carpenter, reportedly the wealthiest man in the village with savings of at least 70 tonnes of paddy. The seventy poor households faced serious difficulties, since the expected monthly food supply of 15 kilograms per capita from the basic rice-field allotment *(ruong khau)* would have to be partially reinvested in the purchase of seeds, fertilizer, and plowing services. Secondary occupational opportunities were quite limited, except at the village market reopened in the late summer of 1988 and at the private furniture factory with twenty-five to thirty-five employees, mostly from outside the village. Approximately ten households also wove mosquito net cloth. The socioeconomic differentiation among village households had increased markedly since 1982, although land, as the most important basis of production, was still largely collectivized. The radical collectivistic emphasis of the 1960s and 1970s has clearly shifted in favor of the hierarchical sociocultural model centering on the kinship unit.

The hierarchical model had persisted to a remarkable degree in the structuring of kinship and gender relations in Son-Duong village. Within the communal framework, the equal access of female villagers to educational opportunities and their significant role in the agricultural production process notwithstanding, the executive committee of the local party branch included no female party member. The enlarged party leadership committee counted only two women out of seventeen members (11.8 percent), in comparison to the high proportion of 31 percent (four of thirteen) in 1977. None of the five members of the cooperative management committee *(ban quan tri)* was a woman and only 40 percent of the production team leaders were female, in contrast to 20 percent and 70 percent, respectively, in 1977. The percentage of women rose to 22 percent on the village people's council, which, however, possessed only nominal power in the system. Village leaders explained the decline of women's public status despite their significant labor contribution in terms of the women's lack of rhetorical skills and the return of war veterans in the 1980s.

In the familial context, junior adult males were visibly present at the central table in front of the ancestral altar at the expense of their senior female relatives (mother and paternal aunt), who either sat at the side of the room or ate separately in a side room of the house. The only exception involved the frequent insistence among guests and hosts that a widow of truly advanced years, most often the mother of the household head, join the men for the meal at the central table. The desire to have sons for the continuation of the patriline still formed a fundamental part of villagers' sociocultural reality, as pointed out by the secretary of the local Communist Party branch in his earlier discussion of population control. Similarly, patrilocal residence was taken for granted as part of the local reality. In order to reduce the rate of conversion of rice fields into residential land, for example, the Son-Duong village administration specified that it would no longer grant a request for residential land unless a household head had more than three *daughters-in-law* in residence within the same compound. The percentage of patrilineally extended families in Son-Duong was estimated to exceed 44 percent in 1987 (see Luong 1989:750). Polygamy still existed, despite its prohibition in the 1960 legal code. One of Bang's nephews (his half-brother's son) had three wives in 1987–1988, following Bang's father and grandfather in their tradition of polygyny. After giving birth to a daughter, the nephew's third wife daily entrusted the baby to his second wife when she went to work at the office of the local agricultural cooperative (see also Luong 1989:749–753).

Bang's continued narrative on his extended visits to the land of his youth opens another window on the continuity in the texture of the village fabric:

On learning of my visit to the Ngu-Xa market and my presence in the area, my former wife Lan, who had been living in the village of Ngu-Xa, hurriedly left for Son-Duong to see me. She had been remarried to a man in Ngu-Xa. She had done so in 1936 only at my suggestion. I had written to her earlier from South America with this suggestion, because I was not released with my two brothers and many other political prisoners during the first year of the Popular Front government in France. By this time, our second son had also died in infancy.

*Did your three adopted sons stay on in your household after your deportation to South America?*

My wife could not raise all three by herself. They all returned to live with their parents. Lan had bad luck in life. Her [second] husband did not live long. Neither did her child with him. She has since lived with the daughter of her second husband in a very big house. She wept all the time during our first encounter after half a century. I told her maybe she could go to Canada, but she said she was too old. We met during both of my extended visits to my homeland. . . .

I also met Lu, my first love, during the first of my two extended Vietnam visits. When we saw each other, she cried and cried. She had wanted to marry me but, unfortunately, to no avail. She then became the concubine of another person. On my second trip, I brought back ten meters of French silk for her —the French silk she had asked me to bring on my next Vietnam trip. But she would never receive the gift. She had died by the time of my return. Her son came to see me. With him, I made a visit to her grave. . . . I can never forget my first love. Relationships and mutual obligations in the past were quite significant, not like nowadays [in the West]. It is part of our national character. . . .

[During my two visits to Son-Duong in 1979 and 1983] the news of my return traveled far and fast. My adopted children, those among my pupils who had been adopted because of the poverty of their families, came immediately from other villages in the district on hearing the news of my return. The descendants of some of my comrades who had passed away in South America also invited me to come over so that they could learn more about the lives of their ancestors in that land. I also saw former schoolmates, especially during the second Vietnam visit, and even former gambling partners. During my weeklong visit to Phu-Ho, one of my nephew's daughters also rode me on her bicycle to my maternal land in Xuan-Lung by the Red River, where I had many emotional encounters with my cousins on my mother's side. I was invited to many banquets by relatives within my patrilineage, by my adopted children, and especially by my former pupils, dozens of whom were still alive at the time and some of whom had achieved high-ranking provincial and district positions in the socialist government. I received so many invitations, at times as many as three on the same day, that I told a nephew of mine to handle my social calendar. Otherwise, the specially prepared food would remain untouched and be wasted.

I organized together with my senior brother Gia a family reunion on the anniversary of our father's death. I also attended quite a few engagement and wedding ceremonies of relatives both within and outside the patrilineage.

"This year on father's death anniversary, you can tell our nieces and nephews or their children that I will pay for the entire anniversary event. They simply need to come to help with the purchase and the preparation of foods," I told Gia. Normally, the sons and daughters of the deceased make financial contributions to the gathering held on the anniversary of a parent's death. The deceased's grandchildren would make the contributions on their parents' behalf if the latter had passed away. A few days before the anniversary, the children or grandchildren would have to contact the chief of the patrilineage branch to inquire about how he planned to organize the anniversary and what they needed to contribute. The contributions were usually in the form of uncooked rice, regular or glutinous. If the anniversary was small, only chickens and ducks were cooked. In the case of a bigger anniversary, a pig might be slaughtered. [At my father's anniversary] my senior brother Gia had to kowtow first three times before the altar, praying to my father as the head of the lineage branch and asking him to enjoy the food offerings. Other relatives and our close associates followed him before the altar. We then divided ourselves up four to a tray, with the four senior relatives in the middle. Although large banquets [to which all relatives could be invited] were no longer given, there still existed a spirit of kinship, at least within the branch.

During my second Vietnam visit, as it had been planned to coincide with the New Year, my senior brother's eldest son, as the branch chief, and I had to bring offerings to the altar of our patrilineage-founding ancestors. The genealogies of my lineage and my branch are still maintained and updated. In my father's branch, genealogical records with the listing of both sons and daughters and descendants through sons date back at least four generations. During the second visit I even returned [to Xuan-Lung] for my maternal grandfather's death anniversary in my mother's patrilineage. Attendance at the Xuan-Lung anniversary easily totaled fifty to sixty, because my maternal grandfather had quite a few children.

In other words, the process of transformation in the village of Son-Duong from 1954 to 1988 was not free of tension. It involved a dialectical relation between the principle of radical collectivism espoused by the Marxist state and a hierarchical model for sociocultural reality centering on the kinship unit. The official collectivist ideology of the state emerged dominant in the northern social formation and underlay a radical transformation of the village political economy. However, the pace of change was not uniform. These fluctuations notwithstanding, the sense of progress in Son-Duong village was unmistakable, especially to the poor villagers of the darker colonial days. The sense of gratitude and optimism that pervaded the narrative of the former landless laborer and party member Te's summed up well the views of numerous less articulate villagers:

After thirty-two years of public service, from the days in the armed forces to my final year as a credit cooperative president, I think that our victory over French imperialism in spite of our primitive weapons had to do with our strong will to free ourselves of foreign oppression and enslavement as well as with the leadership of Uncle Ho and the Party. Other fellow countrymen had risen up before then, but their vision did not appeal as well to the masses.

Having gone through the struggle for national independence and the revolution, I see clearly what it has brought to people, especially to the poor. Before the revolution we had to wade in the mud on the village roads during the rainy season, because many young men had to work elsewhere for the entire year and could not stay long enough in the village to repair the roads. In terms of health care, in the old days we had to rely on traditional medicine and prayers. As far as education was concerned, the village school had thirty or forty pupils, and continuation beyond the third grade was possible only for the children of well-off families. Personally, I still remember so vividly the famine of 1945, when we had to substitute manioc and sweet potatoes for rice. I still recall how for ten piasters owed to a village landlord, a relative and an acquaintance of mine had to mortgage the services of their children as live-in domestic servants and dung-collecting and grass-cutting services for two or three years until the loans were paid off. Nowadays we have widened roads, a village clinic staffed by nurses and physicians, and a village school through to the secondary level with a thousand students. Some villagers have rising expectations and feel discontented with their present conditions: having bicycles, they demand motorcycles, and they will eventually want automobiles. But it is simply greed.

Personally, I feel content with having my own house, my own bicycle, my own cow, and an oxcart. After the harvest, we can transport the grain back to the house in the oxcart and have it polished with the cooperative's machines. Although our house does not have much furniture, I do not care as long as we have warm clothes and sufficient food. It is more important to foster in one's children collectivism and ethical standards. I only wish to see my sons fulfill well their military duties to the state and their moral obligations to the community. As our traditional proverb puts it: "A monument will be eroded within one century. A reputation will last for millennia." I do not agree at all with some brothers in the village who are better off and who still grumble about their living conditions. I find the present expectations of young people unreasonable. In the old days, even at the Hung King shrine festival, we did not dress as fancily and colorfully as the youth do nowadays. In our brown cotton pajamas, we readily waded in the mud to complete our work in the fields. In their white shirts, they walk around gingerly to avoid dirtying their clothes. We worked hard and saved pennies in our day. The youth of today spend almost without limits, hundreds of piasters for a shirt and a pair of trousers. We care about sufficient food and warm clothes, while they think of good tastes and a nice appearance. They simply take for granted what we had to struggle so hard for. They do not even want to believe our stories of the old days. Our country is still poor. However, compared to my youth, we have come a long way. On the ceiling of my house up there are parallel sentences carved at the time when our house was built in 1977. It sums up my thoughts: "Owing to ancestors, the new house is constructed; thanks to the Party and Uncle [Ho], the present conditions are achieved" *(On to tien xay nha moi, nho bac dang co ngay nay).*

≪   ≪   ≪

# CHAPTER 6

•

# Theoretical Reflections

THE PAST CENTURY has witnessed violent turns in the encounter between capitalist imperialism and the social formations of agrarian societies at the periphery of the capitalist world system. In many respects, the dynamics of this encounter are epitomized in the Vietnamese revolution. The Vietnamese transformation has influenced important theoretical models embedded in the major traditions of contemporary Western social theory represented by John Stuart Mill, Karl Marx, and Emile Durkheim. In the following analysis of their relative strengths and weaknesses, I seek to make a small contribution to their refinement on the basis of empirical data on the Vietnamese revolution and the village of Son-Duong in particular. More specifically, I suggest that the revolutionary processes in modern Vietnam cannot be understood primarily in terms of a material cost-benefit analysis of historical agents. Rather, these processes must be situated with regard to both the structure of capitalist imperialism and the local indigenous framework.

A major problem of the rational choice framework (Popkin 1979; Olson 1965) remains how to incorporate historically and socioculturally specific values into its model of revolutionary processes. Without such an incorporation, the framework simply projects Western utilitarian ideology onto a radically different sociocultural landscape, where it encounters numerous empirical anomalies. For example, on which matrix of material costs and benefits did a large number of young Son-Duong villagers from different social strata volunteer for the Vietminh armed forces in the 1946–1950 period, when Vietminh troops faced an enemy of overwhelming technological superiority and before the poor recruits could foresee any substantial socioeconomic reforms in their favor? On which universal grid of values did one half million to two million northern Vietnamese peasants accept starvation in the spring of 1945 instead of revolting spontaneously and seizing rice that would have given them a chance of survival? It would likewise be an oversimplification to explain Son-Duong villagers' redirection of labor input to their household garden plots in the 1978–1981 period exclusively in terms of the diminishing returns from cooperative work. In the 1965–1975 period the cooperative labor input had remained high in spite of the diminishing returns to cooperative members. These low returns had resulted from the cooperative's low-priced paddy sale to the state as a part of its contribution to the war effort.

To label irrational such behavioral choices on the Vietnamese political landscape is to explain them away in the face of the inadequacy of the theoretical model. I do not deny the significance of material costs and benefits in the analysis of human action. Many behavioral choices in the course of the Vietnamese revolution are amenable to such a "rational choice" analysis, most notably the suspension of active resistance to French colonialism and Son-Duong villagers' instrumental, short-termed conversion to Catholicism in the 1930s in the hope of gaining the release of their politically active family members. Similarly, the strengthened support for the Vietminh in the 1950–1954 period among the poorer social strata can be explained within the rational choice framework: the Vietminh had placed greater emphasis on the socioeconomic revolution at that time to the advantage of poorer peasants. However, the needs for survival, sexual reproduction, and material well-being are always refracted to a certain extent by a historically situated and socioculturally constructed matrix of meanings. To reduce the rich texture of the native system of rules and meanings to a supposedly universal grid of material costs and benefits is to fail to explain a wide range of historical events and human acts. While appropriately stressing the dynamics of collective action in the revolutionary processes, the rational choice framework has focused on agency at the expense of structures—structures that constrain human action both through external sanctions and through actors' acceptance of certain ideological premises constitutive of these structures.

Through its close attention to the dynamics of capitalism, the Marxist approach has enhanced our understanding of the encounter between world capitalism and local indigenous systems. However, in paying limited attention to the active role of indigenous precapitalist traditions in revolutionary processes, the approach is not without its share of empirical anomalies.

In the Vietnamese context, as pointed out by world system theorists (Wallerstein 1979; Murray 1980), the unequal exchange between the colonizing core and the colonized periphery constitutes a major structural parameter within which revolutionary processes in the periphery are embedded. This unequal exchange emerged in the nineteenth century as an integral part of the global competition among different states within the capitalist core not necessarily for the immediate profits to be gained from colonial conquests, but out of concern for being denied access to possible markets and resource bases in Africa and Asia (Murray 1980:10–15). In order to recoup the costs of the colonial adventure, once a pax colonia was established in Vietnam, the metropolitan and colonial state apparatuses began using coercive measures to lay the groundwork for capitalist operations and to strengthen the revenue sources of the colonial state. As pointed out by Murray and as briefly discussed in chapter 1, these measures included the concession of indigenous land to colonial settlers for the development of major cash crops; the introduction of direct and indirect taxes, and the conversion of tax payments from kind to cash to facilitate capitalist growth; and the oppressive appropriation of labor through the corvée system, the maintenance of rural labor reserves (to be elaborated on shortly), and repressive labor laws to hold down labor costs for capitalist agro-mineral ventures.

In the interaction between capitalism and the local precapitalist sector in colonial Vietnam, the impact of world capitalism was far from uniform. It was most striking in the south, which emerged as one of the top three rice-exporting areas in the world, where approximately two-thirds of the rural population was separated from the means of agricultural production, where land and labor became strictly commoditized, and where classes became increasingly differentiated. In contrast, in the north and center, although the rural population was increasingly drawn into market relations, the majority still tenaciously held on to their minuscule land holdings, buffered in many communities by their small shares of communal land. Although the institution of communal land in the village of Son-Duong was not significant in the colonial period, in northern and central Vietnam, the proportions of inalienable communal land averaged respectively 21 percent and 25 percent of the cultivated acreage. Murray suggests that the persistence of communal land in the north and the center contributed to the formation of noncapitalist labor reserves for the plantations, mines, and factories within French Indochina and beyond. Such reserves allowed workers to rely on kinship and communal ties for survival in times of recession and during the preproductive and postproductive periods (youth and old age). It has been suggested that the cost of capitalist production was consequently held down because capitalist firms had to pay only the cost of short-term labor reproduction (the cost to sustain workers physically during the period of employment) and not the cost of long-term labor renewal (the cost of replacing a physically debilitated work force with a new generation of laborers and of maintaining a temporarily idle work force during economic downturns) (Murray 1980: ch. 5; see also Meillassoux 1981; Wolpe 1972). Within the confines of northern and central rural communities, the noncapitalist sector of the colonial social formation absorbed part of the cost of labor reproduction for the capitalist sector through the partially effective social insurance mechanisms and thus contributed to the process of capital accumulation. The noncapitalist system persisted to a considerable extent in northern and central Vietnamese villages, since land was available for purchase primarily within communal boundaries, and since most of the mining, industrial, and plantation labor force would re-enter the communal framework whenever possible (Gourou 1936: 360–361; Vu-Quoc-Thuc 1951:67–78). The high turnover rate among plantation and industrial workers had to do not merely with the vicissitudes of the capitalist world economy, but also with the desire of many workers to return to the noncapitalist communal framework. To world system theorists the uneven spread of capitalism in colonial Vietnam actually contributed to the process of capital accumulation in the colonial context, at least in the short run.

> In the Red River delta and the coastal lowlands [of Annam], the social differentiation of village inhabitants, the disintegration of owner-occupancy and petty-proprietorship as the principal social relations of

production, and the consequent growth of the home market evolved relatively slowly during the colonial era. The preservation of the apparently "traditional" structures of northern village communities became an absolute requirement for the labor-force renewal of landless or virtually landless wage-laborers who were compelled by economic necessity to migrate from their natal village communities in search of seasonal and temporary employment at the European-dominated points of production. Metropolitan capital recognized the historical manner in which these northern agricultural village communities fulfilled the functions of social security for unemployed or partially employed wage-laborers. Hence, colonial policies deliberately aimed at the conservation of particular elements of village organization as one means of ensuring the survival of the migrant labor system beneficial to the large-scale metropolitan concessionary enterprises that organized agro-mineral export production directly under the sway of capital.

In contrast, the historic process of native settlement and village formation had hardly begun in the Mekong delta when it was interrupted by French colonial occupation. Consequently, the patterns of land tenure and ownership, class relations and village organization in the Mekong delta developed in direct response to colonial rule and the politico-economic influences of the capitalist world economy rather than through extensive contact with traditional indigenous social and economic organization. In the Mekong delta, the spread of commodity exchange and circulation, the growth of the home market, and the dissolution of the elements of the non-capitalist mode of production evolved at a relatively rapid pace.   (Murray 1980:8–9)

In the long run, Murray suggests, "these 'blockages' [in northern and central Vietnam] to the homogeneous spread and deepening of the extended reproduction of capital coincided with economic stagnation, declining productivity, and the vicious cycle of rural poverty associated with the 'underdeveloped' regions of the globe" (Murray 1980:x; cf. Geertz 1963).

The insights provided by the Wallersteinian theoretical framework regarding the macrostructure of the world system notwithstanding, I would suggest that although class constitutes an important element in the examination of colonial policies, the native sociocultural framework also plays an important role in shaping the encounter between capitalist imperialism and the indigenous system. The dynamics of the Vietnamese revolution cannot be seen merely in terms of local class struggle (cf. Paige 1975). Neither can the remarkable persistence of the noncapitalist sector in northern and central Vietnam be analyzed primarily in terms of its contribution to capital accumulation.

First of all, the active resistance to French colonialism did gain support among many members of the native elite. It can be clearly seen in the history of Vietnamese anticolonialism in Son-Duong, and it is attested to by the necessity of the special category "resistance-supporting landlord" in the land reform campaign in the north after independence (cf. Murray 1980:36–37; Ngo-Vinh-Long 1978b). The active support of these members of the indigenous elite for anticolonial movements cannot be mechanically explained in terms of the struggle by the working classes of the periphery against the capitalists of the core. As discussed in the preceding chapters, the nationalist aspirations among many members of the native intelligentsia were rooted partly in the contradiction between the racial inequality of colonial Vietnam and the metropolitan discourse of "liberty, equality, and fraternity" and partly in the divergence between local tradition and capitalist imperialism. The sharp contrast between the meaningful structure of the colonial racial diarchy and the official metropolitan discourse is highlighted in the French-educated novelist Nhat-Linh's account of his journey from Vietnam to France, quoted in chapter 2:

> The farther the ship got from Vietnam and the closer it got to France, to the same degree the more decently the people aboard the ship treated me. In the China Sea they did not care to look at me. By the Gulf of Siam they were looking at me with scornful apprehension, the way they would look at a mosquito carrying malaria germs to Europe. When we entered the Indian Ocean, their eyes began to become infected with expressions of gentleness and compassion . . . and when we crossed the Mediterranean, suddenly they viewed me as being civilized like themselves, and began to entertain ideas of respecting me. At that time I was very elated. But I still worried about the time when I was going to return home!   (translated in Woodside 1976:4)

The liberty to which the colonial masters claimed to uplift the indigenous masses did not stand up to close scrutiny, as indicated by the expulsion of Vietnamese students (including naturalized French citizens) in the spring of 1930 simply for having demonstrated in Paris against the French execution of participants in the Yen-Bay movement (see chapter 3). In Vietnam, in combination with the symbols of anticolonialism nurtured from earlier waves of resistance and the indigenous belief in racial or ethnic competition and survival, the contradictions within the colonial system viewed through native lenses led a minority of the young intelligentsia to engage in acts of active resistance for the cause of national independence. The organizational efforts of many of the children of the traditional elite provided a crucial link among the rural communities. As seen in the massive 1944–1945 Tonkin famine, the discontent among indigenous masses was seldom transformed into a major movement without a leadership that could effectively mobilize the masses (see also Luong 1985:170; cf. Scott 1976: chs. 5 and 7). As the historian Woodside remarks:

> It does not slander the political contributions of one of the most hardworking and resourceful peasantries in all Asia to point out . . . that the Vietnamese revolution was led for the most part by the sons of the traditional intelligentsia, and that this was the section of Vietnamese society which found itself earlier and most often in demeaning circumstances of cultural and political conflict with the colonial power. The peasantry were also exploited by the colonial power, and cherished extensive memories of a national tradition of resistance to outside aggression. *But peasants did not have to make enormous immediate cultural concessions* to the French colonialists in order to survive. (Woodside 1976:303; emphasis added)

If nationalist appeals propelled many children of the traditional elite (including Ho Chi Minh) toward a path of political activism, their conflict with the French masters hardened many of them and launched them on a leftward political trajectory. Underground and prison experiences under the colonial yoke shattered the elitism among many nonleftist activists, beginning a process of transformation toward socialism as seen in the political trajectory of the exiled Son-Duong native Nguyen Dac Bang. Bang's case was not an isolated incident, although this process of transformation was not universal. As remarked in a contemporary Vietnamese source, "In the specific conditions of our country, the ideological and political trajectory of the majority of [Communist Party] members involved a move from nationalism to class awareness, or the inextricable relation between the two" (Hoang-Uoc 1968:194).

The regional variations in revolutionary strength and socioeconomic conditions in Vietnam present the Marxist models with a second major anomaly. In colonial Vietnam the peasantry was most heavily dispossessed of the means of production in Cochinchina (South Vietnam), where approximately two-thirds of the rural population was landless. However, Paige's model notwithstanding, from the mid-nineteenth century to 1975, the armed resistance to French colonialism and capitalism was *generally* more limited in the south than in the north and the center. With the sole exception of the 1940 armed insurrection in certain areas of Cochinchina (Nguyen-Cong-Binh et al. 1985:318–319; cf. Paige 1975:323–324), at no point did the anticolonial armed movement in the south exceed or even approach the intensity of the unrest in the center and the north. In the pre–World War II period, it was in Annam (central Vietnam) that the 1930–1931 unrest posed the greatest threat to the colonial order (see Luong 1985; Brocheux 1977; and Ngo-Vinh-Long 1978a). During the first Indochinese war (1946–1954), the French encountered considerably greater resistance in Annam and Tonkin.[1] During the period of direct and massive U.S. intervention (1964–1975), it was not in the former Cochinchina but in the southern part of central Vietnam that the National Liberation Front developed its strongest roots (Mitchell 1968). This pattern of regional variation constitutes a striking anomaly to Paige's model, which predicts the greatest socialist revolutionary potential in Cochinchina (with noncultivators deriving their incomes from the land and a large class of cultivators dependent on wages and sharecropping arrangements). In the face of this empirical anomaly, Paige suggests that the more mountainous terrain of north and central Vietnam provides a more favorable condition for guerilla warfare strategy. Paige also argues that north and central Vietnam are closer to supply base areas (China during the Franco-Vietminh conflict and North Vietnam during the U.S. war) (Paige 1976:326–332). Although the geographical factor is certainly not insignificant, it is not as important as Paige suggests. Even if Paige's geographical explanation were adequate, his model would still encounter another major anomaly: the considerably slower pace of socialist agricultural development in southern Vietnam after the end of the U.S. war. By 1980, 83 percent of households in the coastal plains of southern central Vietnam had joined labor exchange teams and agricultural cooperatives that involved 76 percent of the cultivable acreage. In contrast, the percentages in south Vietnam reached only 31 percent and 24 percent, respectively (Nguyen-Huy 1983:113; cf. Ngo-Vinh-Long

1988:165). It is a historical fact that north and central Vietnam, despite the lesser degree of class polarization, constituted the areas with both stronger resistance to Western intervention and greater socialist revolutionary potential.

I hypothesize that the precapitalist tradition of north and central Vietnam provided stronger ideological and organizational resources for the active resistance to French colonialism in particular and to capitalist imperialism in general. Despite a considerable internal tension between class-structured hierarchy and communal collectivism, this tradition nurtured values conducive to the growth of nationalism, to collectivism in a relatively mild form, and to a hierarchical organizational framework. This tradition differs fundamentally from capitalism, which, as defined by Wallerstein, is oriented toward "the maximization of surplus creation" (1979:285).

On one level, the indigenous precapitalist framework was characterized by both class cleavages, and a male-oriented and kinship-centered hierarchy. These features were reinforced, respectively, through linguistic socialization within familial contexts and by the rigid Confucian distinction between mental and manual labor in society at large. Within the family, children were (and continue to be) socialized at an early age into discursive practices that rendered salient the authoritarian structure of the kinship unit, the distinction between patrilineal and nonpatrilineal kin, and the male-centered hierarchy. For example, even in late adulthood a person must continue to use *con* (child) for self-reference in speech interaction with his or her parents. Such a linguistic usage highlights the hierarchical nature of the interaction. In the village of Son-Duong, as part of the androcentric principles of descent, the term *chu* (paternal uncle) is used in reference only to the father's *paternal* junior uncle's sons (patrilineal relatives) and not to the father's *maternal* junior uncle's sons (nonpatrilineal kin, called *cau*). In the pre-twentieth-century sociocultural system in which the mastery of Confucian literature was the main route to power, it is no coincidence that the most popular male middle name, van, means literature. The exclusive use of van for males reinforced the legitimacy of male power in the political structure of the larger society (see Luong 1990:92–93).

Beyond familial contexts, as related by the Son-Duong villager Bang, educated men could not engage in manual labor without incurring social stigma. In the village of Son-Duong, the class distinction was further accentuated by the pervasive commoditization of status as part of the colonial encounter—a process that exempted the exclusively male purchasers of honorary titles from corvée for their lifetimes. Villagers paid utmost attention to one another's class standing in establishing marital alliances. The class-based and male-oriented hierarchical order was rendered salient both in the seating order at communal house ceremonies and in daily speech interaction, in which ranking villagers and their spouses had to be constantly addressed with their formal titles (e.g., Mr. Mayor, Mrs. Canton Chief) (see also Luong 1988). I suggest that the hierarchical structure of the local tradition, maintained partly through the socialization process, accounts for numerous features in Vietnamese anticolonialism and the Vietnamese revolution: the male-centered elitism in the VNP recruitment and organizational methods, the Vietminh's reliance on male members of the intelligentsia for local leadership in the early period of anti-French resistance, and the male dominance in both domestic and public relations in postcolonial Son-Duong.

On another level, the growth of nationalism and a collectivistic vision of political economy are facilitated by important communal institutions and corresponding conceptual categories in the local tradition of the north and the center. Northern and central villages maintained sharp boundaries through villagers' participation in the collective worship of tutelary deities, an extraordinary degree of village endogamy, the institution of communal land, and their nucleated settlement pattern. In Son-Duong it is no coincidence that in villagers' consciousness both of its tutelary deities had played important roles in defending the country against foreign invaders. In terms of community structure, the rate of intracommunity marriages frequently exceeded 80 percent for colonial northern villages (Nguyen-Xuan-Nguyen 1942; Luong 1990:52–53), whereas community exogamy was preferred in the south (Hickey 1964:100). In Tonkin and Annam the percentages of communal land in total cultivated acreage remained 21 percent and 25 percent, respectively, well into the colonial period, compared to 3 percent for Cochinchina (Ngo-Vinh-Long 1973:15–16). Correspondingly, in each northern and central rural community, "insiders" and "outsiders" among village residents (referred to as *noi tich* and *ngoai tich*) were sharply distinguished. It might take three to four generations for the descendants of outsiders (i.e., those not born in the community) to gain the full membership status of *noi tich*, especially where communal land was sufficiently abundant to be redistributed periodically among all the adult male insiders. The categories of *noi tich* and *ngoai tich* constituted part of the general and sharp distinction between the members and nonmembers of a social unit, be it kinship, communal, ethnic, or racial. In contrast, group boundaries were considerably less rigid in southern Vietnamese communities, where settlements were nonnucleated and where significant geographical mobility existed in the frontier environment (see Rambo 1973: ch. 2). The sharp conceptual distinction between members and nonmembers in Tonkin and Annam underlies the northern and central tradition of great formality in interaction with outsiders. In the face of outside forces, it also fostered a sense of unity and collectivism among members of the same category.

Both within and beyond the indigenous communal context, the tension between interclass solidarity and class differentiation in the precapitalist framework was mediated on the one hand by the Confucian high valuation of moral cultivation at the expense of wealth accumulation and mercantile activities and on the other by the norm of noblesse oblige for educated men in their relations with other social strata. The latter was manifested in the precolonial practice of tax reduction for cultivators in times of natural calamity (Ngo-Vinh-Long 1973:33–34; Scott 1976:54). In other words, the tension between class differentiation and interclass unity was partly mediated, in James Scott's terminology, by a subsistence ethic constitutive of the indigenous precapitalist order (Scott 1976). In Vietnam this precapitalist ideology was considerably stronger in the earlier-settled north and center than in the frontier south. It stood in sharp contrast to the rigid and onerous fiscal policy of the colonial state, which contributed heavily to the process of capital accumulation at the expense of the dominated native classes. Not only did higher taxes and state monopolies significantly increase the tax burden on the indigenous population; in a departure from the precolonial practice and in direct violation of the subsistence ethic, the colonial state offered no tax deferral or reduction in times of natural disaster (Scott 1976: ch. 4).

The precapitalist tradition of northern and central Vietnam has proved a fertile ground for the growth of both nationalism and a mild collectivism, on the one hand, and for anticolonial resistance, on the other. Through a sharp distinction between insiders and outsiders in the native conceptualization of kinship, communality, ethnicity, and nationality, the northern and central tradition has intensified the negative reaction of many Vietnamese to any foreign intrusion on the indigenous landscape and to the French domination in the colonial racial diarchy. Modern Vietnamese anticolonial movements capitalized heavily on this salient conceptual dichotomy of Vietnamese and non-Vietnamese races as well as on the symbols of active native resistance to foreign intruders in previous centuries. In northern and central Vietnam, the relatively strong institution of communal land in particular and the subsistence ethic of the precolonial period in general heightened many native actors' sense of colonial and capitalist exploitation. They nurtured a collectivist vision of political economy among many VNP members in the 1920s well before their exposure to Marxism. The existence of communal lands and the subsistence ethic also facilitated the process of land collectivization in northern and central villages, in comparison to its slow progress in the south since 1975. Even during the difficult 1978–1981 period for the collectivistic economy in Son-Duong, villagers resisted a radical collectivism at the expense of their community and households but not the concept of collective land ownership per se. Finally, within the bamboo hedges of the corporate rural community, extensive kinship and communal ties have facilitated the mobilization of resources by local revolutionary leaders, especially the generally well-regarded members of the native intelligentsia.

In the modern history of Vietnamese anticolonialism two sets of factors have led to the triumph of the Marxist-led movement against major Western powers. On the surface, the conflict among the states within the capitalist core during the course of World War II facilitated the Marxists' rise to power (cf. Skocpol 1979: ch. 2). The vulnerability of the French was first exposed with the advance of Japanese forces into Indochina in September 1940 and then laid bare with the French colonial government's subsequent collaboration with Japanese military authorities and the Japanese termination of French administrative powers in March 1945. On a deeper level, the Marxist-led anti-imperialist movement succeeded both through the Vietminh's effective combination of nationalism and equality-oriented socioeconomic reforms and their skillful selective use of the indigenous precapitalist tradition. In the process of revolutionary mobilization, Vietnamese Marxist leaders drew upon the symbols, discursive practices, and values of the indigenous precapitalist tradition that had been nurtured within the corporate rural communities of the north and the center. Ho Chi Minh's Declaration of Independence on September 2, 1945, for example, appealed strongly to the indigenous conceptions of national unity and a subsistence ethic that French capitalism had severely strained. In chastising the French for their historic failure in their role as a protector, Ho's declaration also drew upon the notion of a change in the Mandate of Heaven (see also Mus 1952). In their organizational efforts in the village of Son-Duong, the Vietminh often chose teachers as transitional district and village administrators, drawing upon the dominance of the distinction between mental and manual labor and the general command of authority by members of the intelligentsia in the precapitalist framework. The Chinese-influenced and indigenous noncapitalist tradition thus cannot be ignored in any analysis of the Vietnamese encounter with French colonialism and the capitalist world system in general (see Marr 1971:97; Luong 1985; Boudarel 1984).

In the final analysis, the Vietnamese revolution involved a dynamic interplay between local tradition and capitalist imperialism in the colonial context. In the encounter between the two systems, the persistence of the noncapitalist labor reserves in north and central Vietnam did not merely contribute to capitalist accumulation (cf. Murray 1980; Mellaissoux 1981). It also provided ideological and organizational support for the anticolonial resistance (cf. Smith 1984 and Nash 1979: 330). In the long run, the encounter between the Vietnamese tradition, on the one hand, and Western colonialism and capitalist imperialism, on the other, both adversely affected capitalist accumulation and ushered in a new era in the indigenous social formation.

# NOTES

## Introduction

1. The shrine to the Hung kings is only fourteen kilometers from Son-Duong. The names of many villages near the present provincial capital Viet-Tri reflect the location of the capital of the Hung dynasty in this part of northern Vietnam: Van-Doi and Cam-Doi were army barracks (*doi* means "soldiers"), Minh-Nong and Phu-Nong were agricultural stations (*nong* means "agriculture"), and Lau-Ha and Lau-Thuong were palaces for the king's concubines (*lau* means "palace") (Pham-Xuan-Do 1939:9–10). The capital of Vietnam moved farther south and east, reaching its present location, Hanoi, by the eleventh century as the Vietnamese gradually built up an extensive dike and irrigation system in the lower Red River delta.

2. The village population figure does not include a small number of school teachers from other communities or industrial workers affiliated with the Lam-Thao phosphate factory residing in the village.

3. The figure of 300 *mau* represents my own estimate. It is based partly on the actual ownership of 230 *mau* by twelve households that were still classified as landlord and rich peasant households after the rectification in 1956 of earlier land reform errors. The reclassified households had some of their previously appropriated properties returned.

4. In the past decade Vietnamese Marxist theoreticians have increasingly used the phrase *thoi ky qua do* (period of transition [toward socialism]) to refer to the current period of the Vietnamese social formation—a period that, in their conception, will last into the foreseeable future. The phrase highlights a departure from the earlier, decade-long emphasis on an accelerated process of socialist construction. Its frequent usage is linked to the wide-ranging eco-

nomic reforms away from tight central planning, and to the more open intellectual atmosphere that has emerged since 1981. This terminology and the reforms notwithstanding, the northern Vietnamese social formation since 1954 is still dominated by socialism in that the means of production are largely collectivized, and the achievement of socialism remains the ultimate official goal of the state. In this book the term "socialist" is used as an abbreviation for "socialism-oriented" for the period since 1954 in northern Vietnam.

5. Hickey's (1964) *Village in Vietnam* is a landmark ethnographic study of a village in the Mekong delta of South Vietnam in the late 1950s. Houtart and Lemercinier's (1981) *La sociologie d'une commune vietnamienne* provides valuable statistical data on a Catholic village in the Red River delta of northern Vietnam in 1979. Pham-Cuong and Nguyen-van-Ba's (1976) *Revolution in the Village* focuses on the socioeconomic structure of a northern village in the socialist era, and Trullinger's (1981) *Village at War* is a historical examination of the sociopolitical processes in a central Vietnamese village through the Franco-Vietminh conflict (1946–1954) and especially the American war (to 1975).

6. Dr. Vu Huy Phuc of the Vietnam Institute of History has suggested that Vietnamese Marxists do not emphasize class conflict in their analysis of the nationalist democratic revolution (against the French), which lasted until 1954. However, in the Leninist thesis on colonialism, nationalist revolution in a colonial context constitutes an integral part of the struggle against world capitalism.

7. Wallerstein emphasizes the vital importance of semiperipheral states in the functioning of the capitalist world system. In Wallerstein's conceptual framework, semiperipheral states such as Brazil stand between the core and the periphery in terms of economic power. In the case of rapidly rising labor costs in the core, the semiperiphery serves as an alternative zone for capitalist investment. It also weakens the opposition coming from social formations outside the core of the capitalist world system since semiperipheral formations such as Japan may emerge as core states (Wallerstein 1979:29ff.).

8. However, for Emerson, democracy in the new nation-states tends to be fragile. First, despite the dominance of nationalism, such nations are far from consolidated. Internal crises often lead to centralization of power. Second, these new nations tend to lack the preconditions for the success of democracy, which, for Emerson, include "mass literacy, relatively high living standards, a sizable and stable middle class, a sense of social equality, and a tradition both of tolerance and of individual self-reliance." (Emerson 1962:277–278)

9. To Sahlins, historically situated acts function as signs, thus existing in a dual mode of valuation: in a relation of opposition to other signs within an

integrated indigenous conceptual system and in a relation of indexicality within individual social actors' varied instrumental schemes of practice (see Sahlins 1981:68; cf. Barth 1966).

## Chapter 1

1. In its reports to the Ministry of Colonies in Paris, the Indochinese colonial government initially attributed certain VNP-organized incidents of unrest to communist involvement (cables 260 and 273 to the Ministry of Colonies, respectively on February 11, and February 13, 1930, AOM-P-NF, 322-2614). Thirty years later some analysts, including the French minister of colonies at the time of the VNP-organized revolt, still linked the Yen-Bay incident to the communist movement (Pietri 1960:278–281).

2. There have been numerous studies in both Vietnam and the West on the ICP-led movement of 1930–1931. Among recent Western-language sources, see Luong 1985; Brocheux 1977; and Ngo-Vinh-Long 1978a.

3. Nguyen Khac Nhu was referred by the title *xu*, because he ranked first in a provincial screening test for the Confucian regional examination.

4. The final French report estimated the size of the Phu-Tho contingent at fifty to sixty on the basis of the number of fourth-class tickets sold on February 9 for the Phu-Tho–Yen-Bay trip (Wintrebert report, p. 11, AOM-P-NF, 323-2626). A VNP participant and the French Résident in Yen-Bay at the time reported approximately two hundred party members and sympathizers from Phu-Tho (Nguyen-Hai-Ham 1970; Report of Résident Massimi, AOM-P-NF, 323-2626).

5. The provision of information to the French by a ranking VNP informer, Pham Thanh Duong, dealt a severe blow to the VNP insurrection plan on the eve of the uprising. For example, in early November 1929, Duong fully reported to the French military intelligence on his November 1, 1929, strategy meeting with Hoc, the party president, in a well-guarded locality in Bac-Ninh province. At this meeting Hoc reportedly asked for the map of the Bach-Mai airfield barracks and delegated to Duong the task of recruitment for the planned attack there. Hoc reportedly revealed that other centers such as Nam-Dinh, Bac-Ninh, Hai-Phong, Lang-Son, and Mong-Cay were ready, while Hanoi was not. He promised to provide Duong with three to six hundred civilians for the Bach-Mai airfield attack as well as with arms and food for this civilian contingent. He showed Duong the method of manufacturing bombs and indicated that forty could be produced every day. In a meeting of the party general assembly in the same village two days later, Hoc discussed his plan to hold on to the attacked localities for five or six days in order to await the arrival of the VNP émigré armed forces from China. Hoc reportedly emphasized the need to recruit veterans of the colonial forces as well as

the necessity to launch the attack simultaneously in Annam and Cochinchina. At the next meeting on November 24, 1929, in the La-Hao area of Phu-Tho, a provisional government was reportedly formed with the concurrence of representatives from thirteen provinces. Hoc was elected president; Xu Nhu, vice-president; Pho Duc Chinh, interior affairs minister; Duong, military affairs minister; and the mayor of neighboring Vong-La village (Phu-Tho), finance minister (AOM-AP-I, 7F-57).

6. Insurrection plans were compromised in the provinces of Bac-Giang, Bac-Ninh, Ha-Dong, Kien-An, Hai-Duong, and Vinh-Yen (AOM-P-NF, 323-2626). After the outbreak of the movement in Yen-Bay, the colonial authorities also arrested suspects in the provinces of Hai-Duong and Bac-Ninh, including VNP collaborators in the colonial armed forces.

7. In Yen-Bay the collaboration between military and civilian authorities did not occur because the military commander considered the base and military personnel quarters off-limit to the civilian police. The relation between military and civilian authorities in Yen-Bay was also complicated by the civilian résident's background as a former officer with lower rank than the military commander (Robin report 1930, 37–39, AOM-P-NF, 323-2626).

8. The four other districts were Quang-Oai, Quoc-Oai, Bat-Bat, and Vinh-Tuong (Dang-Huy-Van 1967:49).

9. The catalyst for the event was the list of demands by the French general de Courcy to the Hue court, which the Vietnamese considered both contemptuous and provocative. For example, de Courcy insisted that not only he but also his troops enter the royal palace through the central door, which constituted a royal prerogative (Truong-Buu-Lam 1967:43–44).

10. Hoang-Ke-Viem, the former governor general of Hung-Hoa, Son-Tay, and Tuyen-Quang, was appointed troop commander (Kieu-Huu-Hy et al. 1961:10). However, he played little role in the anticolonial movement from this point onward.

11. Other major centers of resistance in northern Vietnam were situated in the provinces of Hung-Yen, Hai-Duong, and Bac-Ninh (see Marr 1971:71ff.) An excellent general analysis of Vietnamese anticolonialism in this period is provided in chapter 3 of Marr 1971.

12. The dates in brackets represent the dates of the original administrative formation. The dates of provincial reformation are in parentheses.

13. After the establishment of pax colonia, land temporarily abandoned because of warfare or flooding was granted in large plots to colonial enterprises. The commercial firm Bourgoin Meiffre, for example, was reportedly granted 8500 hectares seized from fifty-seven villages in three provinces along the Black River. The Saint Frères Company took over 523 hectares from indigenous cultivators in Doan-Hung district (Le-Tuong and Vu-Kim-Bien

1981:130). In the pre–World War I period little capital was invested in these colonial agricultural ventures.

14. In Lam-Thao the group had its strongest base in the villages of Xuan-Lung (Bang's maternal ancestral village) and Tien-Kien (approximately nine kilometers from Son-Duong) (Le-Tuong and Vu-Kim-Bien 1981:145).

### Chapter 2

1. Of the 8826 villages in the northern delta and midlands in the late 1920s, 29.12 percent had populations less than 300 (5.17 percent had fewer than 100 inhabitants). Only 24.41 percent of the villages had populations greater than 1000 (Bui-Thiet 1985:32).

2. The French-created lineage representative council replaced a council of notables *(hoi dong ky muc)* whose membership was based not on the principle of patrilineage representation but on past and present administrative services at the deputy mayor rank or above, equivalent honorary ranking, and academic achievements. Because of the old notables' discontent with the 1921 reform, the French resurrected the council of notables in 1927. Important decisions made by the lineage representative council were then subject to veto by the *hoi dong ky muc* (Toan-Anh 1969:89; Son-Duong 1987:7; Gourou 1936:266; Tran-Tu 1984:64).

3. Son-Duong, Dung-Hien, and Thuy-Son had already formed three separate villages according to the national list compiled around 1810 (Duong-thi-The and Pham-thi-Thoa 1981). However, my village sources insisted that Dung-Hien and Thuy-Son did not secede until the 1830s (Son-Duong 1987:5).

4. Son-Duong villagers identified General Quy Minh as the god of Tan-Vien Mountain on the other side of the Red River. The worship of General Quy Minh in Son-Duong started well before the colonial period. A local historian reported that in the 1830s, in preparing a royal decree recognizing the tutelary deities of Son-Minh village, Vietnamese court officials discovered one overlapping element in the village name and its deity's name. The overlap violated a Vietnamese naming taboo that prohibited the use of a superior party's name. The name of the village had to be changed from Son-Minh to Son-Duong.

5. After repelling the Mongols, the Tran court decreed that eighteen villages in the surrounding area worship General Lan Ho on the anniversary of his death (Ngo-Quang-Nam and Ta-Huy-Duc 1986:191).

6. At the time of my field research elderly villagers still remembered the location of the former literary shrine at what was then the village clinic. The shrine had reportedly been larger when Son-Duong was the administrative seat for Son-Vi district in the early nineteenth century.

7. The official records of Confucian doctorate degree holders in the nineteenth and early twentieth centuries (Cao-Xuan-Duc 1974) do not list any person from Nguyen Dac Bang's maternal grandfather's native village or from Bang and the grandfather's district.

8. No information is available on the settlement pattern of the third wife and her son.

9. The commoditization of status had certain precedents in Vietnamese history. In the nineteenth century donors to public causes were either granted honorary mandarin titles or exempted from taxes for a number of years (Nguyen-The-Anh 1971:141–142; Tran-Trong-Kim 1964:477–478).

10. The Tan-Viet was formed by a group of modern-educated young men (Ton Quang Phiet, Tran Mong Bach, Ngo Duc Dien) and Confucian scholars released from imprisonment for their political activism in the 1908–1912 period (Le Huan). The name Tan Viet Cach Mang Dang was adopted only in 1928 after a quick succession of names: Hung Nam and Phuc Viet, both meaning Restoration of Vietnam; Viet Nam Cach Mang Dang (Vietnam Revolutionary Party); and Viet Nam Cach Mang Dong Chi Hoi (Vietnam Revolutionary League) (GGI-DAP 1.1, 11, 15, 23, 41).

11. The other twelve party cells were concentrated in the large urban centers of northern and southern Vietnam (GGI-DAP 1.33–34).

12. In its platform the Vietnamese Nationalist Party also referred obliquely to the postcolonial construction of a democratic socialist system (GGI-DAP 2.7).

13. The main exception involved female party members who had been given full memberships in the Confucian scholar Nhu's group in Bac-Giang and who were consequently admitted as full-standing VNP members at the time of the merger.

14. According to a founder of the Vietnamese Nationalist Party, negotiations foundered when the New Vietnam Revolutionary Party objected to what it considered loosely organized activities of the VNP. The VNP in turn objected to maintaining revolutionary headquarters overseas, which the Vietnamese Revolutionary Youth League insisted upon, citing the minimal risk of French repression to the top revolutionary leadership (Hoang-Pham-Tran 1949:39–43).

15. The accounts by ranking VNP members differed regarding whether the assassination was sanctioned by the top party leadership or independently conducted by local party members despite Hoc's veto (Hoang-Pham-Tran 1949:57–59; Hoang-van-Dao 1970:54–58).

### Chapter 3

1. In the first Yen-Bay trial on February 27, 1930, fifteen defendants were convicted, thirteen of whom were sentenced to death. Four of these death-

row inmates were beheaded on March 8, 1930 (Hoang-van-Dao 1970:155–156).

2. The golden stream is a Sino-Vietnamese allusion to the world of the deceased.

3. In 1942 the partnership came to an end when Gia's partner killed the district chief of Cam-Khe. Gia returned to Son-Duong as a cultivator.

### Chapter 4

1. By August 1945 the Vietminh had seized all Vietnamese provinces except for four provinces in the north: Vinh-Yen, Ha-Giang, Lao-Kay, and Lai-Chau (listed in Huynh-Kim-Khanh 1982:326).

2. The Indochinese Communist Party began its activities in this region first in Vinh-Yen, where the ICP predecessor, the Vietnamese Revolutionary Youth League, had organized a progressive youth organization as early as 1928 (Cao-Tien-Phung et al. 1985:34). In Phu-Tho, from the first cell in Cat-Tru (Cam-Khe district) formed in 1939, party membership expanded to three other localities (the paper factory in Viet-Tri, Phu-Ho plantation in Lam-Thao district, and Thai-Ninh village in Thanh-Ba) and increased to approximately a dozen cells by 1940. A provincial committee was formed in Phu-Tho in the same year (ibid.:57).

3. As early as 1930 in Vinh-Yen and Phuc-Yen provinces (which later merged with Phu-Tho into Vinh-Phu), a small number of party members had organized prospective political recruits into both ostensibly nonpolitical groups (e.g., groups devoted to sports, music, women, literacy, mutual aid, wood gathering, and transplanting and harvesting) and explicitly political associations (e.g., Communist Youth and Democratic Youth) (Le-Tuong and Vu-Kim-Bien 1981:153–158; Cao-Tien-Phung et al. 1985:37–45). The former groupings served as a channel for the recruitment of political activists and the diffusion of party ideology. The nature and activities of the latter organizations varied with the tactical shifts in ICP policy during the 1930–1945 period, ranging from class conflict (1930–1936), to "bourgeois democratic" reforms within the colonial framework (1936–1939), to nationalist and anti-imperialist struggle (1939–1945). For example, when the party emphasized class conflict within both national and global contexts, the ICP-organized Red Peasant, Communist Youth, Red Student, and Women's Liberation associations in Vinh-Phuc-Yen provinces mobilized the populace to concentrate on peasants' and workers' concrete needs against the dominating classes. They charged notables with corruption and demanded rent deferrals, reductions, or an end to rent increases; protested physical abuse and demanded higher wages for workers; and hung anti-French and pro-Soviet banners and distributed leaflets denouncing the brutal repression of workers and peasants in the Nghe-Tinh soviet movement by the French (Le-Tuong and Vu-Kim-

Bien 1981:154–155; Cao-Tien-Phung et al. 1985:38, 43, 44). With the emergence of the Popular Front government in France and the release of a number of political prisoners in Indochina in 1936, the party switched its activities from class conflict and anticolonial struggle to "bourgeois" democratic reforms, i.e., pardons for political prisoners and assistance to released prisoners; freedom of speech, association, organization, and movement; abolition and reduction of taxes (e.g., the market tax and license fees); and ending the corruption of notables, ostentatious ceremonies and expensive festivals (Le-Tuong and Vu-Kim-Bien 1981:156–158; Cao-Tien-Phung et al. 1985:45–52). In the province of Phu-Tho, Democratic Youth members from Hanoi also canvassed the electorate to elect a progressive candidate to the Tonkin Chamber of Representatives (Cao-Tien-Phung et al. 1985:52).

4. In the period from September 1940 to March 1945 the Japanese occupied Indochina militarily. The French colonial administrative apparatus was left in place but subject to Japanese command.

5. See Huynh-Kim-Khanh 1982:299 and Ngo-Vinh-Long 1973:131–132 for a discussion of the economic effects of the Japanese military occupation on the Vietnamese rural population.

6. Another source reports that six Son-Duong villagers were arrested on that day and that the thirteen arrested Son-Duong and Kinh-Ke villagers included three Vietminh sympathizers (Le-van-Thu 1973:166). It is possible that the official Communist Party history of the Communist revolution in Son-Duong (Son-Duong 1987) does not take into account the arrest of three Vietminh sympathizers by the French.

7. During the tax season of 1944 administrative guards from Lam-Thao district struck a villager, instead of the village deputy mayor, for the delay in tax submission. Kinh-Ke villagers beat up the guards and managed not to pay taxes that year through extensive arguments with a low-ranking district official (Le-van-Thu 1973:168).

8. After the Japanese-organized coup on March 9, 1945, the Japanese reportedly assisted such anticommunist parties as the Dai Viet Nationalist Party to organize in Phu-Tho and neighboring provinces. They also set up youth associations as one organizational base for anti-Vietminh activities.

9. From 1943 to early 1945, at the instruction of the ICP Central Committee and on the basis of the organizational infrastructure from the 1940–1941 anti-imperialist youth movement, party cadres had built up an important base in this hilly area near the neighboring province of Yen-Bay. They reportedly relied on influential local notables and their own networks to provide protective cover for sixty fugitive party members passing through the area at various points and for other party activities (Cao-van-Luong 1960:144). Such Vietminh organizations as notables' and mandarins' national salvation associ-

ations were set up in the area. A platoon of guerillas armed with modern weapons was subsequently formed in early 1945.

10. The three Thanh-Thuy units came from the villages of La-Hao, Vong-La, and Thuong-Thi, the first two of which, interestingly, also constituted the earliest VNP bases in Phu-Tho in the pre-1930 phase of the VNP. The four other Lam-Thao units came from the villages of Cao-Mai, Ban-Nguyen, Chu-Hoa, and Tien-Kien (Le-van-Thu 1973:172).

11. With the cooperation of the provincial security unit, the Vietminh leadership in Phu-Tho first made a plan to seize arms, money, and medical supplies for the guerilla bases on the other side of the Red River (in Thanh-Son and Yen-Lap). However, the plan did not materialize, because on the day of the uprising, most Vietminh sympathizers among the security force leaders were assigned to duties outside the provincial capital. An alternative plan by the provincial party leadership was also caught up in the chain of quickly unfolding events, beginning with the Japanese surrender in mid-August 1945 (Cao-van-Luong 1960:154–157).

12. Other demands included the transfer of Japanese-confiscated arms from the provincial security unit and the withdrawal of Japanese troops from the province of Phu-Tho, which had served as a gathering point for Japanese troops withdrawn from the neighboring Yen-Bay and Tuyen-Quang. The Japanese agreed to the immediate transfer of power, promised to return the five hundred guns removed from provincial security forces and French troops, and then withdrew to their own barracks to wait for orders from higher authorities on the disarmament question.

13. On August 23, 1945, an armed conflict broke out when a Vietminh patrol was fired upon when stopping a convoy of Japanese arms and troops from the neighboring province of Tuyen-Quang. With emphasis on political and diplomatic struggle, the Vietminh leadership organized a big demonstration in the provincial capital. Mandarins in the Japanese-supported administration, serving as mediators at the time between the Japanese and the Vietminh, were invited to the demonstration only to encounter protests against the mandarinate and the monarchy (Cao-van-Luong 1960:160–161). Unlike in neighboring Vinh-Yen and Phuc-Yen, however, armed conflict did not break out between Vietminh forces and the competing pro-Japanese Dai Viet and the pro-Chinese Vietnamese Nationalist Party. After the unification of provincial Vietminh forces under one command and two more days of tense negotiation, the mandarins in the pro-Japanese government officially transferred power to the Vietminh front on August 25 (Cao-van-Luong 1960: 158–162).

14. Stationed above the sixteenth parallel, between October 1945 and April 1946, Chinese troops reportedly *averaged* 125,000 (McAlister 1971:209).

15. A ranking VNP member reported that in Phu-Tho the VNP platoon succeeded in forcing the Vietminh garrison out of its barracks only through a ruse to gain support from the Chinese: caught in an ambush and pushed into a corner of the Vietminh barracks by Vietminh troops occupying a stockhouse, the VNP commander ordered his troops to fire into the neighboring Chinese garrison in order to provoke Chinese fire on the Vietminh barracks. The ruse succeeded, and the Vietminh stockhouse was heavily damaged by Chinese fire, forcing the Vietminh troops to retreat from their own compound (Hoang-van-Dao 1970:397–398). This source did not report any Chinese help in the VNP attack on Viet-Tri in December 1945.

16. In order to preserve national unity, the 1945 governmental decree of a 25 percent land rent reduction was rarely carried out. In December 1945 Ho agreed to delay elections until January 6, 1946, in order to allow for electoral participation by the opposition and, as an unusual concession, allowed it 70 nonelected seats in the 350-member National Assembly. The ten ministers in Ho's new national coalition government in March 1946 included two Vietminh members, two from the Vietminh-allied Democratic Party, two independents, two from the VNP, and two from the rightist faction under Nguyen Hai Than (Hoang-van-Dao 1970:294–299). The VNP troops, according to a short-lived agreement between Ho's government and the VNP leadership, were to be merged into the army of the Democratic Republic of Vietnam. In Phu-Tho, according to a local Communist Party source, despite the coalition agreement at both the national and provincial levels, the VNP forces still launched an attack on Vietminh troops on January 23, 1946 (Cao-Tien-Phung et al. 1985:134).

17. In exchange for this agreement the French gave up their special territorial rights in Shanghai, Hankou, and Canton, returned Kwangchouwan to China, sold the Yunnan rail line to the Chinese, granted duty exemption to Chinese goods in transit through northern Vietnam, modified the statute regarding Chinese immigrants in Vietnam, and created a tax-free zone in Haiphong, where there existed a sizable Chinese community (Hoang-van-Dao 1970:300).

18. Another village president was forced to resign over the abuse of the village's medical supplies. The reason for the third resignation is not known.

19. On March 6, 1946, facing the prospect of returning French troops, Ho Chi Minh signed an agreement with France that recognized the Democratic Republic of Vietnam (DRV) in North and Central Vietnam as a free state within a French Union and granted the native population in South Vietnam the right to merge with the DRV through referendum. In return, France could station 15,000 troops in northern Vietnam to complete the task of disarming the Japanese and to help with the maintenance of order for a limited period. As soon as it was signed, the agreement was sabotaged by the creation

of a separate Republic of Cochinchina (South Vietnam) by French colonialists in Indochina and hawkish elements in the mother country. The Fontainebleau negotiations between France and the DRV broke down in the summer of 1946 over the Cochinchina issue and the nature of the relations between the DRV and the French Union.

20. The Vietminh destroyed three gunboats in their ambushes of French boats on the Clear River.

21. The Vietminh only allowed the export of tea, turpentine, bamboo shoots, and brown tubers and the import of salt, cloth, and Western medicine. In Son-Duong a Communist Party member was demoted for exporting cattle and another expelled for selling eggs (Son-Duong 1987:35).

22. In 1948 the ICP national leadership had called for the strict enactment of limited land reforms, including the appropriation of French and Vietnamese collaborators' land, communal land redistribution, a 25 percent rent reduction and the abolition of secondary rents, as well as the encouragement of labor exchange and the formation of agricultural cooperatives (Hoang-Uoc 1968:56ff.). In many communities, landlords exerted pressures on combative tenants by demanding back the land and draft animals in order to rent them out at lower rates to more compliant peasants, and demanding the payment of old loans and threatening peasants with a suspension of credit extension (Hoang-Uoc 1968:66–67). In Son-Duong village cadres did not promptly carry out the land reform policy in 1948 out of concern that landlords would demand land back from sharecroppers (Son-Duong 1987:34).

23. Among other changes in the village of Son-Duong by the end of the first phase of the Franco-Vietminh war were the resumption of regular education up to grade three and health improvement through smallpox vaccination, a village medication cabinet, and the establishment of a maternity clinic operated by a midwife with modern training.

24. At the end of 1949 the Vietminh front was merged with the broader Lien Viet (Viet Alliance) front and was officially referred to as the Lien Viet. The Lien Viet membership in the provinces of Phu-Tho, Vinh-Yen, and Phuc-Yen increased from 200,000 in 1947 to half a million by the end of 1949 (Cao-Tien-Phung et al. 1985:160). For the sake of simplicity, I refer to the front during the 1950–1954 period as the Vietminh.

25. Five of the thirty-nine purged members were expelled specifically for adding three kilograms of paddy to every hundred kilograms of village tax obligation during the Vietminh's first land tax season in 1951. Another member had been expelled earlier for violating the Vietminh's food trade embargo on French-occupied territory. Data are not available from the local party branch to perform an analysis of how many expulsions had to do directly with members' class backgrounds.

26. Between the Chrisalide and Lorraine campaigns the French launched a

three-thousand-troop operation in Thanh-Thuy district and neighboring Son-Tay province as part of the larger campaign to take back the midland and the Muong ethnic province of Hoa-Binh. They also heavily bombarded Hac-Tri, Lam-Thao, Tam-Nong, and Thanh-Thuy districts, and dropped bombs in other areas of Phu-Tho province. Vietminh provincial troops and guerillas in Phu-Tho launched a counteroffensive to hold down and wear out French forces in the area in order to facilitate the Vietminh campaign in neighboring Hoa-Binh province (Cao-Tien-Phung et al. 1985:231–232).

## Chapter 5

1. Owing to a combination of bad weather and insect infestation, the average rice yield per *mau* dropped to 1 tonne in the spring of 1987 and 0.6 tonne for the following fall crop.

2. The secretary of the Son-Duong Communist Party branch cited the figure of 1.7 percent as the village birth rate for 1986. I arrived at the higher figure of 2.3 percent from the raw birth data that the village cadre in charge of statistics provided for 1986 and the first half of 1987. The secretary's figure, in my opinion, involved a confusion of the village birth rate with population growth rate.

3. Enrollment in the village school was 700 in 1960 and 980 in 1965. However, these figures include some junior high school students from neighboring villages. When the school was first established, it was attended by students from six other villages in the area (Son-Duong 1987:52).

4. Rural Vietnamese still calculate the number of banquet guests in terms of how many trays are served. A tray of banquet food serves six regular guests or four honored guests.

5. In September 1989 Vietnam officially withdrew its troops from Cambodia. The state reportedly demobilized half a million troops as of 1989.

6. The land reform campaign in the village of Son-Duong constituted part of the fifth rent reduction enforcement wave and the second land reform campaign in northern Vietnam. The policy of alliance with rich peasants was formulated in the light of experimental programs in 1953 (Hoang-Uoc 1968:97–108).

7. In the earlier rent reduction and land reform phases, the first category included "French-collaborating landlords." However, as the Geneva Agreements banned trials of those collaborating with the other side during the war, the focus of land reform was changed to brutal landlords who "violated criminal and civil laws" (Hoang-Uoc 1968:105).

8. A distinction was made between confiscation *(tich thu)* and appropriation *(trung thu)* in the land reform campaign in North Vietnam. Confiscation implied political punishment whereas appropriation did not. Appropriated

lands included those of non-French foreign landlords and village associations as well as any land illegitimately acquired by the church or the pagoda. Other religious lands, according to the land reform policy, would be purchased by the state for redistribution to landless, poor, and middle peasants (Hoang-Uoc 1968:162ff.).

9. In most agricultural cooperatives in the province of Vinh-Phu, households had long contracted with the cooperatives for the care of draft animals. However, they obtained only labor-day credits (*Vinh-Phu,* December 13, 1968, 2). The Dong-Xuan innovation involved the introduction of production targets and incentives to households to exceed these targets.

10. Initially adopted in certain northern agricultural cooperatives on an experimental basis in 1977, the household contract system was sanctioned by the party central committee at its sixth plenum in 1979. By 1983 this contract system had spread rapidly to the entire country, including already cooperativized southern central Vietnam and the two-hundred-plus lower-level cooperatives in the Mekong delta (*Nhan Dan,* May 30, 1983, 1; April 21, 1983, 1).

## Chapter 6

1. In Cochinchina millenarian movements such as the Cao Dai and the Hoa Hao attempted more a restoration of the status quo ante than a fundamental transformation of the Vietnamese social formation. They hardly qualify as revolutionary movements (cf. Paige 1975:325–326; Popkin 1979: ch. 5; Tai 1983).

# GLOSSARY

Ái
Ái Ân [Mrs.]
Ân [late mayor]
An-Lạc
anh

ba cùng
bác
Bắc, Nguyễn thị
Bắc-Cạn
Bắc-Giang
Bắc-Ninh
Bắc-Thái
Bạch, Trần Mộng
bạch đinh
Bạch-Mai
Bản-Nguyên
ban quản trị
Bằng, Nguyễn Đắc
Bảo-Đại
Bất-Bạt
Báu, Mã thị
Bích, Nguyễn Quang
binh điền
Bình-Xuyên

bộ đội địa phương
Bổn (Đội)
Bùi-Thiết

cách mạng
Cẩm-Đội
Cẩm-Khê
Căn, Bùi Thiện
cảnh vệ
Cao-Bằng
Cao-Đài
Cao-Mại
Cao-Tiền-Phùng
Cao-văn-Lượng
Cao-Xuân-Dục
Cát-Trù
cậu
chánh hương hội
Châu, Phan Bội
Chê, Mã thị
chèo
chi
Chi (Chánh)
chị
Chính, Phó Đức

247

chú
Chu-Hoá
Chùa Thông (Thông pagoda)
Chung-Chính
Cổ-Am
Cô-Nhi-Tân
con
Côn [canton chief]
Cứu Quốc

Dẫn
Dật, Lương văn
Di [deputy mayor]
Diên, Bùi Hữu
Diễn, Ngô Đức
Dục-Mỹ
Dụng-Hiền
Dương, Phạm Thành
Dương-thị-The
Duyên [Mrs.]

Đà (sông)
Đại-Đình
Đại-Tụ
Đại Việt
Đặng-Huy-Vận
đảng ủy
Đào [Doctor]
đầu
Đậu
Điếc (Đỗ)
Điện-Biên-Phủ
đình
Định, Lê văn
Đinh-Lục
Đinh-Thu-Cúc
Đoan-Hùng
đội
đồng chí
Đông Kinh Nghĩa Thục

Đồng-Xuân
đường Chè

Gia, Nguyễn Khắc
giáo
giáp
Giáp, Nguyễn văn
Giáp, Võ Nguyên

Hạ-Bì
Hà-Đông
Hà-Giang
Hạ-Hòa
Hà-Nam
Hà-Nội
Hạ-Nông
Hà-Tuyên
Hạc-Trì
Hải-Dương
Hải-Phòng
Hàm-Nghi
hàng Da
Hiển, Kiều
Hiền-Lương
họ
Hồ
Hồ [mayor]
họ cổ
họ gạo
họ tiền
Hòa-Bình
Hòa-Hảo
Hỏa Lò
Hoàng-Liên-Sơn
Hoàng-Phạm-Trân
Hoàng-Ước
Hoàng-văn-Đạo
Học, Nguyễn Thái
học điền
hội chư bà
hội đồng kỳ mục

hội đồng tộc biểu
hội mẹ chiến sĩ
hội phản đế
hội văn thân
Hòn-Gay
Hồng (sông)
Hồng-Lạc
Hồng-Phúc
Huân, Lê
Huề
Hùng [kings]
Hưng-Hóa
Hưng Nam
Hưng-Yên
Hữu-Bổ
Hựu [mayor]
huyền thoại khai hoá
huyền thoại Pháp Việt đề huề
Huỳnh-Kim-Khánh

khu
Kiểm [deputy mayor]
Kiến-An
Kiều (Đề)
Kiều-Hữu-Hỷ
Kim-Anh
Kính, Nguyễn Quang
Kinh-Kệ

La-Hào
Lai-Châu
Lâm-Thao
Lân Hồ
Lạng-Sơn
Lao Động
Lào-Kay
Lập, Bùi Khắc
Lập-Thạch
lâu
Lâu-Hạ
Lâu-Thượng

Lê [dynasty]
lễ hạ điền
Lê-Tượng
Lê-văn-Thụ
Liên, Nguyễn Như
Liên, Nguyễn văn
Liên Việt
Lĩnh, Bùi Kim
Lô (sông)
Lư [Mrs.]
lúa chiêm
lúa mùa
Luân, Mai thị
lý quyền
lý trưởng

Mai
Mai (Lãnh)
Mai (Lý)
Mai-Hanh
Mãng, Tôn
mẫu
mày
Minh, Hồ Chí
Minh-Nông
Mòn
Móng-Cáy
Mương
Mường

Nam-Định
Nam-Hà
Ngân [Miss]
ngày cầu
Nghệ-Tĩnh
Nghiệp, Đặng Trần
Ngô-Quang-Nam
Ngô-Vi-Liên
Ngô-Vĩnh-Long
ngoại tịch
Ngọc, Đỗ Kim [district chief]

Ngữ (Đốc)
ngũ đại đồng đường
Ngũ-Xã
Nguyễn [dynasty]
Nguyễn-Công-Bình
Nguyễn-Hải-Hàm
Nguyễn-Huy
Nguyễn-Khắc-Đạm
Nguyễn-Khắc-Viện
Nguyễn-Khắc-Xương
Nguyễn-Thế-Anh
Nguyễn-Thiệu-Lâu
Nguyễn-văn-Bá
Nguyễn-văn-Trung
Nguyễn-Xuân-Nguyên
Nhân Dân
Nhân Hòa
Nhất-Linh
Nhu, Nguyễn Khắc (Xứ)
Nhượng-Tống
Ninh-Bình
Nội-Bài
nội tịch
nông

ông

Phạm-Cường
Phạm-Gia-Đức
Phạm-thị-Thoa
Phạm-Xuân-Độ
phe
Phiệt, Tôn Quang
phó bảng
phó hương hội
phó lý tiền
Phong-Châu
Phủ-Dực
Phú-Hộ
Phú-Lạng-Thương
Phủ-Lý
Phù-Ninh

Phù-Nông
Phú-Thọ
Phúc, Lưu Vĩnh
Phúc-Khánh
Phục Việt
Phúc-Yên
Phùng-Nguyên

Quảng-Oai
Quang Phục Quân
Quảng-Yên
Quốc, Nguyễn Ái
Quốc-Anh
quốc ngữ
Quốc-Oai
Quý Minh
Quyền, Nguyễn Tôn
Quỳnh-Lâm

ruộng khẩu
ruộng lao động
ruộng tăng sản

Sảng, Trần Quốc
sào
Sĩ
Sơn-Dương
Sơn-La
Sơn-Lưu
Sơn Minh
Sơn-Tây
Sơn-Vi
Sông-Thao

Tạ-Huy-Đức
Tạ-Long
Tam-Đảo
Tam-Nông
Tam-Thanh
Tản Viên
Tân Việt Cách Mạng Đảng
Tăng, Nguyễn Doãn
tao

Tập

Tây-Sơn

Tế, Nguyễn Doãn

Thạch-Sơn

Thái-Bình

Thái-Nguyên

Thái-Ninh

Thám (Đề)

Thẩm, Nguyễn Doãn

Thần, Nguyễn Hải

Thăng-Long

Thanh (Phó)

Thành [old lady]

Thanh-Ba

Thanh-Hóa

Thanh-Hòa

Thanh-Mai

Thanh-Sơn

Thanh-Thủy

Thọ [Mrs.]

thời kỳ quá độ

Thục [teacher]

Thượng-Thị

thường vụ đảng ủy

Thúy (Đỗ)

Thụy, Nguyễn Khắc

Thụy-Sơn

tịch thu

Tiêm, Lê văn

Tiên-Kiên

Tín

Tín Quãy

Toại, Nguyễn văn (Đồ)

Toan-Ánh

Trần [dynasty]

Trần-Huy-Liệu

Trần-Trọng-Kim

Trần-Từ

Trần-Yên

Trí Tri

Trinh, Phan Chu

Trọng, Tôn

Trung-Bắc-Tân-Văn

trưng thu

Trương-Bửu-Lâm

tuần phủ

Tuyên-Quang

Ty (Chánh)

Ty, Nguyễn Doãn

Văn

Văn-Chấn

văn chỉ

Vân-Đội

Vĩ (Councillor/Hội)

Viêm, Hoàng Kê

Việt

Việt Nam Cách Mạng Đảng

Việt Nam Cách Mạng Đồng Chí Hội

Việt Nam Độc Lập Đồng Minh Hội

Việt Nam Quốc Dân Đảng

Việt Nam Thanh Niên Đồng Chí Hội

Việt-Cường

Việt-Trì

Vĩnh-Bảo

Vĩnh-Lạc

Vĩnh-Lại

Vĩnh-Phú

Vĩnh-Phúc

Vĩnh-Phúc-Yên

Vĩnh-Tường

Vĩnh-Yên

Võng-La

Vũ-Kim-Biên

Vũ-Quốc-Thúc

Vũ-văn-Tính

Vỹ, Quách

xã tiền

Xuân-Lũng

Yên-Báy

Yên-Lãng

Yên-Lập

Yên-Thế

# REFERENCES

Archives nationales, Section d'outre-mer. AOM-P-NF. Paris. Indochine–
Nouveaux fonds. Files 267, 322, 323.

————. AOM-AP-I. Aix-en-Provence. Indochine. Files 2, 7F, 9.

————. AOM-AP-RST. Aix-en-Provence. Résidence supérieure du Tonkin.
Files 27, 53.

*Avenir du Tonkin, L'.* 1930–1931.

Ballof, Daniel. 1979. "La déportation des Indochinois en Guyane et les
établissements penitentiares spéciaux, 1931–1945." *Equinoxe* 10:1–
25.

Barth, Fredrik. 1966. *Models of Social Organization.* London: Royal Anthropological Institute.

Boudarel, Georges. 1984. "Marxisme et Confucianisme." In *Les aventures du
marxisme,* edited by René Gallissot, 321–356. Paris: Syros.

Brocheux, Pierre. 1977. "L'implantation du mouvement communiste en
Indochine française: Le cas du Nghe-Tinh, 1930–1931." *Revue d'histoire moderne et contemporaine* 24:49–77.

Bui-Thiet. 1985. "Quy mo lanh tho, dan cu lang xa Bac bo dau the ky XX"
(The Populations and Territories of Northern Villages in the Early
Twentieth Century). *Tap chi Dan toc hoc* (Journal of Ethnology) 2-
1985:29–38.

*Bulletin économique de l'Indochine.* 1890–1940.

Cao-Tien-Phung et al. 1985. *Lich su dang bo tinh Vinh-Phu (1930–1954)* (History of the Party in the Province of Vinh-Phu, 1930–1954). Viet-
Tri: Ban Tuyen giao Tinh uy Vinh Phu.

Cao-van-Luong. 1960. "Phu-Tho: Thanh lap chi bo dau tien va su phat trien
co so dang" (Phu-Tho: The Establishment of the First Party Cell

and the Development of Party Organizations). In *Cach mang thang tam* (The August Revolution), vol. 1, edited by Tran-Huy-Lieu, 143–162. Hanoi: Nha xuat ban su hoc.

Cao-Xuan-Duc, comp. 1974. *Quoc trieu dang khoa luc* (Records of Successful Examination Candidates of This Dynasty). Translated into modern Vietnamese by Le-Manh-Lieu. Second edition. Saigon: Trung tam hoc lieu.

Chaliand, Gérard. 1968. *The Peasants of North Vietnam.* New York: Penguin.

Co-Nhi-Tan. 1969. *Nguyen Thai Hoc.* Saigon: Pham Quang Khai.

Dang-Huy-Van. 1967. "Them mot so tai lieu ve Doc Ngu va phong trao chong Phap o vung ha luu song Da cuoi the ky XIX" (Additional Documents on General Ngu and the Anti-French Movement in the Lower Da Valley at the End of the Nineteenth Century). *Nghien cuu lich su* 96:45–56.

Dinh-Thu-Cuc. 1985. "Nhung buoc dau tren con duong di len chu nghia xa hoi cua giai cap nong nhan Viet Nam" (The First Steps of the Vietnamese Peasantry on the Path toward Socialism). *Nghien cuu lich su* 223:28–38.

Duong-thi-The and Pham-thi-Thoa, eds. 1981. *Ten lang xa Viet Nam dau the ky XIX* (The Nomenclature of Vietnamese Villages in the Early Nineteenth Century). Hanoi: Khoa hoc xa hoi.

Emerson, Rupert. 1960. *From Empire to Nation.* Boston: Beacon.

Fforde, Adam. 1989. *The Agrarian Question in North Vietnam, 1974–1979.* Armonk, N.Y.: M. E. Sharpe.

Geertz, Clifford. 1963. *Agricultural Involution.* Berkeley: University of California Press.

Goubeaux, J. 1928. "Etude agronomique et économique de la Province de Phu-Tho (Tonkin)." *Bulletin économique de l'Indochine* 31 (n.s.):389–412.

Gourou, Pierre. 1936. *Les paysans du delta tonkinois.* Paris: Ecole française d'Extrême-Orient.

Gouvernement général de l'Indochine, Direction des affaires politiques et de la sûreté générale (GGI-DAP). 1930–1933. *Contribution à l'histoire des mouvements politiques de l'Indochine française.* 6 vols. Hanoi.

Gran, Guy. 1975. *Vietnam and the Capitalist Road to Modernity: Village Cochinchina, 1880–1940.* Ph.D. dissertation, University of Wisconsin at Madison.

Harrison, James P. 1982. *The Endless War: Fifty Years of Struggle in Vietnam.* New York: Free Press.

Henry, Yves. 1932. *L'économie agricole de l'Indochine.* Hanoi: Extrême-Orient.

Hickey, Gerald. 1964. *Village in Vietnam.* New Haven: Yale University Press.

Hoang-Pham-Tran (pseudonym of Nhuong-Tong). 1949. *Nguyen Thai Hoc.* Second edition. Saigon: Tan Viet.

Hoang-Uoc. 1968. "Cach mang ruong dat o Viet Nam, Phan I and II" (The Land Revolution in Vietnam, Parts I and II"). In *Cach mang ruong dat o Viet Nam* (The Land Revolution in Vietnam), edited by Tran-Phuong, 1–217. Hanoi: Nha Xuat Ban Khoa Hoc Xa Hoi.

Hoang-van-Dao. 1970. *Viet Nam Quoc Dan Dang* (The Vietnamese Nationalist Party). Second edition. Saigon: Nguyen Hoa Hiep.

Houtart, Françoise, and Geneviève Lemercinier. 1981. *La sociologie d'une commune vietnamienne.* Louvain-la-Neuve: Catholic University of Louvain.

Hunt, David. 1982. "Village Culture and the Vietnamese Revolution." *Past and Present* 92:131–157.

Huynh-Kim-Khanh. 1982. *Vietnamese Communism, 1925–1945.* Ithaca: Cornell University Press.

Indochine, Gouvernement général de l'. 1930–1983. *Contribution à l'histoire des mouvements politiques de l'Indochine française.* 6 vols. Hanoi: Direction des affaires politiques et de la sûreté générale.

———. 1931. *Le Tonkin scolaire.* Hanoi: Direction générale de l'instruction publique.

Kelly, Raymond. 1977. *Etoso Social Structure.* Ann Arbor: University of Michigan Press.

Kieu-Huu-Hy et al. 1961. *Tho van Nguyen Quang Bich* (The Poetry and Prose of Nguyen Quang Bich). Hanoi: Van Hoa.

Knudsen, John Chr. 1990. "Cognitive Models in Life Histories." *Anthropological Quarterly* 63:122–133.

Le-Tuong. 1967. "Gop them y kien ve Doc Ngu va phong trao chong Phap o vung ha luu song Da cuoi the ky XIX" (Additional Ideas on General Ngu and the Anti-French Movement in the Lower Da Valley at the End of the Nineteenth Century). *Nghien cuu lich su* 101:51–57.

Le-Tuong and Nguyen-Khac-Xuong. 1987. *Truyen thuyet Hung Vuong.* Fifth edition. Viet-Tri: Hoi Van hoc nghe thuat Vinh Phu.

Le-Tuong and Vu-Kim-Bien. 1981. *Lich su Vinh-Phu* (The History of Vinh-Phu). Viet-Tri: Ty van hoa va thong tin Vinh Phu.

Le-van-Thu. 1973. "Phong trao Viet Minh xa Kinh-Ke" (The Vietminh Movement in Kinh-Ke Village). In *Nhung ngay cach mang thang tam —Hoi ky* (The Days of the August Revolution: Memoirs), vol. 1. Viet-Tri: Ban Nghien cuu lich su dang Vinh Phu.

Luong, Hy Van. 1984. " 'Brother' and 'Uncle': Rules, Structural Contradictions, and Meaning in Vietnamese Kinship." *American Anthropologist* 86:290–315.

————. 1985. "Agrarian Unrest from an Anthropological Perspective: The Case of Vietnam." *Comparative Politics* 17:153–174.

————. 1988. "Discursive Practices, Ideological Oppositions, and Power Structure: Person-referring Forms and Sociopolitical Struggles in Vietnam." *American Ethnologist* 15:239–253.

————. 1989. "Vietnamese Kinship: Structural Principles and the Socialist Transformation in Twentieth-Century Vietnam." *Journal of Asian Studies* 48:741–756.

————. 1990. *Discursive Practices and Linguistic Meanings: The Vietnamese System of Person Reference.* Philadelphia and Amsterdam: John Benjamins.

————. 1991. "Vietnamese Life-History Narratives: Discursive Practices and Ideological Oppositions." Unpublished manuscript.

McAleavy, Henry. 1968. *Black Flags in Vietnam: The Story of a Chinese Intervention.* London: George Allen and Unwin.

McAlister, John, Jr. 1971. *Vietnam: The Origins of Revolution.* Garden City, N.Y.: Doubleday.

Mai-Hanh. 1967. "Doc Ngu va luc luong nghia quan song Da trong phong trao chong ngoai xam cua nhan dan Viet Nam thoi cuoi the ky XIX" (General Ngu and the Da River Resistance Force in the Vietnamese Movement against Foreign Invasions at the End of the Nineteenth Century). *Nghien cuu lich su* 97:27–42.

Marr, David. 1971. *Vietnamese Anticolonialism, 1885–1925.* Berkeley: University of California Press.

————. 1981. *Vietnamese Tradition on Trial, 1920–1945.* Berkeley: University of California Press.

Marx, Karl. 1963. *The Eighteenth Brumaire of Louis Bonaparte.* Translated from the German. New York: International Publishers.

Meillassoux, Claude. 1981. *Maidens, Meal and Money: Capitalism and the Domestic Community.* Cambridge: Cambridge University Press.

Mintz, Sidney. 1977. "The So-called World System: Local Initiative and Local Response." *Dialectical Anthropology* 2:253–270.

Mitchell, Edward J. 1968. "Inequality and Insurgency: A Statistical Study of South Vietnam." *World Politics* 20:421–438.

Mitrany, David. 1951. *Marx Against the Peasant.* Chapel Hill: University of North Carolina Press.

Murray, Martin. 1980. *The Development of Capitalism in Colonial Indochina (1870–1940).* Berkeley: University of California Press.

Mus, Paul. 1949. "The Role of the Village in Vietnamese Politics." *Pacific Affairs* 22:265–271.

————. 1952. *Vietnam: La sociologie d'une guerre.* Paris: Editions du Seuil.

*Nhan-Dan.* 1954–1955, 1983–1988.

Nash, June. 1979. *We Eat the Mines and the Mines Eat Us: Dependency and Exploitation in Bolivian Tin-Mines.* New York: Columbia University Press.

Ngo-Quang-Nam and Ta-Huy-Duc. 1986. "My thuat dan gian" (Folk Arts). In *Dia chi Vinh Phu: Van hoa dan gian vung dat to* (The Geography of Vinh-Phu: Folk Culture in the Ancestral Land), edited by Ngo-Quang-Nam and Xuan-Thiem, 173–209. Viet-Tri: So van hoa thong tin Vinh Phu.

Ngo-vi-Lien. 1928. *Nomenclature des communes du Tonkin.* Hanoi: Le van Tan.

Ngo-Vinh-Long. 1973. *Before the Revolution: Vietnamese Peasants under the French.* Cambridge, Mass.: MIT Press.

————. 1978a. "The Indochinese Communist Party and Peasant Rebellion in Central Vietnam, 1930–1931." *Bulletin of Concerned Asian Scholars* 10:15–34.

————. 1978b. *Peasant Revolutionary Struggles in Vietnam in the 1930's.* Ph.D. dissertation, Harvard University.

————. 1988. "Some Aspects of Cooperativization in the Mekong Delta." In *Postwar Vietnam: Dilemmas in Socialist Development,* edited by David Marr and Christine White, 163–173. Ithaca: Cornell University Southeast Asia Program.

Nguyen-Cong-Binh et al. 1985. *Lich su Viet Nam* (History of Vietnam). Vol. 2. Hanoi: Khoa hoc xa hoi.

Nguyen-Hai-Ham. 1970. *Tu Yen Bay den Con Lon* (From Yen Bay to Poulo Condore). Saigon: Khai-Tri.

Nguyen-Huy. 1980. "Ve cac hinh thuc khoan trong hop tac xa trong lua" (On the Types of Contract Systems in Rice-growing Cooperatives). *Nghien cuu kinh te* (Economic Research) 118:9–23.

————. 1983. *Dua nong nghiep tu san xuat nho len san xuat lon xa hoi chu nghia* (To Bring Agriculture from Small-Scale Production to the Large-Scale Production of the Socialist Era). Vol. 2. Hanoi: Khoa hoc xa hoi.

Nguyen-Khac-Vien. 1971. "Confucianisme et marxisme." In *Tradition et révolution au Vietnam,* edited by J. Chesneaux et al., 21–57. Paris: Anthropos.

Nguyen-The-Anh. 1971. *Kinh te va xa hoi Viet Nam duoi cac vua trieu Nguyen* (Vietnamese Economy and Society under the Nguyen Rulers). Saigon: Lua Thieng.

Nguyen-Thieu-Lau. 1951. "La reforme agraire de 1839 dans le Binh Dinh." *Bulletin de l'Ecole française d'Extrême-Orient* 45:119–129.

Nguyen-Xuan-Nguyen. 1942. "Enquêtes démographiques sur deux agglomerations annamites." *Bulletin de l'Institut Indochinois pour l'étude de l'homme* 5:2:129–136.

Nguyen-van-Trung. 1963. *Chu nghia thuc dan Phap o Viet Nam: Thuc chat va huyen thoai* (French Colonialism in Vietnam: Reality and Myths). Saigon: Nam Son.

Olson, Mancur. 1965. *The Logic of Collective Action.* Cambridge, Mass.: Harvard University Press.

Paige, Jeffery. 1975. *Agrarian Revolution: Social Movements and Export Agriculture in the Underdeveloped World.* New York: Free Press.

———. 1983. "Social Theory and Peasant Revolution in Vietnam and Guatemala." *Theory and Society* 12:699–737.

Pham-Cuong and Nguyen-van-Ba. 1976. *Revolution in the Village: Nam Hong (1945–1975).* Hanoi: Foreign Languages Publishing House.

Pham-Gia-Duc. 1986. *Lich su cuoc khang chien chong thuc dan Phap 1945–1954* (The History of the Resistance to French Colonialism, 1945–1954). Hanoi: Quan doi nhan dan.

Pham-Xuan-Do. 1939. *Phu-Tho tinh dia chi* (Geography of Phu-Tho Province). Hanoi: Nam Ky.

Phuc-Khanh and Dinh-Luc. 1986. *Cuoc khang chien chong thuc dan Phap xam luoc (9.1945–7.1954)* (The Resistance against French Invaders, 9/1945–7/1954). Hanoi: Su that.

*Phu-Tho.* 1960–1968.

Piétri, François. 1960. "L'affaire de Yen Bay." *La revue des deux mondes,* July 15, 1960, 278–288.

Popkin, Samuel. 1979. *The Rational Peasant: The Political Economy of Rural Society in Vietnam.* Berkeley: University of California Press.

Porter, Gareth, ed. 1981. *Vietnam: A History in Documents.* New York: New American.

Pouvourville, A. 1892. *Deux années de lutte (1890–1891).* Paris: Albert Savine.

———. 1923. *Chasseur de pirates.* Paris: Monde moderne.

Quoc-Anh. 1975. "Mot vai y kien ve moi quan he giua cac khuynh huong chinh tri tieu tu san voi phong trao cong nhan trong phong trao giai phong dan toc Viet Nam truoc 1930" (A Few Ideas on the Relation between the Political Trends among the Petite Bourgeoisie and Workers' Movements in the pre-1930 Vietnamese National Independence Movement). *Nghien cuu lich su* 160:28–48.

Rambo, A. Terry. 1973. *A Comparison of Peasant Social Systems of Northern and Southern Vietnam: A Study of Ecological Adaptation, Social Succession, and Cultural Evolution.* Carbondale: Southern Illinois University Center for Vietnamese Studies.

Rouband, Louis. 1931. *Vietnam: La tragédie indochinoise.* Paris: Valois.

Sahlins, Marshall. 1981. *Historical Metaphors and Mythical Realities.* Ann Arbor: University of Michigan Press.

———. 1985. *Islands of History.* Chicago: University of Chicago Press.

Scott, James C. 1976. *The Moral Economy of the Peasant.* New Haven: Yale University Press.

Scott, James George. 1885. *France and Tongking: A Narrative of the Campaign of 1884 and the Occupation of Further India.* London: Fisher Unwin.

Skocpol, Theda. 1979. *States and Social Revolutions.* Cambridge: Cambridge University Press.

Smith, Carol. 1984. "Local History in Global Context: Social and Economic Transitions in Western Guatemala." *Comparative Studies in Society and History* 26:193–228.

Son-Duong. 1987. *Lich su xa Son-Duong: So thao* (A Preliminary History of Son-Duong Village). Published under the editorship of the [Communist] Party Executive Committee in Son-Duong Village. Viet-Tri: So Van hoa Thong tin Vinh Phu.

Ta-Long. 1976. "Doi net ve cac nghi le trong mot nam o Vinh Phu truoc cach mang thang tam" (Certain Features of Annual Rituals in Vinh-Phu before the August [1945] Revolution). *Tap chi Dan toc hoc* (Journal of Ethnology) 2-1976:74–84.

———. 1983. "Tinh biet lap va tinh cong dong trong sinh hoat ton giao cua mot so lang xa o Bac Bo truoc cach mang" ([Community] Isolation and Relations through Religious Activities of a Number of Northern Villages before the [1945] Revolution). *Tap chi Dan toc hoc* (Journal of Ethnology) 2-1983:27–38.

Tai, Hue-Tam Ho. 1983. *Millenarianism and Peasant Politics in Vietnam.* Cambridge, Mass.: Harvard University Press.

Toan-Anh. 1969. *Mien Bac khai nguyen.* Saigon: Dai Nam.

Tran-Huy-Lieu, Van-Tao, and Nguyen-Khac-Dam. 1957. *Phong trao Van than khoi nghia* (The Aid-the-King Movement). Hanoi: Van su dia.

Tran-Trong-Kim. 1964. *Viet Nam su luoc* (A Summary History of Vietnam). Saigon: Khai Tri.

Tran-Tu. 1984. *Co cau to chuc cua lang Viet co truyen o Bac Bo* (The Organizational Structure of Traditional Vietnamese Villages in North Vietnam). Hanoi: Nha xuat ban khoa hoc xa hoi.

Trullinger, James Walker. 1980. *Village at War.* New York: Longman.

*Trung-Bac-Tan-Van.* 1930–1931.

Truong-Buu-Lam. 1967. *Patterns of Vietnamese Response to Foreign Intervention, 1858–1900.* New Haven, Conn.: Yale University Southeast Asia Studies.

Viollis, Andrée (pseudonym of A. F. C. d'Ardenne de Tizac). 1935. *Indochine: S.O.S.* Paris: Gallimard.

*Vinh-Phu.* 1968–1975.

Vinh-Phu Research Committee on Party History. 1971. *Bon muoi nam hoat dong cua dang bo Vinh Phu* (Forty Years of Activities of the Vinh Phu Provincial Party Organization). Viet-Tri: Ban nghien cuu lich su dang Vinh Phu.

Vu-Quoc-Thuc. 1951. *L'économie communaliste du Vietnam.* Hanoi: Presses universitaires du Vietnam.

Vu-Van-Tinh. 1970a. "Nhung thay doi ve dia ly hanh chinh cac tinh Bac ky trong thoi ky Phap thuoc" (Administrative Geographical Changes of Tonkinese Provinces in the French Colonial Period), Part 1. *Nghien cuu lich su* 133:43–51.

———. 1970b. "Nhung thay doi ve dia ly hanh chinh cac tinh Bac ky trong thoi ky Phap thuoc" (Administrative Geographical Changes of Tonkinese Provinces in the French Colonial Period), Part 2. *Nghien cuu lich su* 134:53–63.

Wallerstein, Immanuel. 1979. *The Capitalist World-Economy.* Cambridge: Cambridge University Press.

White, Christine. 1981. *Agrarian Reform and National Liberation in the Vietnamese Revolution: 1920–1957.* Ph.D. dissertation, Cornell University.

———. 1983. "Peasant Mobilization and Anti-colonial Struggle in Vietnam: The Rent Reduction Campaign of 1953." *Journal of Peasant Studies* 10:187–213.

———. 1988. "Alternative Approaches to the Socialist Transformation of Agriculture in Postwar Vietnam." In *Postwar Vietnam: Dilemmas in Socialist Development,* edited by David Marr and Christine White, 133–146. Ithaca: Cornell University Southeast Asia Program.

Wolf, Eric. 1969. *Peasant Wars of the Twentieth Century.* New York: Harper and Row.

Wolf, Margery. 1972. *Women and the Family in Rural Taiwan.* Stanford: Stanford University Press.

Wolpe, Harold. 1972. "Capitalism and Cheap Labour-Power in South Africa: From Segregation to Apartheid." *Economy and Society* 1:425–456.

Woodside, Alexander. 1976. *Community and Revolution in Modern Vietnam.* Boston: Houghton Mifflin.

# INDEX